Mark Twain

THE ADVENTURES OF HUCKLEBERRY FINN

[Edited with Introduction, Author's Information, Complete Text, Summary and Analysis and Study Questions]

Anshu Mallika Sawhney
M.A. English, Delhi University
M. Phil., Himachal Pradesh University

ANMOL PUBLICATIONS PVT. LTD.
NEW DELHI - 110 002 (INDIA)

ANMOL PUBLICATIONS PVT. LTD.

H.O.: 4374/4B, Ansari Road, Darya Ganj,
New Delhi-110 002 (India)
Ph.: 23278000, 23261597

B.O.: No. 1015, Ist Main Road, BSK IIIrd Stage
IIIrd Phase, IIIrd Block
Bangalore - 560 085 (India)
Visit us at: www.anmolpublications.com

The Adventures of Huckleberry Finn

First Published, 2009

PRINTED IN INDIA

Printed at Balaji Offset Press, Delhi.

Mark Twain

THE ADVENTURES OF HUCKLEBERRY FINN

Contents

Preface

Mark twain was born Samuel Langhorne Clemens in the town of Florida, Missouri, in 1835. American writer, journalist, and humorist, who won a worldwide audience for his stories of youthful adventures of Tom Sawyer and Huckleberry Finn. When he was four years old, his family moved to Hannibal, a town on the Mississippi River much like the towns depicted in his two most famous novels, The Adventures of Tom Sawyer (1876) and The Adventures of Huckleberry Finn (1884).Clemens spent his young life in a fairly affluent family that owned a number of household slaves.

Sensitive to the sound of language, Twain introduced colloquial speech into American fiction. In Green Hills of Africa, Ernest Hemingway wrote: "All modern American literature comes from one book by Mark Twain called Huckleberry Finn..."

Author

Chapter 1

Introduction

Mark Twain was born Samuel Langhorne Clemens in the town of Florida, Missouri, in 1835. When he was four years old, his family moved to Hannibal, a town on the Mississippi River much like the towns depicted in his two most famous novels, The Adventures of Tom Sawyer and The Adventures of Huckleberry Finn. Clemens spent his young life in a fairly affluent family that owned a number of household slaves. The death of Clemens's father in 1847, however, left the family in hardship. Clemens left school, worked for a printer, and, in 1851, having finished his apprenticeship, began to set type for his brother Orion's newspaper, the Hannibal Journal. But Hannibal proved too small to hold Clemens, who soon became a sort of itinerant printer and found work in a number of American cities, including New York and Philadelphia.

While still in his early twenties, Clemens gave up his printing career in order to work on riverboats on the Mississippi. Clemens eventually became a riverboat pilot, and his life on the river influenced him a great deal. Perhaps most important, the riverboat life provided him with the pen name Mark Twain, derived from the riverboat leadsmen's signal—"By the mark, twain"—that the water was deep enough for safe passage. Life on the river also gave Twain material for several of his books, including the raft scenes of Huckleberry Finn and the material for his autobiographical Life on the Mississippi.

Clemens continued to work on the river until 1861, when the Civil War exploded across America and shut down the Mississippi for travel and shipping. Although Clemens joined a Confederate cavalry division, he was no ardent Confederate, and when his division deserted en masse, he did too. He then made his way west with his brother Orion, working first as a silver miner in Nevada and then stumbling into his true calling, journalism. In 1863, Clemens began to sign articles with the name Mark Twain.

Throughout the late 1860s and 1870s, Twain's articles, stories, memoirs, and novels, characterized by an irrepressible wit and a deft ear for language and dialect, garnered him immense celebrity. His novel The Innocents Abroad was an instant bestseller, and The Adventures of Tom Sawyer received even greater national acclaim and cemented Twain's position as a giant in American literary circles. As the nation prospered economically in the post-Civil War period—an era that came to be known as the Gilded Age, an epithet that Twain coined—so too did Twain. His books were sold door-to-door, and he became wealthy enough to build a large house in Hartford, Connecticut, for himself and his wife, Olivia, whom he had married in 1870.

Twain began work on Huckleberry Finn, a sequel to Tom Sawyer, in an effort to capitalize on the popularity of the earlier novel. This new novel took on a more serious character, however, as Twain focused increasingly on the institution of slavery and the South. Twain soon set Huckleberry Finn aside, perhaps because its darker tone did not fit the optimistic sentiments of the Gilded Age. In the early 1880s, however, the hopefulness of the post-Civil War years began to fade. Reconstruction, the political programme designed to reintegrate the defeated South into the Union as a slavery-free region, began to fail. The harsh measures the victorious North imposed only embittered the South. Concerned about maintaining power, many Southern politicians began an effort to control and oppress the black men and women whom the war had freed. Meanwhile, Twain's personal life began to collapse. His wife had long been sickly, and the couple lost their first son after just nineteen months. Twain also made a number of poor investments and financial decisions and, in 1891, found himself mired in debilitating debt. As his personal fortune dwindled, he continued to devote himself to writing. Drawing from his personal plight and the prevalent national troubles of the day, he finished a draft of Huckleberry Finn in 1883, and by 1884 had it ready for publication. The novel met with great public and critical acclaim.

Twain continued to write over the next ten years. He published two more popular novels, A Connecticut Yankee in King Arthur's Court and Pudd'nhead Wilson, but went into a considerable decline afterward, never again publishing work that matched the high standard he had set with Huckleberry Finn. Personal tragedy also continued to hound Twain: his finances remained troublesome, and within the course of a few years, his wife and two of his daughters passed away. Twain's writing from this period until the end of his life reflects a depression and a sort of righteous rage at the injustices of the world. Despite his personal troubles, however, Twain continued to enjoy immense esteem and fame and continued to be in demand as a public speaker until his death in 1910.

The story of Huckleberry Finn, however, does not end with the death of its author. Through the twentieth century, the novel has become famous not merely as the crown jewel in the work of one of America's preeminent writers, but also as a subject of intense controversy. The novel occasionally has been banned in Southern states because of its steadfastly critical take on the South and the hypocrisies of slavery. Others have dismissed Huckleberry Finn as vulgar or racist because it uses the word "nigger," a term whose connotations obscure the novel's deeper themes—which are unequivocally antislavery—and even prevent some from reading and enjoying it altogether. The fact that the historical context in which Twain wrote made his use of the word insignificant—and, indeed, part of the realism he wanted to create—offers little solace to some modern readers. Ultimately, The Adventures of Huckleberry Finn has proved significant not only as a novel that explores the racial and moral world of its time but also, through the controversies that continue to surround it, as an artifact of those same moral and racial tensions as they have evolved to the present day.

Chapter 2

Biography

Mark Twain (1835-1910) - pseudonym of Samuel Langhorne Clemens

American writer, journalist, and humorist, who won a worldwide audience for his stories of youthful adventures of Tom Sawyer and Huckleberry Finn. Sensitive to the sound of language, Twain introduced colloquial speech into American fiction. In Green Hills of Africa, Ernest Hemingway wrote: "All modern American literature comes from one book by Mark Twain called Huckleberry Finn..."

"When I was a boy, there was but one permanent ambition among my comrades in our village on the west bank of the Mississippi River. That was, to be a steamboatman." (from 'Old Times on the Mississippi', 1875)

Samuel Langhorne Clemens (Mark Twain) was born in Florida, Missouri, of a Virginian family. The family soon moved to Hannibal, Missouri, where Twain was brought up. At school, accroding to his own words, he "excelled only in spelling". After his father's death in 1847, Twain was apprenticed to a printer. Her also started his career as a journalist by writing for the Hannibal Journal. Later Twain worked as a licensed Mississippi river-boat pilot (1857-61). His famous penname Twain adopted from the call ('Mark twain!' - meaning by the mark of two fathoms) used when sounding river shallows. But this isn't the full story: he had also satirized an older writer, Isaiah Sellers, who called himself Mark Twain. In 1861 Twain served briefly as a confederate irregular. The Civil War put an end to the steamboat traffic, and during a period when Twain was out of work, he lived in a primitive cabin on Jackass Hill and tried his luck as a gold-miner. "I would have been more or less than human if I had not gone mad like the rest," he confessed.

Twain moved to Virginia City, where he edited two years Territorial Enterprise. On February 3, 1863, 'Mark Twain' was born when he signed a humorous travel account with that pseudonym. In 1864 Twain left for California, where worked in San Francisco as a reporter. After hearing a story about a frog, Twain made an entry in his notebook: "Coleman with his jumping frog - bet a stranger $50. - Stranger had no frog and C. got him one: - In the meantime stranger filled C's frog full of shot and he couldn't jump.

The stranger's frog won." From these lines he developed 'Jim Smiley and his Jumping Frog' which was published in The Saturday Press of New York on the 18th of November in 1865. It was reprinted all over the country and became the foundation stone of the celebrated jumping frog of calaveras county, and other sketches. This work marked the beginning of twain's literary career.

In 1866 Twain visited Hawaii as a correspondent for The Sacramento Union, publishing letters on his trip. He then set out world tour, travelling in France and italy. His experiences twain recorded in the innocents abroad. The work, which gained him wide popularity, poked fun at both american and european prejudices and manners. Throughout his life, twain frequently returned to travel writing - many of his finest novels, such as the adventures of tom sawyer, dealt with journeys and escapes into freedom.

The success of The Innocents Abroad gave Twain enough financial security to marry Olivia Langdon in 1870, after writing about 189 love letters during his courtship. William Dean Howells praised the author in The Atlantic Monthly, and Twain thanked him by saying: "When I read that review of yours, I felt like the woman who was so glad her baby had come white."

Olivia, Twain's beloved Livy, served and protected her husband devotedly. They moved to Hartford, where the family remained, with occasional trips abroad, until 1891. Twain continued to lecture in the United States and England. Between 1876 and 1884 he published several masterpieces. Tom Sawyer was originally intended for adults. Twain had abandoned the work in 1874, but returned to it in the following summer and even then was undecided if he were writing a book for adults or for young readers. Eventually he declared that it was "professedly and confessedly a boy's and girl's book". The prince and the pauper was about edward vi of england and a little pauper who change places.

The book was dedicated "to those good-mannered and agreeable children, susie and clara clemens." Life on the mississippi contained an attack on the influence of sir walter scott, whose romanticism have caused according to twain 'measureless harm' to progressive ideas. From the very beginning of his journalistic career, twain made fun with the novel and its tradition. Although twain enjoyed magnificent popularity as a novelist, he believed that he lacked the analytical sensibility necessary to the novelist's art.

Huckleberry finn, an american odysseus, was first considered adult fiction. Huck, who could not possibly write a story, tells us the story: "You don't know about me without you have read a book by the name of the adventures of tom sawyer, but that ain't no matter. That book was made by mr. Mark twain and he told the truth, mainly." Both tom sawyer and huckleberry finn stand high on the list of eminent writers like stevenson, dickens, and saroyan who honestly depicted young people. Huck's debate whether or not he will turn in jim, an escaped slave and a friend, probed the racial tensions of the national conscience. Later twain wrote in the man that corrupted hadleyburg: "I have no race prejudices... All that i care to know is that a man is a human being - that is enough for me; he can't be any worse."

One of twain's major achievements is the way he narrates huckleberry finn, following the twists and turns of ordinary speech, his native missouri dialect. Shelley fisher fishkin has noted in was huck black? That the book drew upon a vernacular formed by black voices as well as white. The model for huck finn's voice, according to fishkin, was a black child instead of a white one. The character of huck was based on a boy named tom blankenship, twain's boyhood friend.

'"Who is your folks?" He questions me.

"The phelpses, down yonder."

"Oh," he says, "how'd you say he got shot?"

"He had a dream," i says, "and it shot him."

"Funny dream," the doctor says.'

(From huckleberry finn)

In the 1880s twain wrote also such books as the tragedy of pudd'head wilson, a murder mystery and a case of transposed identities, but also an implicit condemnation of a society that allows slavery, and personal recollections of joan of arc, published under the pseudonym of sieur louis de conte. In the 1890s twain lost most of his earnings in financial speculations and in the downhill of his own publishing firm, c.l. Webster, which he had established in 1884 in new york city. In 1894 he had invested in the infamous paige typesetter, which never worked. "Paige and i always met on elusively affectionate terms," twain said, "and yet he knows perfectly well that if i had him in a steel trap i would shut out all human succor and watch that trap until he died..." Twain closed hartford house. To recover from the bankrupt, he started a world lecture tour. By 1898 he had repaid all debts. From 1896 to 1900 he resided mainly in europe. During the tour susy, his favourite daughter, died of spinal meningitis.

Twain traveled new zealand, australia, india, and south africa, and returned to the u.s. In 1900. Twain's travel book, following the equator, appeared in 1897. In 1902 twain made a trip to hannibal, his home town which had inspired several of his works. His plans for a peaceful and quiet visit were ruined when more than 100 newspapers chronicled his every move.

The death of his wife in 1904 in Florence and his second daughter darkened the author's life, which is also seen in writings and his posthumously published autobiography. Twain's view of the human nature had never been very optimistic, but during final years, he become even more bitter: "I believe that our Heavenly Father invented man because he was disappointed in the monkey." Especially hostile Twain was towards Christianity: "If men neglected 'God's poor' and 'God's stricken and helpless ones' as He does, what would become of them? The answer is to be found in those dark lands where man follows His example and turns his indifference back upon them: they get no help at all; they cry, and plead and pray in vain, they linger and suffer, and miserably die." (from 'Thoughts of God') Twain died on april 21, 1910. His autobiography twain dictated to his secretary a.b. Paine; various versions of it have been published. In 1916 appeared the mysterious stranger, set in the 16th-century austria, in which satan reveals the hypocrisies and stupidities of the village of eseldorf. "

The first man was a hypocrite and a coward, qualities which have not yet failed in his line; it is the foundation upon which all civilizations have been built." The work was composed between 1897 and 1908 in several, quite different versions, one of which was set in Hannibal, another in a print shop. Albert Bigelow Paine, Mark Twain's authorized biographer, apparently added to it a concluding chapter from another version altogether. Mark Twain's colorful life inspired the film The Adventures of Mark Twain, directed by Irving Rapper and starring Fredric March. In Philip José Farmer's Riverworld epic Mark Twain was one of the central characters.

During his long writing career, Twain produced a considerable number of essays, which appeared in various newspapers and in magazines, including the Galaxy, Harper's, the Atlantic Monthly, and North American Review. In his 'Sandwich Islands' letters Twain described how the missionaries and American government have corrupted the Hawaiians, 'Queen Victoria's Jubilee' presented the pomp and pageantry of an English royal procession, and 'King Leopold's Soliloquy' revealed in a dramatic monologue the political evils caused by despotism.

The King complains: "Blister the meddlesome missionaries! They write tons of these things. They seem to be always around, always spying, always eye-witnessing the happenings; and everything they see they commit to paper... One of these missionaries saw eighty-one of these hands drying over a fire for transmission to my officials—and of course they must go and set it down and print it... nothing is too trivial for them to print..." Twain's finest satire of imperialism was perhaps 'To the Person Sitting in Darkness', in which the author wrote that the people in darkness are beginning to see "more light than... was profitable for us."

Chapter 3

Major Works

Samuel langhorne clemens, for nearly half a century known and celebrated as "Mark Twain," was born in Florida, Missouri, on November 30, 1835. He was one of the foremost American philosophers of his day; he was the world's most famous humorist of any day. During the later years of his life he ranked not only as America's chief man of letters, but likewise as her best known and best loved citizen.

The beginnings of that life were sufficiently unpromising. The family was a good one, of old Virginia and Kentucky stock, but its circumstances were reduced, its environment meager and disheartening. The father, John Marshall Clemens—a lawyer by profession, a merchant by vocation—had brought his household to Florida from Jamestown, Tennessee, somewhat after the manner of judge Hawkins as pictured in The Gilded Age.

Florida was a small town then, a mere village of twenty-one houses located on Salt River, but judge Clemens, as he was usually called, optimistic and speculative in his temperament, believed in its future. Salt River would be made navigable; Florida would become a metropolis. He established a small business there, and located his family in the humble frame cottage where, five months later, was born a baby boy to whom they gave the name of Samuel—a family name—and added Langhorne, after an old Virginia friend of his father.

The child was puny, and did not make a very sturdy fight for life. Still he weathered along, season after season, and survived two stronger children, Margaret and Benjamin. By 1839 Judge Clemens had lost faith in Florida. He removed his family to Hannibal, and in this Mississippi River town the little lad whom the world was to know as Mark Twain spent his early life. In Tom Sawyer we have a picture of the Hannibal of those days and the atmosphere of his boyhood there.

His schooling was brief and of a desultory kind. It ended one day in 1847, when his father died and it became necessary that each one should help somewhat in the domestic crisis. His brother Orion, ten years his senior, was already a printer by trade. Pamela, his sister; also considerably older, had acquired music, and now took a few pupils. The little boy Sam, at twelve, was apprenticed to a printer named Ament. His wages consisted of his board and clothes—"more board than clothes," as he once remarked to the writer.

He remained with Ament until his brother Orion bought out a small paper in Hannibal in 1850. The paper, in time, was moved into a part of the Clemens home, and the two brothers ran it, the younger setting most of the type. A still younger brother, Henry, entered the office as an apprentice. The Hannibal journal was no great paper from the beginning, and it did not improve with time. Still, it managed to survive—country papers nearly always manage to survive—year after year, bringing in some sort of return.

It was on this paper that young Sam Clemens began his writings—burlesque, as a rule, of local characters and conditions— usually published in his brother's absence; generally resulting in trouble on his return. Yet they made the paper sell, and if Orion had but realized his brother's talent he might have turned it into capital even then. In 1853 (he was not yet eighteen) Sam Clemens grew tired of his limitations and pined for the wider horizon of the world. He gave out to his family that he was going to St. Louis, but he kept on to New York, where a World's Fair was then going on. In New York he found employment at his trade, and during the hot months of 1853 worked in a printing- office in Cliff Street. By and by he went to Philadelphia, where he worked a brief time; made a trip to Washington, and presently set out for the West again, after an absence of more than a year.

Onion, meanwhile, had established himself at Muscatine,

Iowa, but soon after removed to Keokuk, where the brothers were once more together, till following their trade. Young Sam Clemens remained in Keokuk until the winter of 1856-57, when he caught a touch of the South-American fever then prevalent; and decided to go to Brazil. He left Keokuk for Cincinnati, worked that winter in a printing-office there, and in April took the little steamer, Paul Jones, for New Orleans, where he expected to find a South-American vessel.

In Life on the Mississippi we have his story of how he met Horace Bixby and decided to become a pilot instead of a South American adventurer—jauntily setting himself the stupendous task of learning the twelve hundred miles of the Mississippi River between St. Louis and New Orleans—of knowing it as exactly and as unfailingly, even in the dark, as one knows the way to his own features. It seems incredible to those who knew Mark Twain in his later years—dreamy, unpractical, and indifferent to details—that he could have acquired so vast a store of minute facts as were required by that task. Yet within eighteen months he had become not only a pilot, but one of the best and most careful pilots on the river, intrusted with some of the largest and most valuable steamers. He continued in that profession for two and a half years longer, and during that time met with no disaster that cost his owners a single dollar for damage. Then the war broke out. South Carolina seceded in December, 1860 and other States followed. Clemens was in New Orleans in January, 1861, when Louisiana seceded, and his boat was put into the Confederate service and sent up the Red River. His occupation gone, he took steamer for the North—the last one before the blockade closed. A blank cartridge was fired at them from Jefferson Barracks when they reached St. Louis, but they did not understand the signal, and kept on. Presently a shell carried away part of the pilot-house and considerably disturbed its inmates. They realized, then, that war had really begun.

In those days Clemens's sympathies were with the South. He hurried up to Hannibal and enlisted with a company of young fellows who were recruiting with the avowed purpose of "throwing off the yoke of the invader." They were ready for the field, presently, and set out in good order, a sort of nondescript cavalry detachment, mounted on animals more picturesque than beautiful. Still, it was a resolute band, and might have done very well, only it rained a good deal, which made soldiering disagreeable and hard. Lieutenant Clemens resigned at the end of two weeks, and decided to go to Nevada with Orion, who was a Union abolitionist and had received an appointment from Lincoln as Secretary of the new Territory.

In 'Roughing It' Mark Twain gives us the story of the overland journey made by the two brothers, and a picture of experiences at the other end —true in aspect, even if here and there elaborated in detail. He was Orion's private secretary, but there was no private-secretary work to do, and no salary attached to the position. The incumbent presently went to mining, adding that to his other trades.

He became a professional miner, but not a rich one. He was at Aurora, California, in the Esmeralda district, skimping along, with not much to eat and less to wear, when he was summoned by Joe Goodman, owner and editor of the Virginia City Enterprise, to come up and take the local editorship of that paper. He had been contributing sketches to it now and then, under the pen, name of "Josh," and Goodman, a man of fine literary instincts, recognized a talent full of possibilities. This was in the late summer of 1862.

Clemens walked one hundred and thirty miles over very bad roads to take the job, and arrived way-worn and travel-stained. He began on a salary of twenty-five dollars a week, picking up news items here and there, and contributing occasional sketches, burlesques, hoaxes, and the like. When the Legislature convened at Carson City he was sent down to report it, and then, for the first time, began signing his articles "Mark Twain," a river term, used in making soundings, recalled from his piloting days. The name presently became known up and down the Pacific coast. His articles were, copied and commented upon. He was recognized as one of the foremost among a little coterie of overland writers, two of whom, Mark Twain and Bret Harte, were soon to acquire a world-wide fame.

Chapter 4

Chronology

1835	Nov. 30-Samuel Langhorne Clemens is born in Florida, Missouri to John M. and Jane L. Clemens (5th surviving child)
1839	*Clemens family moves to Hannibal, Missouri*
1840	*Begins school*
1845	*Takes first steamboat to St. Louis*
	Olivia Langdon, future wife, born in Elmira, New York
1847	John M. Clemens, father, dies. Begins delivering papers and working as an errand boy for Hannibal Gazette, ending formal education at the age of 11(5th Grade)
	Works as a printer's apprentice for Hannibal Courier.
1850	Works for brother Orion as reporter and printer at Hannibal Journal, runs paper when Orion away.
1851	"A Gallant Fireman", Clemens' earliest known sketch appears in Hannibal Journal.
	Sketches appear in Philadelphia's Saturday Evening Post.
1853	Works as itinerant printer in St. Louis, New York City and Philadelphia.
	Corresponds for Iowa's Muscatine Journal from Philadelphia.
1854	Works in brother Orion's Ben Franklin Book and Job Office, Keokuk, Iowa.
1856	Gives first public speech at printers banquet in Keokuk, Iowa.
	Cub (apprentice) riverboat pilot on Mississippi River under Horace Bixby.

1858 Brother Henry Clemens dies from injuries sustained in explosion of riverboat Pennsylvania.

1859 Earns steamboat pilot license. Works steadily as a river pilot on the Mississippi River between St. Louis and New Orleans.

1861 Piloting career ends with closing of Mississippi River due to Civil War. Joins band of Confederate irregulars around Marion Country for a few weeks. Brother Orion is appointed Secretary to the Nevada Territory. Sam travels with him by stagecoach to Virginia city. Prospects unsuccessfully for silver in Nevada.

1862 Writes for the Territorial Enterprise in Virginia City Nevada.

Adopts pen name "Mark T ʌain," an old riverboat term which means the line between safe water and dangerous water.

Visits San Francisco.

1864 Works as a reporter for San Francisco Morning Call and the Sacramento Union.

1865 Visits Angels Camp in Calaveras Country, California.

Writes "Jim Smiley and His Jumping Frog."

1866 Goes to Sandwich Islands (Hawaii) as a reporter for Sacramento Union.

Arrested for disorderly conduct in New York City. Spends the night in jail.

Visits Europe and the Holy Land of the Quaker City as a reporter.

Meets Olivia Langdon in New York City. Attends a reading by Charles Dickens with her family.

Publishes The Celebrated Jumping Frog of Calaveras County and Other Stories.

Visits San Francisco.

1868 Visits Hartford, Connecticut to see publisher, The American Publishing Company.

Meets Harriet Beecher Stowe.

Formally engaged to marry Olivia (livy) Langdon.

Publishes The Innocents Abroad.

Meets Frederick Douglass.

Marries Olivia Langdon in Elmira, New York, on February 2. Couple settles in Buffalo, New York. Partial owner of Buffalo Express. A son, Langdon Clemens is born.

Visits San Francisco.

1871 Moves family to Hartford, Connecticut, leases a home in Nook Farm neighborhood.

March 19-Olivia Susan (Susy) Clemens, daughter, born in Elmira, New York.

June 2-Langdon dies in Hartford.

Publishes Roughing It.

Clemens family buys property on Farmington Avenue and commissions E. T. Potter, architect, to design their house.

Lectures and travels with family in England.

Patents Self Pasting Scrapbook.

Publishes The Gilded Age with Charles Dudley Warner.

Clara Langdon Clemens, daughter, born in Elmira.

Clemens family moves to new Hartford home.

Publishes The Adventures of Tom Sawyer.

Starts to work on Adventures of Huckleberry Finn as sequel to Tom Sawyer, but stops several months later.

1878 *Travels with family in Europe for neariy 2 years.*

1879 Resumes work on Adventures of Huckleberry Finn. Stops at chapter 21.

Publishes A Tramp Abroad.

Jane Lampton (Jean) Clemens, daughter, born in Elmira.

Begins modest investments in Paige Compositor.

1881 Hires Louis Comfort Tiffany and Associated Artists to decorate public rooms of Hartford home.

Publishes The Prince and the Pauper.

1882 Travels down the Mississippi River to do research for Life on the Mississippi.

Witnessing the failure of Reconstruction in the south, Twain returns to work on Adventures of Huckleberry Finn.

Publishes Life on the Mississippi.

	Finishes Adventures of Huckleberry Finn.
1884	*Founds Charles L. Webster Publishing and Co.*
	Lectures throughout United States.
1885	*Publishes Adventures of Huckleberry Finn.*
	Charles L. Webster and Co. issues first volume of Personal Memoirs of U.S. Grant.
1886	Forms partnership with James Paige to further develop Paige Compositor. Buys half-interest in invention.
1888	Awarded honorary Master of Arts degree at Yale University.
	Publishes A Yankee in King Arthur's Court.
1890	*Jane Lampton Clemens, mother, dies.*
	Olivia L. Langdon, mother-in-law, dies.
1891	Financial hardship forces family to leave Hartford home for less expensive life in Europe.
1892	*Travels in Europe.*
	Meets Kaiser Wilhelm II and Prince Edward, Prince of Wales.
	Returns to United States briefly on business.
	Publishes The American Claimant.
	Publishes Pudd'nhead Wilson.
	Travels in Europe and United States.
	Charles L. Webster and Co. fails.
	Paige Compositor tested and found impractical commercial device.
	Declares bankruptcy.
	Publishes Tom Sawyer Abroad
1895	Beigns world lecture tour to Canada, India, Australia, New Zealand, Ceylon and South Africa to pay off debts. Clara and Livy travel with him.
1896	*Meets Mahatma Gandhi.*
	Completes world lecture tour, returning triumphantly to England.
	Susy Clemens dies of Spinal Meningitis in Hartford home.
	Publishes Personal Recollections of Joan of Arc. Publishes Following the Equator (based on the world tour).
	Lives and lectures in Europe.

1898 *Meets Sigmund Freud.*
Pays off creditors.

1899 Private audience with Emperor Franz Josef I of Austria-Hungary.
Meets Booker T. Washington.

1900 *Returns to United States to live in New York City.*
Introduces Winston Churchill to his first American lecture audience.

1901 Rents house in Riverdale, New York.
Receives honorary Doctor of Letters from Yale University.
Serves as Vice President for Anti-Imperialist League for the next 9 years.
Publishes "To the Person Sitting in Darkness."
Writes "The United States of Lyncherdom."

1902 *Visits Hannibal for last time.*
Receives honorary degree from University of Missouri.
Summers in York Harbor, Maine.
Livy becomes seriously ill.
Lives in New York and Italy.
Sells Hartford home to Bissell Family.

1904 *Livy dies in Florence, Italy.*
Twain returns to New York City.

1905 Dines at White House with President Theodore Roosevelt. *Publishes "The Czar's Soliloquy."*
Publishes "King Leopold's Soliloquy."
Summers in Dublin, New Hampshire.

1906 *Publishes Eve's Diary.*
Testifies before Congress for Copyright legislation. (Wearing white suit-beginning trademark of wearing the white suit year-round in public).
Lives in New York City.
Continues to travel extensively
Awarded honorary Doctor of Letters by Oxford University (along with Rudyard Kipling, Auguste Rodin and Camille Saint-Saens).
Moves to "Stormfield" his new home in Redding, Connecticut.

1909 *Travels to Bermuda.*
Publishes "Is Shakespeare Dead?"
Clara Clemens marries Ossip Gabrilowitsch (Russian musician) at "Stormfield".
Dec. 24-Jean dies at "Stormfield".
Last writing: "Turning Point of My Life".
Travels to Bermuda for last time.

April 21-Samuel Clemens/Mark Twain dies at "Stormfield" at age 74.
"I came in with Halley's comet in 1835...I expect to go out with it"

Chapter 5

Historical Context

Slavery

The issue of slavery threatened to divide the nation as early as the Constitutional Convention of 1787, and throughout the years a series of concessions were made on both sides in an effort to keep the union together. One of the most significant of these was the Missouri Compromise of 1820. The furor had begun when Missouri requested to enter the union as a slave state. In order to maintain a balance between free and slave states in the union, Missouri was admitted as a slave state while Maine entered as a free one. And although Congress would not accept Missouri's proposal to ban free blacks from the state, it did allow a provision permitting the state's slaveholders to reclaim runaway slaves from neighboring free states. The federal government's passage of Fugitive Slave Laws was also a compromise to appease southern slaveholders. The first one, passed in 1793, required anyone helping a slave to escape to pay a fine of $500.

But by 1850, when a second law was passed, slaveowners had become increasingly insecure about their ability to retain their slaves in the face of abolitionism. The 1850 Fugitive Slave Law increased the fine for abetting a runaway slave to $1000, added the penalty of up to six months in prison, and required that every U.S. citizen assist in the capture of runaways. This law allowed southern slaveowners to claim their fugitive property without requiring them to provide proof of ownership. Whites and blacks in the North were outraged by the law, which effectively implicated all American citizens in the institution of slavery. As a result, many who had previously felt unmoved by the issue became ardent supporters of the abolitionist movement.

Among those who were outraged into action by the Fugitive Slave Law was Harriet Beecher Stowe, whose novel Uncle Tom's Cabin galvanized the North against slavery. Dozens of slave narratives — first hand accounts of the cruelties of slavery — had shown white Northerners a side of slavery that had previously remained hidden, but the impact of Stowe's novel on white Northerners was more widespread. Abraham Lincoln is reported to have said when he met her during the Civil War, "So you're the little lady who started this big war." White southerners also recognized the powerful effect of the national debate on slavery as it was manifested in print, and many southern states, fearing the spread of such agitating ideas to their slaves, passed laws which made it illegal to teach slaves to read. Missouri passed such a law in 1847. Despite the efforts of southerners to keep slaves in the dark about those who were willing to help them in the North, thousands of slaves did escape to the free states. Many escape routes led to the Ohio River, which formed the southern border of the free states of Illinois and Indiana. The large number of slaves who escaped belied the myths of contented slaves that originated from the South.

Reconstruction

Although The Adventures of Huckleberry Finn takes place before the Civil War, it was written in the wake of Reconstruction, the period directly after the Civil War when the confederate states were brought back into the union. The years from 1865 to 1876 witnessed rapid and radical progress in the South, as many schools for blacks were opened, black men gained the right to vote with the passage of the Fifteenth Amendment in 1870, and the Civil Rights Act of 1875 desegregated public places. But these improvements were quickly undermined by new Black Codes in the South that restricted such rights. White southerners felt threatened by Republicans from the North who went south to help direct the course of Reconstruction. Most galling was the new authority of free blacks, many of whom held political office and owned businesses. While prospects did improve somewhat for African Americans during Reconstruction, their perceived authority in the new culture was exaggerated by whites holding on to the theory of white superiority that had justified slavery.

In response to the perceived threat, many terrorist groups were formed to intimidate freed blacks and white Republicans through vigilante violence. The Ku Klux Klan, the most prominent of these new groups, was formed in 1866. Efforts to disband these terrorist groups proved ineffective. By 1876, Democrats had regained control over the South and by 1877, federal troops had withdrawn. Reconstruction and the many rights blacks had gained dissipated as former abolitionists lost interest in the issue of race, and the country became consumed with financial crises and conflicts with Native Americans in the West. Throughout the 1880s and 1890s, new Jim Crow laws segregated public spaces in the South, culminating in the Supreme Court's decision in the case Plessy v. Ferguson in 1896, which legalized segregation.

Minstrel Shows

As the first indigenous form of entertainment in America, minstrel shows flourished from the 1830s to the first decade of the twentieth century. In the 1860s, for example, there were more than one hundred minstrel groups in the country. Samuel Clemens recalled his love of minstrel shows in his posthumously published Autobiography, writing, "If I could have the nigger show back again in its pristine purity and perfection I should have but little further use for opera." His attraction to black-face entertainment informed The Adventures of Huckleberry Finn, where, many critics believe, he used its humorous effects to challenge the racial stereotypes on which it was based.

Minstrel shows featured white men in black-face and outrageous costumes. The men played music, danced, and acted burlesque skits, but the central feature of the shows was the exaggerated imitation of black speech and mannerisms, which produced a stereotype of blacks as docile, happy, and ignorant. The shows also depicted slavery as a natural and benign institution and slaves as contented with their lot. These stereotypes of blacks helped to reinforce attitudes amongst whites that blacks were fundamentally different and inferior. The minstrel show died out as vaudeville, burlesques, and radio became the most popular forms of entertainment.

Compare and Contrast

1840s: Under the Slave Codes, enacted by individual southern states, slaves could not own property, testify against whites in court, or make contracts. Slave marriages were not recognized by law.

1884: As the result of Black Codes enacted by states during Reconstruction, African Americans could now legally marry and own property, but the codes also imposed curfews and segregation. The Fifteenth Amendment granted black men the right to vote, but individual states prohibited them from doing so.

Today: The right to vote is universal for all citizens above the age of eighteen, and other rights are not restricted by race.

1840s: The steamboat was the most popular mode of travel and the Mississippi and Ohio Rivers were the main thoroughfares in the West.

1884: The railroad had taken over as the means of mass transportation all across America.

Today: Most goods are transported within the U.S. by truck, and airplanes and cars allow people to travel long distances in short periods of time.

1840s: Means of entertainment were beginning to flourish in America. Among the many new kinds of literature available were slave narratives and romantic adventures. The first minstrel show was staged in 1843.

1884: The field of literature, in the form of books and periodicals, had become the province of the masses.

The minstrel show continued to be popular, as did the music of ragtime which was associated with it.
Today: Entertainment, especially film, television, and music, is a multi-billion-dollar industry.

1840s: The Mississippi River ran freely, making travel dangerous, due to snags, large pieces of trees lodged in the river.

1884: The Mississippi River Commission had been founded in 1879 to improve navigation. Over the next decades, a series of levees were built which also alleviated flooding problems.
Today: The level of the Mississippi River and its banks are tightly controlled so that navigation is very safe and floods are less frequent.

Chapter 6

Character List

Adolphus: Huck's name when the King pretends to be the British brother of Peter Wilks.

Levi Bell: The lawyer who tries to ascertain the true heirs to the Wilks's fortune.

Rev. Elexander Blodgett: The false name the King uses when addressing Tim Collins, the young man bound for Orleans who tells the King everything about the Wilks family.

Boggs: A drunk man who insults Colonel Sherburn and is later killed by him. The action takes place in the same town where the Duke and the King put on their Shakespearean show.

Tim Collins: A young man who reveals the entire story about the Wilks's fortune to the King.

The Dauphin: See The King

Widow Douglas: The widow who takes Huck into her home and tries to "civilize" him. It is her home that he leaves when Pap kidnaps him and takes him to the log cabin.

The Duke: The younger of the two con men and the man who invents the Royal Nonesuch. He is later tarred and feathered in Pikesville.

Huckleberry Finn: The main character of the story. He runs away and travels down the Mississippi River on a raft with a runaway slave, Jim, as his companion.

Bob Grangerford Buck: A son of Col. Grangerford.

Grangerford: The youngest son of Col. Grangerford who becomes good friends with Huck but is later killed in the feud.

Miss Charlotte Grangerford: A daughter of Col. Grangerford.

Col. Grangerford: The father of the Grangerford house and the man who invites Huck to live with the family. He is killed in the feud.

Emmeline Grangerford: A daughter of the Grangerford's. She passed away before Huck's arrival, but used to create wonderful paintings and poetry.

Miss Sophia Grangerford: The daughter of Col. Grangerford who runs off with Harney Shepherdson and rekindles the feud.

Tom Grangerford: The eldest son of the Grangerford family.

Buck Harkness: The man who starts rallying a mob to kill Colonel Sherburn after Sherburn shoots and kills Boggs.

Joe Harper: A member of Tom's robber band.

George Jackson: The false name Huck uses when he lives with the Grangerford's.

Jim: A runaway slave who accompanies Huck Finn down the Mississippi River.

The King: The elder of the two con men with whom Huck is forced to travel. He plays the naked man in the Royal Nonesuch and is the man who sells Jim as a runaway slave. He is later tarred and feathered along with the Duke.

Mrs. Judith Loftus: The woman whom Huck visits to gather news while pretending to be a girl. She tells him that she suspects Jim is hiding on Jackson's Island. Huck barely has time to get back to Jim and get them both off the island.

Sally Phelps: Tom Sawyer's aunt. She is married to Silas Phelps and initially mistakes Huck for Tom Sawyer.

Silas Phelps: Tom Sawyer's uncle, and the farmer who purchases Jim from the King for forty dollars.

Aunt Polly: Tom's aunt who shows up at the end to find out what tricks Tom has been playing on her kinfolk. She reveals the true identities of Tom and Huck to her sister and spoils their attempt to steal Jim out of slavery by explaining he is already free.

Doctor Robinson: The only man who recognizes that the King and Duke are frauds when they try to pretend to be British. He warns the town but they ignore him.

Ben Rogers: A member of Tom's robber band.

Sid Sawyer: Tom Sawyer's younger brother. Tom pretends

to be Sid while he and Huck Finn are living with Sally Phelps.

Tom Sawyer: Huck Finn's best friend. Tom loves make believe games and sets up a band of robbers. Later he and Huck live together with Tom's Aunt Sally and Huck pretends to be Tom while Tom pretends to be his younger brother Sid.

Harney Shepherdson: The young man who runs away with Miss Sophia Grangerford.

Colonel Sherburn: Colonel Sherburn

Judge Thatcher: An eminent citizen in the town who is respected and well-liked. He fights to protect Huck's money when Pap returns to claim Huck and steal his money.

Jim Turner: One of the robbers on the shipwrecked steamboat.

Miss Watson: The sister of the Widow Douglas. She tries to teach Huck how to read and write properly. Jim is her slave. He runs away from her after hearing that she wanted to sell him to a trader from down south.

Harvey Wilks: The British brother of Peter Wilks whom the King impersonates until the real Harvey Wilks arrives.

Joanna Wilks: The youngest daughter of the deceased George Wilks, she is distinguishable by her harelip.

Mary Jane Wilks: The eldest daughter of the deceased George Wilks, a red-headed girl whom Huck starts to fall in love with. She becomes convinced that the King is her real uncle and not a fraud until Huck tells her the truth.

Peter Wilks: The dead man whose brother the King impersonates.

Susan Wilks: The second eldest daughter of the deceased George Wilks.

William Wilks: The British brother of Peter Wilks whom the Duke impersonates until the real William Wilks arrives.

Pap: Huck's abusive, alcoholic, broke father who returns early in the book to claim custody over him. When Huck can no longer take his father's abuse, he runs away and begins his journey down the river with Jim.

Chapter 7

Analysis of Major Characters

Huck Finn

From the beginning of the novel, Twain makes it clear that Huck is a boy who comes from the lowest levels of white society. His father is a drunk and a ruffian who disappears for months on end. Huck himself is dirty and frequently homeless. Although the Widow Douglas attempts to "reform" Huck, he resists her attempts and maintains his independent ways. The community has failed to protect him from his father, and though the Widow finally gives Huck some of the schooling and religious training that he had missed, he has not been indoctrinated with social values in the same way a middle-class boy like Tom Sawyer has been. Huck's distance from mainstream society makes him skeptical of the world around him and the ideas it passes on to him.

Huck's instinctual distrust and his experiences as he travels down the river force him to question the things society has taught him. According to the law, Jim is Miss Watson's property, but according to Huck's sense of logic and fairness, it seems "right" to help Jim. Huck's natural intelligence and his willingness to think through a situation on its own merits lead him to some conclusions that are correct in their context but that would shock white society. For example, Huck discovers, when he and Jim meet a group of slave-hunters, that telling a lie is sometimes the right course of action.Because Huck is a child, the world seems new to him. Everything he encounters is an occasion for thought. Because of his background, however, he does more than just apply the rules that he has been taught—he creates his own rules. Yet Huck is not some kind of independent moral genius. He must still struggle with some of the preconceptions about blacks that society has ingrained in him, and at the end of the novel, he shows himself all too willing to follow Tom Sawyer's lead. But even these failures are part of what makes Huck appealing and sympathetic. He is only a boy, after all, and therefore fallible. Imperfect as he is, Huck represents what anyone is capable of becoming: a thinking, feeling human being rather than a mere cog in the machine of society.

Jim

Jim, Huck's companion as he travels down the river, is a man of remarkable intelligence and compassion. At first glance, Jim seems to be superstitious to the point of idiocy, but a careful reading of the time that Huck and Jim spend on Jackson's Island reveals that Jim's superstitions conceal a deep knowledge of the natural world and represent an alternate form of "truth" or intelligence. Moreover, Jim has one of the few healthy, functioning families in the novel. Although he has been separated from his wife and children, he misses them terribly, and it is only the thought of a permanent separation from them that motivates his criminal act of running away from Miss Watson. On the river, Jim becomes a surrogate father, as well as a friend, to Huck, taking care of him without being intrusive or smothering. He cooks for the boy and shelters him from some of the worst horrors that they encounter, including the sight of Pap's corpse, and, for a time, the news of his father's passing.

Some readers have criticized Jim as being too passive, but it is important to remember that he remains at the mercy of every other character in this novel, including even the poor, thirteen-year-old Huck, as the letter that Huck nearly sends to Miss Watson demonstrates. Like Huck, Jim is realistic about his situation and must find ways of accomplishing his goals without incurring the wrath of those who could turn him in. In this position, he is seldom able to act boldly or speak his mind. Nonetheless, despite these restrictions and constant fear,

Jim consistently acts as a noble human being and a loyal friend. In fact, Jim could be described as the only real adult in the novel, and the only one who provides a positive, respectable example for Huck to follow.

Tom Sawyer

Tom is the same age as Huck and his best friend. Whereas Huck's birth and upbringing have left him in poverty and on the margins of society, Tom has been raised in relative comfort. As a result, his beliefs are an unfortunate combination of what he has learned from the adults around him and the fanciful notions he has gleaned from reading romance and adventure novels. Tom believes in sticking strictly to "rules," most of which have more to do with style than with morality or anyone's welfare. Tom is thus the perfect foil for Huck: his rigid adherence to rules and precepts contrasts with Huck's tendency to question authority and think for himself.

Although Tom's escapades are often funny, they also show just how disturbingly and unthinkingly cruel society can be. Tom knows all along that Miss Watson has died and that Jim is now a free man, yet he is willing to allow Jim to remain a captive while he entertains himself with fantastic escape plans. Tom's plotting tortures not only Jim, but Aunt Sally and Uncle Silas as well. In the end, although he is just a boy like Huck and is appealing in his zest for adventure and his unconscious wittiness, Tom embodies what a young, well-to-do white man is raised to become in the society of his time: self-centered with dominion over all.

Chapter 8

Analysis of The Adventures of Huckleberry Finn

Plot Overview

The Adventures of Huckleberry Finn opens by familiarizing us with the events of the novel that preceded it, The Adventures of Tom Sawyer. Both novels are set in the town of St. Petersburg, Missouri, which lies on the banks of the Mississippi River. At the end of Tom Sawyer, Huckleberry Finn, a poor boy with a drunken bum for a father, and his friend Tom Sawyer, a middle-class boy with an imagination too active for his own good, found a robber's stash of gold. As a result of his adventure, Huck gained quite a bit of money, which the bank held for him in trust. Huck was adopted by the Widow Douglas, a kind but stifling woman who lives with her sister, the self-righteous Miss Watson.

As Huckleberry Finn opens, Huck is none too thrilled with his new life of cleanliness, manners, church, and school. However, he sticks it out at the bequest of Tom Sawyer, who tells him that in order to take part in Tom's new "robbers' gang," Huck must stay "respectable." All is well and good until Huck's brutish, drunken father, Pap, reappears in town and demands Huck's money. The local judge, Judge Thatcher, and the Widow try to get legal custody of Huck, but another well-intentioned new judge in town believes in the rights of Huck's natural father and even takes the old drunk into his own home in an attempt to reform him. This effort fails miserably, and Pap soon returns to his old ways. He hangs around town for several months, harassing his son, who in the meantime has learned to read and to tolerate the Widow's attempts to improve him. Finally, outraged when the Widow Douglas warns him to stay away from her house, Pap kidnaps Huck and holds him in a cabin across the river from St. Petersburg.

Whenever Pap goes out, he locks Huck in the cabin, and when he returns home drunk, he beats the boy. Tired of his confinement and fearing the beatings will worsen, Huck escapes from Pap by faking his own death, killing a pig and spreading its blood all over the cabin. Hiding on Jackson's Island in the middle of the Mississippi River, Huck watches the townspeople search the river for his body. After a few days on the island, he encounters Jim, one of Miss Watson's slaves. Jim has run away from Miss Watson after hearing her talk about selling him to a plantation down the river, where he would be treated horribly and separated from his wife and children. Huck and Jim team up, despite Huck's uncertainty about the legality or morality of helping a runaway slave. While they camp out on the island, a great storm causes the Mississippi to flood. Huck and Jim spy a log raft and a house floating past the island. They capture the raft and loot the house, finding in it the body of a man who has been shot. Jim refuses to let Huck see the dead man's face.

Although the island is blissful, Huck and Jim are forced to leave after Huck learns from a woman onshore that her husband has seen smoke coming from the island and believes that Jim is hiding out there. Huck also learns that a reward has been offered for Jim's capture. Huck and Jim start downriver on the raft, intending to leave it at the mouth of the Ohio River and proceed up that river by steamboat to the free states, where slavery is prohibited. Several days' travel takes them past St. Louis, and they have a close encounter with a gang of robbers on a wrecked steamboat. They manage to escape with the robbers' loot.

During a night of thick fog, Huck and Jim miss the mouth of the Ohio and encounter a group of men looking for escaped slaves. Huck has a brief moral crisis about concealing stolen "property"—Jim, after all, belongs to Miss Watson—but then lies to the men and tells them that his father is on the raft suffering from smallpox. Terrified of the disease, the men give Huck money and hurry away. Unable to backtrack to the mouth of the Ohio, Huck and Jim continue downriver. The next night, a steamboat slams into their raft, and Huck and Jim are separated.

Huck ends up in the home of the kindly Grangerfords, a family of Southern aristocrats locked in a bitter and silly feud with a neighboring clan, the Shepherdsons. The elopement of a Grangerford daughter with a Shepherdson son leads to a gun battle in which many in the families are killed. While Huck is caught up in the feud, Jim shows up with the repaired raft. Huck hurries to Jim's hiding place, and they take off down the river. A few days later, Huck and Jim rescue a pair of men who are being pursued by armed bandits. The men, clearly con artists, claim to be a displaced English duke (the duke) and the long-lost heir to the French throne (the dauphin). Powerless to tell two white adults to leave, Huck and Jim continue down the river with the pair of "aristocrats." The duke and the dauphin pull several scams in the small towns along the river. Coming into one town, they hear the story of a man, Peter Wilks, who has recently died and left much of his inheritance to his two brothers, who should be arriving from England any day. The duke and the dauphin enter the town pretending to be Wilks's brothers.

Wilks's three nieces welcome the con men and quickly set about liquidating the estate. A few townspeople become skeptical, and Huck, who grows to admire the Wilks sisters, decides to thwart the scam. He steals the dead Peter Wilks's gold from the duke and the dauphin but is forced to stash it in Wilks's coffin. Huck then reveals all to the eldest Wilks sister, Mary Jane. Huck's plan for exposing the duke and the dauphin is about to unfold when Wilks's real brothers arrive from England. The angry townspeople hold both sets of Wilks claimants, and the duke and the dauphin just barely escape in the ensuing confusion. Fortunately for the sisters, the gold is found. Unfortunately for Huck and Jim, the duke and the dauphin make it back to the raft just as Huck and Jim are pushing off. After a few more small scams, the duke and dauphin commit their worst crime yet: they sell Jim to a local farmer, telling him Jim is a runaway for whom a large reward is being offered. Huck finds out where Jim is being held and resolves to free him. At the house where Jim is a prisoner, a woman greets Huck excitedly and calls him "Tom."

As Huck quickly discovers, the people holding Jim are none other than Tom Sawyer's aunt and uncle, Silas and Sally Phelps. The Phelpses mistake Huck for Tom, who is due to arrive for a visit, and Huck goes along with their mistake. He intercepts Tom between the Phelps house and the steamboat dock, and Tom pretends to be his own younger brother, Sid. Tom hatches a wild plan to free Jim, adding all sorts of unnecessary obstacles even though Jim is only lightly secured. Huck is sure Tom's plan will get them all killed, but he complies nonetheless. After a seeming eternity of pointless preparation, during which the boys ransack the Phelps's house and make Aunt Sally miserable, they put the plan into action. Jim is freed, but a pursuer shoots Tom in the leg.

Huck is forced to get a doctor, and Jim sacrifices his freedom to nurse Tom. All are returned to the Phelps's house, where Jim ends up back in chains. When Tom wakes the next morning, he reveals that Jim has actually been a free man all along, as Miss Watson, who made a provision in her will to free Jim, died two months earlier. Tom had planned the entire escape idea all as a game and had intended to pay Jim for his troubles. Tom's Aunt Polly then shows up, identifying "Tom" and "Sid" as Huck and Tom. Jim tells Huck, who fears for his future—particularly that his father might reappear—that the body they found on the floating house off Jackson's Island had been Pap's. Aunt Sally then steps in and offers to adopt Huck, but Huck, who has had enough "sivilizing," announces his plan to set out for the West.

Critical Overview

When it was first published, responses to Adventures of Huckleberry Finn were fairly nonexistent until the Concord

Public Library in Massachusetts announced that it was banning the book from its shelves. This action set off a public debate over the merits of the book. The most vocal were those who deemed the book to be unsuitable for children, fearing their corruption by exposure to its lower-class hero. Howard G. Baetzhold reports that beloved children's author Louisa May Alcott said about the book, "if Mr. Clemens cannot think of something better to tell our pure-minded lads and lasses, he had best stop writing books for them." Critics who demanded that literature be uplifting cited rough language, lack of moral values, and a disrespectful stance towards authority as the book's faults. But some critics rallied behind the author and wrote reviews that praised the book as a lasting contribution to American literature.

These early reactions are a fair indication of how the book has been received ever since. On the one hand, respected scholars have claimed the book as the core text of an American literary canon, where it has enjoyed a secure position since the 1950s. As Leo Marx claims, "Everyone agrees that Huckleberry Finn is a masterpiece." H. L. Mencken went so far as to dub the novel "perhaps the greatest novel ever written in English." Although some have questioned the formal coherence of the novel, arguing that the ending and Tom's burlesque escapades disrupt the text's quest for freedom, the general consensus has emerged that The Adventures of Huckleberry Finn is one of the most important works of American fiction ever written.

But despite this resounding stamp of approval from the nation's leading literary scholars, secondary schools around the country have at various times questioned its suitability for students, even going so far as to ban the book. Whereas detractors of the novel from the previous century had been primarily concerned with its lack of decency and moral values, in the wake of the Civil Rights movement, the main concern of administrators, parents, and librarians has become that it promotes racism and demeans African American children with its extensive use of the word "nigger." Ultimately, the fear is that the complexity of the racial issues in the text may be too much for schoolchildren to comprehend. As Peaches Henry explains, "Parents fear that the more obvious aspects of Jim's depiction may over-shadow the more subtle uses to which they are put."

Although in the past there have been sharp contrasts between the responses of scholarly and lay readers of The Adventures of Huckleberry Finn, the debate over the book's racial messages has more recently become the cnetre of debate amongst literary scholars as well. The crux of the controversy is whether or not the novel presents an indictment of racism or simply reflects the generally accepted racist attitudes of the time period in which it was written. For most critics, the issue boils down to the depiction of Jim. For some, Jim is nothing more than a minstrel show stereotype, "the archetypal 'good nigger,' who lacks self-respect, dignity, and a sense of self separate from the one whites want him to have," in the words of Julius Lester. In these critics' eyes, Twain reveals his racism when he allows Tom to derail and hence belittle Jim's serious attempts to gain freedom and Huck's efforts to overturn society's view of blacks as property.

But to others, a subtle satire on slavery and racism emerges from the text and takes precedence over any stereotypical depictions of African-Americans. Eric Lott argues, for example, "Twain took up the American dilemma (of race) not by avoiding popular racial presentations but by inhabiting them so forcefully that he produced an immanent criticism of them." According to Lott, the use of minstrel show stereotypes, exaggerated and ridiculous depictions of whites's false perceptions of blacks, has the effect of "making nonsense out of America's racial structures." Many critics agree with Lott, seeing the novel itself as a critique of the racism expressed by its narrator, Huck.

For many critics, however, Twain's conscious intentions about racial messages are not the issue. They see instead a variety of perhaps unconscious effects in the novel that point to new ways to understand the text's complex evocation of America's racial predicament. For example, Forrest G. Robinson sees a depth to Jim that he thinks previous scholars have missed. Jim is both the stereotypical "darky" and the complex human being, wearing a mask of contentment and gullibility that represents the kind of prejudice whites have about him as an African American. But behind the mask, the real Jim is a shrewd agent in his own defence.

In essence, Robinson argues that whether Twain was aware of it or not, Jim is a complex African American character that reflects the situation of slaves at the time as they attempted to survive in a racist society. Such readings draw attention to the complex ways the novel addresses, in Robinson's words, "the nation's most painful and enduring dilemma." These readings accept Twain's ambivalence and contradictory responses to the issue, rather than attempting to vilify the author or insulate him from accusations of racism. In a related vein of argument, Peaches Henry declares that we may not be able to decide once and for all whether the novel is racist or subversive, but the book deserves our attention because "[t]he insolubility of the race question as regards Huckleberry Finn functions as a model of the fundamental racial ambiguity of the American mind-set."

Criticism

The Adventures of Huckleberry Finn has been a source of controversy since its publication in 1884. It was banned from many public libraries on its first appearance for being "trash." Although today it is widely regarded as a — if not the — classic American novel, it still poses problems for its readers. Huckleberry Finn has long been identified as expressing something essentially American: in the words of Bernard De Voto, "the novel derives from the folk and embodies their mode of thought more purely and more completely than any other ever written." In some ways, the debate about the Americanness of Huckleberry Finn reveals the larger struggle to define American identity. Those who first condemned the novel as being "trash" objected to it on grounds of both literary merit and racial, social, and economic class: they rejected its portrayal of a slave and an uneducated, poor boy as the most typical kind of American citizens. The opposite point of view, which celebrates the novel as an expression of the "folk," asserts its subject is the quintessential, or typical, American story: characters without social advantages trying to "make good." Twain creates the impression of American folk culture through his use of dialect and phonetic spelling, which mimics speech, rather than writing. As he points out in his opening notice to the reader, different characters use different dialects; in this world, where not everyone receives the same kind of education, people speak differently from one another. Many critics read Huckleberry Finn as a lesson in the way that identity is formed by social realities. They focus on the fact that Twain uses language to show that access to culture and education defines character. Depending on how you read it, the spoken language can either make characters more believable, complex, and therefore dignified, or it can make them seem merely uneducated, caricatured, and "backward."

Twain's attempt to capture the sounds of vernacular (local) speech is part of the novel's realism, part of its documentary quality. And yet, the novel also has elements of romance, which is the very opposite of realism. For instance, Twain relies on unbelievable coincidences in his plot, like the fact that the Phelpses just happen to be Tom Sawyer's relatives, and he just happens to be arriving on the same day that Huck comes to the farm. Twain manages to merge elements of these two kinds of writing by using a third literary tradition to structure his novel. This literary tradition is called the picaresque — the comedy of the road, the traveling adventure; only here, instead of on a road, the journey takes place on a river. The episodes along the river suggest that the Mississippi winds through a semi-wild frontier.

Twain makes the American landscape a site of endless adventures. The river, symbolizing both the power of nature and the inevitable passing of time, is what keeps the raft, and the story, moving. This picaresque framework, although it is usually associated with romance, makes the novel's realistic, documentary moments possible. As Huck and Jim move down the Mississippi, they encounter a diverse swath of American society. Huck gives firsthand descriptions of feuding families, a camp-meeting religious revival, a lynch mob, and other complex social phenomena. Twain connects the picaresque structure, which leaves room for endless variation and adventures, with the endless variation of America's inhabitants. As in his earlier novel, Life on the Mississippi, Twain draws on his own childhood experience and his knowledge as a river man to give the book its convincing details. Samuel Clemens even took his pseudonym, "Mark Twain," from his life on the river.

If Huckleberry Finn is the authentically American adventure story, it also explores one of America's most lasting problems: racism. Many critics have questioned Twain's portrayal of "the nigger Jim." Twain's consistent use of the word "nigger" is itself troubling to readers today. It is important to notice that Twain uses a great deal of irony in general, and that what Huck thinks is not the same thing that Twain thinks. There are two main questions here: does Twain simply use stereotypes? And if he does, does he do so in order to make those stereotypes seem true, or to show them as false and oversimplified? On the one hand, Jim's humanity makes him the novel's most appealing character. Jim fills a gap in Huck's life: he is the father that Pap is not; he teaches Huck about the world and how it works, and about friendship. But on the other hand, parts of Jim's character belong to a traditional stereotype of the "happy darky" — an imaginary portrayal of the slave as simple, childlike, and contented. Although Jim runs away, he does not strike the reader as overtly "rebellious" or dangerous. Jim never seems to suspect Huck's crisis of conscience about whether or not he should be helping a slave to escape. And, instead of being angry with Tom Sawyer for the trick he plays at the end of the novel, Jim is simply happy to take his forty dollars.

How we read Jim influences how we read the novel's primary structural "problem," its ending. One way of thinking about this problem is to ask whether Huckleberry Finn seems to go in a line, or in a circle. On the journey down the river, Huck learns that Jim has real feelings, recognizes his humanity, and vows not to play any more tricks on him. If the novel is a bildungsroman — a narrative about a character coming of age — this is the moment in which Huck learns his most valuable lesson. Huck seems to be traveling onward, in a line of development. But the ending chapters seem to circle us back into the childlike, irresponsible world of boyish adventure that Huck has supposedly left behind. The long and drawn out trick that Tom Sawyer plays on Jim makes the reader doubt if any real development has taken place.

Which side of the joke is Huck on? Even though he does not know that Jim has been freed, he lets Tom turn the escape into a game, and seems to feel little, if any, remorse for toying with Jim's fate. He seems to have forgotten what he learned about the importance of Jim's feelings. Finally, even though Jim is technically "free," he is not recognized as a man by the other characters, or by the larger social world he inhabits. Toni Morrison argues that the novel needs Jim's enslavement to make the other characters seem free by contrast. She explains, "freedom has no meaning to Huck or to the text without the specter of enslavement, the anodyne to individualism; the yardstick of absolute power over the life of another; the signed, marked, informning, and mutating presence of a black slave." At the end of the novel, for instance, Huck plans to "light out for the Territory" in search of more adventures. But Jim's wife and children are still slaves. Because of his racial identity in a racist society, Jim always remains more confined than Huck does.

Writing The Adventures of Huckleberry Finn took Mark Twain several years. He began the project as a sequel to The Adventures of Tom Sawyer, as another children's book. But as he wrote, it became more complex; it raises questions that make it a challenging book for readers of all ages. To understand the novel's complexity, one has to take its dual historical context into account. Twain locates the action in the past, before the civil war, and before the legal abolition of slavery. But much of the novel speaks to Twain's contemporary audience, who lived during Reconstruction, a time when the South especially was trying to deal with the effects of the Civil War. The "king" and "duke" owe something of their depiction to the post-Civil War stereotype of carpetbaggers (a derogatory stereotype of Northerners come to prey on the defeated South). Jim belongs, at least partially, to a postwar Vaudeville tradition of the "happy darky," played on stage by white men in blackface, who used a parodied version of black dialect. This popular stereotype conveyed a white nostalgia, and enacted an imaginary construction of the slave before Emancipation, before the "disappointments" of Reconstruction. Twain tries to come to terms with this nostalgia, but whether he critiques it, or indulges in it, is up for debate.

During his lifetime, Twain was best known for being a humorist, a user of irony and a writer of satire. In this novel, he uses Huck as a relatively naive narrator to make ironic observations about Southern culture and human nature in general. As usual, Twain finds a likely object of satire in religious fervor, in the cases both of Miss Watson and of the visit the "king" pays to the camp-meeting. But the irony in Huckleberry Finn exists at several levels of narration: sometimes Twain seems to aim his irony at Huck, while other times, Huck himself is an ironic and detached observer. For instance, when the rascally "king" and "duke" come aboard the raft, Huck tells the reader:

It didn't take me long to make up my mind that these liars warn't no kings nor dukes at all, but just low-down humbugs and frauds. But I never said nothing, never let on; kept it to myself; it's the best way; then you don't have no quarrels, and don't get into no trouble. If they wanted us to call them kings and dukes, I hadn't no objections, 'long as it would keep peace in the family; and it warn't no use to tell Jim, so I didn't tell him. If I never learnt nothing else out of Pap, I learnt that the best way to get along with his kind of people is to let them have their own way.

This passage ironically undercuts the way we think Huck has been relating to the two frauds; he does not, in fact, "feel right and kind towards" them. In fact, the connections among the foursome on the raft are extremely tenuous. Huck's choice of metaphor compounds the irony: he compares the two men to his father, and decides to think of them as part of his "family," throwing the whole notion of "family" into an ironic light. Huck thinks he can avoid "trouble" by pretending not to know that they are frauds, but trouble is all they bring. Huck's decision to "let them have their own way" is wishful, because he really has no choice. Finally, although Huck seems to condemn them, he recognizes them as liars partially because he is one himself — he tricks people out of money on more than one occasion. This passage explicitly reminds us that Huck can dissemble and pretend, just as Twain does in his writing. As readers of Huckleberry Finn, we are continually challenged to locate the multiple objects of the novel's satire.

Twain's irony complicates the question of race and racism in the world of Huckleberry Finn. What the novel make clear, though, as their journey continually separates and reunites Huck and Jim — white and black — is that their fate is intertwined. Their destinies must be worked out in relation to each other. For Twain, that is the great, and greatly troubled, American adventure.

Chapter 9

Short Summary

The Adventures of Huckleberry Finn is often considered Twain's greatest masterpiece. Combining his raw humour and startlingly mature material, Twain developed a novel that directly attacked many of the traditions the South held dear at the time of its publication. Huckleberry Finn is the main character, and through his eyes, the reader sees and judges the South, its faults, and its redeeming qualities. Huck's companion Jim, a runaway slave, provides friendship and protection while the two journey along the Mississippi on their raft. The novel opens with Huck telling his story. Briefly, he describes what he has experienced since, The Adventures of Tom Sawyer, which preceded this novel.

After Huck and Tom discovered twelve thousand dollars in treasure, Judge Thatcher invested the money for them. Huck was adopted by the Widow Douglas and Miss Watson, both of whom took pains to raise him properly. Dissatisfied with his new life, and wishing for the simplicity he used to know, Huck runs away. Tom Sawyer searches him out and convinces him to return home by promising to start a band of robbers. All the local young boys join Tom's band, using a hidden cave for their hideout and meeting place. However, many soon grow bored with their make-believe battles, and the band falls apart. Soon thereafter, Huck discovers footprints in the snow and recognizes them as his violent, abusive Pap's.

Huck realizes Pap, who Huck hasn't seen in a very long time, has returned to claim the money Huck found, and he quickly runs to Judge Thatcher to "sell" his share of the money for a "consideration" of a dollar. Pap catches Huck after leaving Judge Thatcher, forces him to hand over the dollar, and threatens to beat Huck if he ever goes to school again. Upon Pap's return, Judge Thatcher and the Widow try to gain court custody of Huck, but a new judge in town refuses to separate Huck from his father. Pap steals Huck away from the Widow's house and takes him to a log cabin. At first Huck enjoys the cabin life, but after receiving frequent beatings, he decides to escape. When Pap goes into town, Huck seizes the opportunity. He saws his way out of the log cabin, kills a pig, spreads the blood as if it were his own, takes a canoe, and floats downstream to Jackson's Island. Once there, he sets up camp and hides out.

A few days after arriving on the island, Huck stumbles upon a still smoldering campfire. Although slightly frightened, Huck decides to seek out his fellow inhabitant. The next day, he discovers Miss Watson's slave, Jim, is living on the island. After overhearing the Widow's plan to sell him to a slave trader, Jim ran away. Jim, along with the rest of the townspeople, thought Huck was dead and is frightened upon seeing him. Soon, the two share their escape stories and are happy to have a companion.

While Huck and Jim live on the island, the river rises significantly. At one point, an entire house floats past them as they stand near the shore. Huck and Jim climb aboard to see what they can salvage and find a dead man lying in the corner of the house. Jim goes over to inspect the body and realizes it is Pap, Huck's father. Jim keeps this information a secret. Soon afterwards, Huck returns to the town disguised as a girl in order to gather some news. While talking with a woman, he learns that both Jim and Pap are suspects in his murder. The woman then tells Huck that she believes Jim is hiding out on Jackson's Island. Upon hearing her suspicions, Huck immediately returns to Jim and together they flee the island to avoid discovery.

Using a large raft, they float downstream during the nights and hide along the shore during the days. In the middle of a strong thunderstorm, they see a steamboat that has crashed, and Huck convinces Jim to land on the boat. Together, they climb aboard and discover there are three thieves on the wreck, two of whom are debating whether to kill the third. Huck overhears this conversation, and he and Jim try to escape, only to find that their raft has come undone from its makeshift mooring. They manage to find the robbers' skiff and immediately take off. Within a short time, they see the wrecked steamship floating downstream, far enough below the waterline to have drowned everyone on board. Subsequently, they reclaim their original raft, and continue down the river with both the raft and the canoe.

As Jim and Huck continue floating downstream, they become close friends. Their goal is to reach Cairo, where they can take a steamship up the Ohio River and into the free states. However, during a dense fog, with Huck in the canoe and Jim in the raft, they are separated. When they find each other in the morning, it soon becomes clear that in the midst of the fog, they passed Cairo.

A few nights later, a steamboat runs over the raft, and forces Huck and Jim to jump overboard. Again, they are separated as they swim for their lives. Huck finds the shore and is immediately surrounded by dogs. After managing to escape, he is invited to live with a family called the Grangerford's. At the Grangerford home, Huck is treated well and discovers that Jim is hiding in a nearby swamp. Everything is peaceful until an old family feud between the Grangerford's and the Shepherdson's is rekindled. Within one day all the men in the Grangerford family are killed, including Huck's new best friend, Buck. Amid the chaos, Huck runs back to Jim, and together they start downriver again.

Further downstream, Huck rescues two humbugs known as the Duke and the King. Immediately, the two men take control of the raft and start to travel downstream, making money by cheating people in the various towns along the river. The Duke and the King develop a scam they call the Royal Nonesuch, which earns them over four hundred dollars. The scam involves getting all the men in the town to come to a show with promises of great entertainment. In the show, the King parades around naked for a few minutes. The men are too ashamed to admit to wasting their money, and tell everyone else that the show was phenomenal, thus making the following night's performance a success. On the third night, everyone returns plotting revenge, but the Duke and King manage to escape with all their ill gotten gains.

Further downriver, the two con men learn about a large inheritance meant for three recently orphaned girls. To steal the money, the men pretend to be the girls' British uncles. The girls are so happy to see their "uncles" that they do not realise they are being swindled. Meanwhile, the girls treat Huck so nicely that he vows to protect them from the con men's scheme. Huck sneaks into the King's room and steals the large bag of gold from the inheritance. He hides the gold in Peter Wilks's (the girls' father) coffin. Meanwhile, the humbugs spend their time liquidating the Wilks family property. At one point, Huck finds Mary Jane Wilks, the eldest of the girls, and sees that she is crying. He confesses the entire story to her. She is infuriated, but agrees to leave the house for a few days so Huck can escape.

Right after Mary Jane leaves, the real Wilks uncles arrive in town. However, because they lost their baggage on their voyage, they are unable to prove their identities. Thus, the town lawyer gathers all four men to determine who is lying. The King and the Duke fake their roles so well that there is no way to determine the truth. Finally, one of the real uncles says his brother Peter had a tattoo on his chest and challenges the King to identify it. In order to determine the truth, the townspeople decide to exhume the body. Upon digging up the grave, the townspeople discover the missing money Huck hid in the coffin. In the ensuing chaos, Huck runs straight back to the raft and he and Jim push off into the river. The Duke and King also escape and catch up to rejoin the raft.

Farther down the river, the King and Duke sell Jim into slavery, claiming he is a runaway slave from New Orleans. Huck decides to rescue Jim, and daringly walks up to the house where Jim is being kept. Luckily, the house is owned by none other than Tom Sawyer's Aunt Sally. Huck immediately pretends to be Tom. When the real Tom arrives, he pretends to be his younger brother, Sid Sawyer. Together, he and Huck contrive a plan to help Jim escape from his "prison," an outdoor shed. Tom, always the troublemaker, also makes Jim's life difficult by putting snakes and spiders into his room.

After a great deal of planning, the boys convince the town that a group of thieves is planning to steal Jim. That night, they collect Jim and start to run away. The local farmers follow them, shooting as they run after them. Huck, Jim, and Tom manage to escape, but Tom is shot in the leg. Huck returns to town to fetch a doctor, whom he sends to Tom and Jim's hiding place. The doctor returns with Tom on a stretcher and Jim in chains. Jim is treated badly until the doctor describes how Jim helped him take care of the boy. When Tom awakens, he demands that they let Jim go free.

At this point, Aunt Polly appears, having traveled all the way down the river. She realized something was very wrong after her sister wrote to her that both Tom and Sid had arrived. Aunt Polly tells them that Jim is indeed a free man, because the Widow had passed away and freed him in her will. Huck and Tom give Jim forty dollars for being such a good prisoner and letting them free him, while in fact he had been free for quite some time.

After this revelation, Jim tells Huck to stop worrying about his Pap and reveals that the dead man in the floating house was in fact Huck's father. Aunt Sally offers to adopt Huck, but he refuses on the grounds that he had tried that sort of lifestyle once before, and it didn't suit him. Huck concludes the novel stating he would never have undertaken the task of writing out his story in a book, had he known it would take so long to complete.

Chapter 10

Chapterwise Summary and Analysis of the Adventures of Huckleberry Finn

Summary and Analysis of Chapter 1 to Chapter 5

Summary: Chapter 1

The Adventures of Huckleberry Finn begins where the The Adventures of Tom Sawyer leaves off. At the end of the previous novel, Huck and Tom find a treasure of twelve thousand dollars, which they divide. Judge Thatcher takes their money and invests it in the bank at six percent interest, so that each boy earns a dollar a day on their money. Huck Finn moves in with the Widow Douglas, who has agreed to care for him.

Huckleberry Finn is the narrator of this story, and he starts off by describing his life to the reader. After moving in with the Widow Douglas, who buys him new clothes and begins teaching him the Bible. Huck is uncomfortable with all of these "restrictions" on his life, and soon runs away to avoid being "civilized". Tom Sawyer goes after Huck and convinces him to return to the Widow's house after promising that they will start a band of robbers together. Huck agrees to return, but still complains about having to wear new clothes and eat only when the dinner bell rings, something he was not used to while growing up with his Pap.

The Widow Douglas teaches Huck the Bible and forbids

him from smoking. Her attentions towards him are complemented by her sister, Miss Watson, who also lives in the house. Miss Watson is a spinster who decides that Huck must get an education. She tries to teach him spelling and lectures him on how to behave well so that he will be welcomed into heaven. Miss Watson warns Huck that if he does not change his ways, he will go to hell. Ironically, Huck finds the description of hell far more enticing and exciting than the description of heaven, and decides he would rather go to hell, but doesn't tell Miss Watson of his decision.

That night, Huck goes into his bedroom and lights a candle before falling asleep. He starts to feel very lonely and equates every night sound, including an owl, dog and whippowill, with death. At one point, Huck flicks a spider away, and accidentally burns it up in the candle flame, which he thinks is a very bad omen. Huck lies awake until midnight, at which time he hears a soft meow from below his window. The meow is a signal from Tom Sawyer, and Huck replies with a similar meow. He climbs out of the bedroom window and drops to the ground to meet his friend.

Chapter 2

While the boys are sneaking away, Huck trips over a root and makes a noise when he falls. Miss Watson's slave Jim hears the sound and comes outside to look around. Huck and Tom hunker down to hide, and Jim ends up sitting down right between them to wait to hear the sound again. At first, Huck thinks they will never get away, but Jim soon gets tired and falls asleep against a tree. While Jim sleeps, Tom wants to play a trick on him. He and Huck climb into the house and steal three candles, for which they leave a nickel as "pay".

Then Tom quietly makes his way to Jim, takes off Jim's hat, and places it on a tree branch above Jim's head. He soon returns and tells Huck what he did. After Jim wakes up, he believes he has been bewitched, and keeps the nickel as a token around his neck for the rest of his life. According to Huck, Jim tells all the other slaves that he had been ridden around the world by some witches, and that the nickel was given to him by the devil. Tom and Huck sneak down to the river and meet some of the other boys who are supposed to be members of Tom's robber band. Together, they steal a skiff and float down the river several miles to an area where Tom has discovered a cave. Tom shows the boys a hidden room in the cave which they make their robber headquarters.

Tom then reads them an oath that he has written, taken mostly from robber books and pirate stories. The boys argue over what Huck Finn's role in the gang will be, because Huck does not have a family for them to kill in case he reveals any of the gang's secrets. Huck finally offers them Miss Watson in place of his real parents, and the boys then sign an oath in blood to join the band. Tom is elected captain.

Tom explains that as robbers, they will only attack carriages and take the things inside. The men will be killed and the women will be brought back to the cave. He also mentions that they will ransom some of the people, because that is what they do in books, although he has no idea what "ransom" means. After that, all the boys agree to meet again soon. They return home exhausted and Huck climbs into bed having muddied up his new clothes, and feeling dead tired.

Chapter 3

The morning after his robber gang adventure, Huck receives a lecture from Miss Watson for dirtying his clothes. She takes him into a closet to pray, and tells him to pray every day so he will get what he wants. Huck tries to pray daily, but becomes disillusioned when all he gets is a fish-line with no hooks, when he prayed extra hard for hooks. When he asks Miss Watson about it, she tells him praying brings spiritual gifts. Unable to see any use for that sort of thing, Huck decides praying is probably not worth his time.

A drowned man is found in the river, and the townspeople believe is Huck's Pap. Huck is unconvinced after he hears the man was found floating on his back. He remarks that everyone knows dead men float face down, so this must have been a woman in man's clothing that looked like his Pap.

Tom Sawyer's robber band falls apart after a few weeks

because the boys get bored of pretending they are robbing people. The only real escapade is when they wreck a Sunday School picnic and chase some of elementary school children away. Tom pretends that during this 'battle' there were Arabs and elephants and that the boys were attacking a large army, but Huck is too practical to follow Tom's fantastical imaginations. When Huck asks why they could not see all the elephants, Tom explains that some magicians must have turned the whole army into a Sunday School picnic. Tom then tells Huck all about genies in bottles, and how the genies must obey whoever rubs the bottle. Huck gets an old lamp and tries to find a genie, but when it fails he decides that the genies were just another of Tom's lies.

Chapter 4

Huck spends the next three months living with the widow and getting acclimated to his new life. He starts to attend school and remarks, "I liked the old ways best, but I was getting so I liked the new ones, too."

Everything goes fairly well until one day when Huck accidentally overturns a salt-shaker at the breakfast table. Miss Watson does not let him throw any salt over his left shoulder (as a way of avoiding the bad luck), and as a result Huck starts to get worried that something bad will happen. As soon as Huck leaves the house, he notices boot prints in the fresh snow. Upon closer inspection he realizes that there is a cross on the left boot-heel, which he has only ever seen in his Pap's. Huck's Pap has returned. Aware that Pap is probably after his money (the $6,000 that he got from sharing the treasure with Tom), Huck goes to Judge Thatcher and begs the Judge to take all his money as a gift. The Judge is quite surprised by the request, but when Huck refuses to reveal why he wants to give away his money, Judge Thatcher agrees to "buy" it for one dollar, saying he will take the money "for a consideration." Huck, still quite worried over what is going to happen now that Pap has returned, goes to the Miss Watson's slave Jim for advice. Jim takes out a hair-ball in order to do some magic with it for Huck. When the hair-ball refuses to work properly, Jim suggest that Huck give it some money. Huck offers a counterfeit quarter, which Jim takes and places under the ball. Jim tells Huck that Pap is torn between two angels, a good white angel and a bad black angel. He also explains that Huck will have considerable pain in his life and at the same time considerable joy. Huck returns to his room that night and finds his Pap sitting there.

Chapter 5

Huck arrives back at his room and sees his Pap sitting in a chair. Huck describes Pap as a filthy, poor man who used to scare him a great deal. Now, however, Huck is no longer scared of Pap, and instead notes how old his father has grown.

Pap harasses Huck for wearing good clothes and going to school. He then accuses Huck of putting on airs and acting better than his own father. Pap remarks that no one in his family could ever read, and that he certainly does not want his son to be smarter than he is. He demands that Huck read him something, and soon becomes quite furious when he realizes that Huck is in fact able to read. Pap threatens to beat Huck if he ever catches him near the school again. He makes Huck hand over the dollar that Judge Thatcher "paid" him and then climbs out the window to go drinking in the town.

The next day, Pap goes to Judge Thatcher and tries to make the Judge give him Huck's money. The Judge refuses, and he and the widow take a case to court in an effort to get Huck legally placed with one of them. The custody judge is unfortunately new to the town and refuses to separate Huck from his father. Judge Thatcher, realizing he cannot win, gives Huck some money, which Huck immediately turns over to Pap. Pap gets extremely drunk and is placed in jail for a week.

The new judge then sympathetically takes Pap into his home, dresses him well, and tries to reform him. After thinking that he has reformed Pap, the Judge goes to bed. That night, Pap sneaks out of the new judge's house and buys some alcohol. By morning he is so drunk that he breaks his arm in two places and nearly freezes to death on the porch. The new judge is livid at this betrayal of his trust and comments that the only way to reform Pap is with a shotgun.

Analysis

The first sentence introduces Huck in a colloquial, friendly manner: "You don't know about me." From the very first words of the novel, Twain makes it clear that Huck is the narrator, and that the reader will hear the story of his adventures directly from him. In addition, to make it clear to readers unfamiliar with The Adventures of Tom Sawyer that this novel exists independently, Huck explains that if they haven't read Twain's earlier work, it "ain't no matter."

The Widow Douglas is an honorable woman who hopes to nurture Huck into a civilized child. Here, the reader immediately understands the main theme of the novel, the conflict between civilization and freedom. In agreement with Rousseau, Twain tends to suggest that civilization corrupts rather than improves human beings. For example, in the first chapter, Huck is forced to change his natural character into the mold the Widow Douglas demands from him. He feels cramped in new clothes, and hates being limited to eating dinner only when the dinner bell rings. Twain cleverly contrasts this new lifestyle with Huck's old way of life. For example, Huck compares eating dinner off a plate to eating from a "barrel of odds and ends," which implies a pig's slop bucket. Here, Twain explains that in his earlier life, Huck competed for food with pigs, but also notes that Huck enjoyed eating from the slop bucket more than eating from the plate. Huck's relationship with food is a prominent theme throughout the novel, and during his time on Jackson's Island and working his way down river, Huck revels in and enjoys his ad hoc dining.

In the first chapter, we observe Huck is ironically trapped in a "civilized" world, when he would prefer to live freely in nature. Irony appears in other areas of the novel as well. For example, Huck explains that the Widow Douglas wouldn't let him smoke, even though, ironically, she secretly uses snuff herself. Irony appears yet again when Miss Watson tries to warn Huck about hell. This warning is juxtaposed by her painful academic lessons. Huck finds spelling very difficult to learn and hates the lessons so much, that he remarks hell sounds more enjoyable. In this ironic reference, Twain reminds the reader of Huck's childhood innocence. Only a child would rationally choose hell over heaven.

Superstition permeates the novel. The first chapter provides several examples of Huck's superstitious side, specifically in his interpretation of the night sounds (as death), and in how he believes the spider burning to death in the flame of his candle is a serious omen of bad luck. After killing the spider, Huck immediately attempts a counter-charm, even though he knows there is no way of undoing bad luck.

Typically, Huck is a very sensible person, making his adherence to superstition slightly ironic. Huck is very logical and reasonable. For example, in determining that he would prefer heaven over hell after Miss Watson describes the two to him, Huck uses very logical reasoning that the reader can understand. Superstition, on the other hand, is completely irrational. Thus, when confronted by superstition Huck behaves contrary to his usual manner, perhaps a reminder that he is just a child, or an allusion to typical sensibilities of the time. Moreover, superstition symbolizes Huck's fear of the unknown; Huck is most superstitious whenever he is extremely worried about his future, such as in this opening chapter and later while on Jackson's Island. Superstition also serves to foreshadow events throughout the novel, as Huck knows the bad luck will return to haunt him. For example, after Huck accidentally brushes the spider into his candle flame, Pap returns to town.

This chapter serves to introduce the other boys in Huck's town. It is important to notice that although Huck Finn and Tom Sawyer are best friends, the other boys are more than willing to cut Huck out of Tom's gang. Understanding that Huck is not very popular helps explain his feelings of isolation in the town; the adults keep trying to "sivilize" him, and the other boys tend to ignore him.

Here, Twain interestingly juxtaposes theft and honour. These contradictory ideas are conveniently merged by Tom Sawyer, who logically explains to the other boys that robbery is honorable. Tom's definition appears to be complete nonsense. However, as the reader will see by the end of the book, this scene actually parallels the novel's ending, where Huck and Tom "steal" Jim out of slavery. Thus, Twain truly demonstrates how honour and robbery can coexist.

Tom Sawyer's gang can be viewed as a childish representation of society as a whole, an example of a synecdoche. Tom creates a set of rules, ideas, and morals that he expects the boys to adhere to, all of which he gets from books. Thus, books form a foundation for civilization; using books, Tom creates a society for his gang of friends. Ironically, Twain mocks the adult world in this chapter by showing that although the adult world relies on books such as the Bible to define civilization, pirate and robber books might also suffice.

Slavery is introduced in this chapter through Tom and Huck's interactions with Miss Watson's slave, Jim. As the novel progresses, slavery gradually becomes a larger issue. It is important to note Huck's views towards slavery at this point so that they may be compared to his views later on. In this chapter, Huck comments that Jim, "was most ruined, for a servant," thus demonstrating he supports the idea of slavery. Only later in the novel does Huck start to question whether Jim should be a servant at all.

Huck's rationality and literalness appear here. Twain goes to great lengths to show that Huck is a logical thinker who only believes what he can see with his own eyes. Thus, Tom's band becomes boring when all they do is attack turnip wagons and Sunday School picnics. Unlike Tom Sawyer, Huck is unable to make-believe that the picnic is really an Arab army. The same thing happens with respect to Huck's Pap; Huck decides that Pap cannot be dead because the dead person was floating on its back rather than its face, meaning that it must have been a woman.

This focus on rationality and literalness is used by Twain to further attack religion. Huck is told to pray for what he wants, but when he prays and does not get anything, he decides that praying is pointless. Huck also thinks about the Christian concept of always helping other people. When he realizes that Christianity seems to offer him no personal advantage in life, he quickly rejects it as quite pointless. Superstition appears again when Huck asks Jim to help him decide what to do about Pap. Jim uses a large hairball he believes to have magical abilities to help Huck.

This is the first time that Twain foreshadows the happenings of the rest of the novel. Jim mentions "two gals flyin'" around Huck's life, a light one and a dark one, a rich one and a poor one. This is of course a reference to Huck and to Jim, since Huck is rich and Jim is poor. Jim's comment that Huck should avoid the water will go unheeded when both of them end up running away downriver. Huck reinforces a split between what can be termed "natural learning" versus "book learning." He has been brought up with only "natural learning," such as how to survive in the wild. This can be contrasted with Tom Sawyer's "book learning," which has little actual application in Huck's life, and which Twain makes fun of by portraying the silliness of Tom's robber band. The usefulness of Huck's type of learning is constantly tested, for instance when he spots Pap's boot marks in the snow. This split between natural and book learning will be brought to a head when Huck encounters Pap directly.

Summary and Analysis of Chapter 6 to Chapter 10

Summary: Chapter 6

Pap begins hanging out around the town and demands Huck give him money every few days. When the widow tells Pap to get away from her property, he kidnaps Huck and takes him three miles upriver to a log cabin. Pap carefully locks the door and never leaves Huck's side without making sure that Huck cannot escape. Huck enjoys being free from school but soon gets upset that he is being beaten so much.

Searching for a way to escape, Huck discovers part of a saw that is missing its handle and starts to saw off a log in the rear corner of the cabin, but is forced to stop when Pap returns. Pap is drunk and makes Huck go outside and bring in all the supplies he has brought from town. Pap proceeds to drunkenly curse everyone he has ever met and spends a significant part of his tirade criticizing the government. Huck hopes to escape after Pap falls asleep, but Pap has a fitful night, and Huck is afraid he might wake up and catch him trying to get out of the cabin. At one point Pap jumps up thinking he is covered with snakes. Later, he dreams that the angel of death is after him and he starts to chase Huck around the cabin with a knife. Huck runs for his life and manages to survive after Pap falls asleep again. Huck then takes down the gun and holds it for protection.

Chapter 7

Pap and Huck go out into the woods to hunt for game. While there, Huck sees an abandoned canoe on the river and jumps in to get it. When he realizes that Pap did not see him snare the canoe, he hides it in a little stream for future use and returns to Pap. Next, Huck fetches a wooden raft from the river with timber that is worth about ten dollars. Pap locks Huck into the cabin and takes the raft to town in order to sell it. Taking advantage of Pap's absence, Huck quickly finishes his sawing and climbs out of the cabin, taking everything worth any money to his canoe. He axes down the front door and goes hunting for game. Huck shoots a wild pig, butchers it inside the cabin, and spreads the blood on his shirt and the floor. He also carefully lays some of his hairs on the now bloody ax to make it appear as if he has been killed.

Huck cuts open a sack of flour and marks a trail indicating that the killer left via a lake that does not connect to the river. Thus, he prevents anyone from searching along the river for anything more than his dead body. As Huck is finishing, a man appears nearby in a skiff. Huck recognizes that it is Pap returning early and that he is sobre. Immediately, Huck jumps into the canoe and pushes off. He floats downstream until he reaches Jackson's Island, a deserted stretch of land in the middle of the river. Huck ties up the canoe and satisfied with his work, settles down to get some sleep.

Chapter 8

Huck wakes up on Jackson's Island late the next day and

hears a cannon being fired. A ferryboat filled with his friends comes down the river firing a cannon in hopes of bringing his dead body to the surface. The search parties have also set loaves of bread filled with mercury afloat, believing the mercury and bread will be attracted to his body. Knowing the loaves will be floating around the area, Huck searches for one and enjoys eating it for lunch.

After a few days, Huck begins exploring the island. While following and hunting a large snake, he accidentally stumbles into a clearing with a still smoking campfire. Out of fear, he retreats to his campsite and paddles over to the Illinois side of the river. However, he soon returns for the night and sleeps poorly as he is overwhelmed with fear for who else might be inhabiting the island.

The next morning Huck decides to find out who else is on the island with him. He paddles his canoe down to the other campsite and hides in the brush. Soon he sees Jim, the slave Tom Sawyer played tricks on. Out of joy for finding a friend on the island, Huck rushes out and greets him. Jim nearly dies of fright when he sees Huck, whom he believes to be dead. Huck tells him the story about how he faked his murder. Jim relates that he overhead Miss Watson telling the widow that she was going to sell him down the river for a good sum of money. To avoid being sold, Jim ran away, and has been hiding out on Jackson's island. Jim starts to tell Huck about various superstitious signs which the slaves watch out for. When some birds go hopping along the ground, stopping every few feet, Jim comments that means it will rain soon. He also tells Huck a story about how he lost a large sum of money, fourteen dollars at the time, by speculating. First, Jim bought a cow that died, and then invested with another slave who was setting up a "bank." Unfortunately, the bank lost all its money and poor Jim had nothing left.

Chapter 9

Jim and Huck explore the island together and discover a cavern atop a hill in the middle of the island. They paddle their canoe to the base of the hill and then haul their equipment into the cave in order to keep it dry. The storm Jim predicted arrives that night, and the river rises for more than twelve days straight. Huck and Jim go out on the river at night to pick up drifting logs and other objects that happen to float downstream. One night, they capture a large raft which they will later use to navigate the river after they leave the island. Later on, they see a whole house floating downstream and climb into it to salvage some of the goods. Jim finds Huck's Pap lying dead on the floor of the house, but refuses to let Huck see the man's face and does not reveal that it is Pap. Jim sees Pap was shot in the back while obviously attempting to rob the house.

Chapter 10

Huck is thrilled with all the things they managed to get from the house and tells Jim that he wishes they could have fun like that more often. Huck is also still curious about the man in the house but Jim refuses to talk about him. Huck mentions that he thought they would have bad luck after he brought a snakeskin into the cave, not great luck like what they were having. Always superstitious, Jim warns Huck that the bad luck is still coming. Three days later, Huck tries to play a trick on Jim by leaving a curled up dead rattlesnake under Jim's blanket. But when Jim crawls into the bed he gets bitten in the ankle by the snake's mate. Huck kills the mate and sheepishly carries both snakes far away from the cave, embarrassed by the results of his behaviour. Jim takes the jug of Pap's whiskey and drinks himself into a drunken stupor to avoid feeling the pain of his swollen leg.

It takes Jim four entire days to recover from the bite and Huck vows to never touch a snakeskin with his hands again. In order to catch up on what is happening in the town, Huck dresses up as a girl and goes to the village. He stops at a house where he sees a woman knitting. Since she is new to the town, Huck figures he can talk to her without being recognized.

Analysis

These five chapters reveal a great deal about Huck as a

person. Huck emerges as a vibrant character who fights powerfully for his life. Huck's capture and escape from Pap demonstrate his genius for innovation, as does his ability to live alone on Jackson's Island. Huck does not need anyone's help to survive, and the only indication that he is not completely happy is his comment that he sometimes gets lonely.

Huck's personality is quite uniquely established throughout these chapters. He exhibits humility in that he constantly underplays his brilliant ideas. Thus, when he fakes his death, he says that even Tom Sawyer would have been proud of the charade, indicating that Tom would have been able to fake it better but that it was a good enough to earn some praise. The innocent side of Huck is also revealed in his encounter with Jim. Jim swears him to secrecy before revealing that he has run away from Miss Watson. Huck is immediately faced with the responsibility of protecting Jim or telling the town the truth. He chooses to stay with Jim because, as a young boy who has lived outside of main stream society for quite some time, he still lacks the prejudices of the older folks in his town. This youthfulness is reinforced by the image of Huck dressing up as a girl at the end of Chapter 10.

The strength of character that leads Huck to refuse to reveal Jim at this juncture of the novel is tested many times during the course of their travels. In a sense, it is Huck's desperate need to not be alone anymore that overcomes his fear of damnation for not turning in a runaway slave. While Tom Sawyer may be his best friend as a playmate, Huck seeks someone who will care about him as a person rather than as a simple play friend. While it is not at all clear that Jim will be able to assume this role, early indications lean towards the development of this relationship as Jim works to get Huck safely inside the cave and out of the rain.

Jim's motive for keeping Pap's death from Huck is unclear. Jim could simply be trying to protect Huck's feelings, but there is also very likely a selfish motive. Jim has just revealed to Huck that he ran away from the widow. Were he to tell Huck that Pap died, there would be no reason for Huck to remain with Jim on the island. Jim fears that Huck might at some point return to town and tell people where he is hiding. Thus, for Jim, it is a life and death decision whether or not to inform Huck of Pap's death.

Summary and Analysis of Chapter 11 to Chapter 15

Summary: Chapter 11

Dressed as a girl, Huck knocks on the door of the house. The woman lets him in, believing him to be a young girl. Huck inquires about the area, and the woman talks for over an hour about her problems. She finally gets to the news about Jim and Huck and tells him that there is a three hundred dollar bounty for capturing Jim. Apparently some of the townspeople believe that Jim killed Huck and ran away, while other people believe that Pap killed Huck. She tells Huck that she personally believes Jim is hiding out on Jackson's Island.

Huck becomes nervous at this news and picks up a needle and thread. He does such a poor job of threading the needle that the woman gets suspicious of his gender. Without Huck knowing he is being tested, the woman has him throw a piece of lead at a rat in order to judge his aim. Afterwards, she reveals where Huck went wrong with his "girl" behaviour and asks him what his real name is, telling him to be honest. Huck cleverly pretends to be an escaped apprentice hiding in women's clothes to avoid detection.

Huck is finally able to extricate himself from the woman and immediately returns to the island. He tells Jim to grab everything and put it in the canoe. Together they shove off, after piling their belongings onto the raft, which they then tow behind them.

Chapter 12

Jim and Huck spend the next few days traveling down the river. They improve the raft by building a wigwam, which will keep them dry and warm. Each night, Huck goes into a nearby town and buys more provisions for the next day. They only travel at night to avoid being seen and questioned.

One night, during a strong storm, they see a wrecked steamboat ahead of them. Huck convinces Jim to tie the raft to the boat and climb on board. They are surprised to hear voices, which Huck goes to investigate. There are three robbers on board, two of whom have tied up the third man. Apparently the bound man had threatened to turn them all in to the state. One of the robbers wants to kill him immediately, but the other man restrains him. The two men finally decide to kill their partner by leaving him on the boat and waiting until it sinks.

At this news, Huck scrambles back to rejoin Jim. Together they discover that their raft has come untied and floated away.

Chapter 13

Having lost their raft, Huck and Jim search along the crashed ferryboat for the robbers' skiff. Just as they find it, the two robbers emerge and place the goods they have looted into the skiff. The robbers then remember that their partner still has his share of the money, so they return to steal it from him. Before they can return back to the boat, Huck and Jim jump into the skiff, cut the rope, and speed away downstream. Before morning, they manage to find their raft again and recapture it.

Huck then goes ashore and finds a ferry night-watchman. To try to save the robbers, because he feels guilty leaving them for dead, he tells the man that his family ran into the wreck while traveling downriver and that they are stuck there. The man immediately gets his ferry moving to try and save them. However, before he gets very far, the wreck floats by, having come loose and sunk even further. Huck realizes that all three men aboard the wreck have surely drowned. Disappointed, but proud of his effort, Huck paddles downriver until he meets up with Jim. Together they sink the skiff and tie up to wait for daylight.

Chapter 14

Huck and Jim spend some time relaxing and discussing various things. Huck tells Jim all about kings and other aristocratic personages, and Jim is very impressed and interested. However, when Huck mentions King Solomon, Jim starts telling him that Solomon was one of the most foolish men who ever lived. Jim comments that any man who had as many wives as Solomon would go crazy, and that the notion of chopping a child in half in order to figure out which woman is the rightful mother is plain stupid. Jim remarks that the issue was about a whole child, not a half a child, and Solomon would have shown more respect for children if he had not had so many. Huck tries to explain the moral lesson Solomon was trying to teach, but Jim hears none of it. Next, Huck tries to explain to Jim that Frenchmen speak a different language. Jim is surprised by this and cannot understand why all men would not speak the same language. Huck tries to make the analogy that a cat and a cow do not speak the same language, so neither should an American and a Frenchman. Jim then points out that a cat and a cow are not the same species, but Frenchmen and Americans are. He concludes that Frenchmen should therefore speak the same language he does. At this point Huck gets frustrated and gives up trying to argue with Jim.

Chapter 15

Jim is hoping to reach Cairo, at the bottom of Illinois where the Ohio river merges with the Mississippi. From there, both he and Huck will be able to take a steamboat upriver and into the free states where Jim will finally be a free man.

As they approaching that section of the river, a dense fog arrives and blankets everything in a murky white. They land on the shore, but before Huck is able to tie up the raft, the raft pulls loose and starts floating downstream with Jim aboard. Huck jumps into the canoe and follows it, but soon loses sight of it in the fog. He and Jim spend several hours tracking each other by calling out, but a large island finally separates them and Huck is left all alone.

The next morning, Huck awakens and luckily manages to catch up with the raft. He finds Jim asleep and wakes him up. Jim is glad to see him, but Huck tries to play a trick on Jim by telling him that the events of the night before were just a dream. After some convincing, Jim starts to interpret the "dream." After some time, Huck finally points out the leaves and debris left from the night before, at which point Jim gets mad at Huck for playing such a mean trick on him. Huck feels terrible about what he did and apologizes to Jim.

Analysis

These chapters provide insight into Jim's character. Jim is sincere and trustworthy, but also stubborn and mature. The chapters test Jim's loyalty to Huck, and vice-versa. For the first time the novel is dealing with the issue of loyalty, which will later have a strong impact on each character's decisions.

Jim's sincerity is established in several ways. The most potent example is his joy at seeing Huck alive again after they are separated by the fog. Jim gets upset with Huck for tricking him into believing it was all a dream precisely because he had invested a great deal of emotional pain into the adventure. In this section, it becomes obvious that Jim would be willing to sacrifice a great deal to ensure Huck's safety.

The problem at this juncture of the novel is that Huck does not yet reciprocate Jim's feelings. Huck is not yet willing to sacrifice part of his life to ensure Jim's safety, and thus leads Jim from one adventure to another, be it on the wrecked steamboat or during the fog. This is important because it is Huck's loyalty to Jim that will be tested later.

The stubborn and mature side of Jim is evidenced by his arguments with Huck and his attitude towards adventures. Huck comments that once Jim gets and idea into his head it is impossible to change it, and proves this to the reader by discussing Jim's opinions of Solomon and Frenchmen. Jim's stubbornness can partially be traced to his maturity. He desperately wishes to avoid any adventures because adventures bring complications. Jim would be happiest if he were able to get to Cairo and take the steamboat upriver with no interruptions.

Twain is famous for his sense of irony, and this section contains several examples. His best use of irony concerns the three robbers on the wrecked steamboat. When Huck and Jim lose their raft, they need to steal the robbers' skiff. However, the robbers return before they can steal it. The robbers then decide that they want all of their money, including their partner's share, and thus head back into the steamboat. Huck and Jim immediately steal the skiff. The irony is two-fold: not only are the robbers "robbed," they are also condemned to die on the steamboat as a result of their greed. Huck attempts to have them rescued, but the river acts faster than he can, by dragging the wreck further and causing it to sink too far for anyone to survive. Thus, the robbers meet the fate they condemned their partner to, namely drowning.

Summary and Analysis of Chapter 16 to Chapter 20

Summary: Chapter 16

As Jim and Huck float downriver, Jim restlessly searches the riverbank for the town of Cairo. Each time Jim mentions how soon he will be free, Huck feels increasingly guilty. Huck knows that helping Jim escape is breaking the law, but Jim is also his friend. Thus, Huck is trapped in a difficult moral dilemma. After a great deal of reasoning, Huck realizes he will feel possibly even worse if he turned Jim into the authorities, and decides it would be best to let him escape.

Huck makes this decision spontaneously, when heading to shore to determine what town they are near and with the intention of reporting Jim. On his way to shore, Huck meets two white men searching for runaway slaves. The men ask him who else is on his raft and rather than telling them about Jim, Huck tells them his Pa, mother, and sister are aboard. Huck pretends to be eager for their help and tells them no one else has been willing to pull the raft to shore. At this news, the men become suspicious and finally conclude that Huck's family must have smallpox. Each man then puts a twenty dollar coin on a log and floats it over to Huck to avoid any interaction with him, but only after making him promise not to land anywhere near their town. Huck's ingenious lie fools the men and saves Jim from capture.

Huck and Jim are thrilled to have received so much extra money, which is enough for several trips up the river. They continue watching for Cairo, but are unable to locate it. After several days, both Huck and Jim begin to suspect that they passed Cairo in the fog several nights prior. The next night, Huck and Jim start to plan to use the canoe to paddle upriver. However, the canoe disappears, forcing them to continue downriver in hopes of buying a new canoe. While drifting downstream, they encounter an oncoming steamboat. Instead of getting out of their way as the steamboats usually do, the boat ploughs directly over the raft. Both Huck and Jim are forced to dive overboard. Huck emerges and grabs a piece of wood with which he paddles to the shore. Jim is nowhere to be seen. Huck is soon surrounded by dogs and stands dripping wet and immobilized.

Chapter 17

Huck knows better than to run when surrounded by dogs, and stands stock still. Within a few moments, a man calls out to him from the house telling him to be still. After several of the men in the house prepare their rifles, Huck is allowed to approach. He cautiously enters the house and when the family sees him, they immediately become friendly. Huck has happened upon the Grangerford household, which is in a drawn out and violent feud with the nearby Shepherdson family. When the Grangerford's recognize that Huck is no relation to the Shepherdson's, they welcome him with open arms. Huck tells the family that he is an orphan named George Jackson from down south who has lost everything, and arrived at their home after falling off of a steamboat. The Grangerford's offer him a place in their home and he agrees to stay.

The youngest son, Buck, is near to Huck's age and they soon become good friends. As Huck grows acclimated to his new home, he learns that the family had a younger daughter named Emmeline who passed away several years earlier. She was a talented poet and painter, and concentrated her work on eulogies for the dead. Huck thinks Emmeline's poetry is very beautiful and wishes that he could compose some lines devoted to Emmeline, but is unable to come up with anything. The family is quite wealthy considering their location. They own a fairly large house with nice furnishings and even have intellectual books in the parlor. Huck is happy to stay there, especially when he discovers their wonderful cooking.

Chapter 18

Huck introduces the reader to most of the Grangerford family. The father of the house is Colonel Grangerford, whom Huck describes as a powerful, well-respected and honored man. The family owns a considerable amount of land and over one hundred slaves, including a slave for each member of the household. The two eldest sons are Tom and Bob, and the youngest is Buck, with whom Huck becomes friends. There are two daughters: Miss Charlotte, who bears herself like her father, and Miss Sophia, who is timid and kind.

While out hunting one day, Huck and Buck hear a horse approaching behind them. Quickly, they run behind a bush and wait to see who arrives. Harvey Shepherdson passes by and Buck takes a shot at him, knocking off his hat. Harvey then follows the two boys into the woods but is unable to catch them. At this point, Buck explains the family feud to Huck. For over thirty years, the men in each family have been committed to killing off the men in the opposing family. No one remembers why the feud started, but several men have been killed each year. When the Grangerford's attend church, all the men carry guns with them, and ironically listen to preaching about brotherly love. After the service and once they have all returned home, Miss Sophia pulls Huck aside and urgently asks him to return to the church and fetch her Testament, which she accidentally left there. Huck does as he is asked and finds the book, but also sees a note that has been slipped into it which reads, "half past two."

Huck returns the Testament to Sophia, and promises that he did not read the note. When Huck goes outside, he realizes that his personal slave is following him very closely. which is unusual. The slave offers to show him some water moccasins, an offer which he had extended the day before as well. Huck realizes that the slave is speaking to him in some kind of code and that something else is going on. Huck agrees to follow him and in the swamp is surprised to find Jim asleep on the ground. Jim has the raft, which he completely repaired, and is waiting for Huck to rejoin him so they can continue their trip downriver. The next day Miss Sophia elopes with Harvey Shepherdson, and the feud is rekindled in full force. Buck's father and both his brothers are killed in an ambush, and Huck arrives at the harbor in time to see Buck and his cousin shooting at five grown men. Eventually the men manage to sneak around Buck and kill both the boys while Huck watches from a tree that he climbed in an attempt to find safety. Once the Shepherdson's have left, Huck pulls Buck and the other boy out of the river and onto dry land where he weeps and covers their faces.

Huck runs back to the house and sees that it is quite silent in the wake of the family tragedy. He goes to the swamp, finds Jim, who is glad to see that Huck lived through the massacre, and together they push the raft into the river and start floating downstream.

Chapter 19

Huck and Jim continue down the river for a few days, enjoying the fresh air and warm breezes. Huck finds a canoe and uses it to paddle up a stream about a mile in search of berries. Two men come running through the woods and beg him for help. Huck makes them cover their tracks and then all three paddle back to the river.

The two men are humbugs and frauds who were running away from townspeople who meant to tar and feather them. One man is about seventy and balding, and the other is in his thirties. The younger man specializes in printing and theater while the older man often "works" camp revivals. The younger man then tells them that he is actually the direct descendent of the Duke of Bridgewater and therefore is a Duke. Both Huck and Jim start to treat him as royalty and cater to his every need. This makes the older man jealous and so he then tells them that he is the Dauphin, or Louis the XVII. Huck and Jim treat both men as aristocracy, although Huck comments that it is pretty obvious neither is true royalty.

Chapter 20

Huck explains to the King and Duke that he is a farmer's son who has lost his father and brother. He tells them that Jim is the last slave the family owns and that he is traveling south to Orleans to live with his Uncle Ben. Huck also says that he and Jim travel at night because they keep getting harassed by people who think Jim is a runaway slave. The Duke tells him that he will figure out a way for them to travel during the daytime. That night, the Duke and King take over Huck and Jim's beds. A large storm causes the river to become choppy, and Huck watches for danger. Soon Jim takes over and Huck falls asleep until he is washed overboard by a large wave. Jim bursts out laughing at the sight of Huck flailing about in the water. The next day, the King and Duke brainstorm money making schemes. The Duke decides that they should put on a play where they perform short scenes from Shakespeare and the King agrees. After dinner, they go into a nearby town to see what luck will bring them. The men find the town deserted, as everyone has gone to a revival meeting. The Duke breaks into a printer's shop and takes orders from some farmers. He collects cash and promises to print advertisements in the paper. In his final project, he makes a handbill showing a runaway slave and describing Jim. He tells the others that this handbill will make it seem as if they are taking Jim back to collect the reward.

The King goes to the revival meeting with Huck and chances upon a crowd being listening to the preacher. The people get inflamed with the spirit of repentance, and in the middle of all their crying and yelling, the King jumps up onto the stage. He tells the audience that he was once a pirate in the Indian Ocean and that their meeting made him regret the actions of his former life. The King says that he would return to the Indian Ocean to convert his former colleagues, if only he had the money to do so. Immediately, a collection is taken up and the King leaves with over eighty-seven dollars.

Analysis

These chapters focus on social commentary of the people

and places along the Southern Mississippi. Each chapter introduces new characters and adventures that highlight particular prejudices or follies. Huck is also forced to play different roles as he tries to assimilate himself into each new situation. Through each of Huck's roles, the reader receives new insight into his personality and character. Twain offers social commentary in three separate escapades in the novel. First, two slave-hunters approach Huck's raft and Huck makes them believe his smallpox ridden family is aboard. Desperate to avoid the plague, each man forks over $20 just to keep the raft away from town. While disease is a valid concern, Twain demonstrates the fear with which people treat other sick people who need assistance and support. Rather than offering to help, the two men try to buy off the family and send them elsewhere.

Second, the Grangerford and Shepherdson families participate in a violent, tragic feud. In fact, the happenings reflect a modern day Romeo and Juliet theme, as a Grangerford daughter and Shepherdson son elope, causing a familial massacre. Ironically, the two lovers are the only ones that survive. Huck explains how civilized, wealthy and respected the Grangerford family is, but then shatters this image by detailing the feud's excessive and tragic killings. Here, Twain demonstrates the utter stupidity of even the most educated and respected families, who can destroy themselves through nonsensical behaviour and excessive pride.

The last escapade in occurs when the King bilks an entire congregation out of money. His story about being a pirate and wishing to convert his brethren is laughable and silly, but at the revival meeting, everyone is so overcome by the love of God and their fellow man that they believe him and donate to his cause. With this anecdote, Twain is commenting on the gullibility of religious zealots, which is consistent with his attack on religion in the very first pages of the novel, when Huck decides that praying and heaven as described by Miss Watson as lousy alternatives to having fun. Twain's view of religion is lucidly set forth in this and other novels, and he tends to express that devotion to religion is simply a waste of time. Throughout these chapters, Huck consistently assumes different characters and roles in order to survive and to protect Jim. At the Grangerford's, he pretends to be an orphan, to the slave-hunters he pretends to be an innocent boy living with a sick family, and to the Duke and Dauphin, he pretends to be an orphan traveling with his only slave. Each of these roles provides great insight into Huck's personality. When Buck is killed, Huck is deeply affected by the entire tragedy and even admits to crying upon pulling his friend's dead body out of the river. He wishes that he had not played a role in causing the death of so many people, and, at the same time, realizes how foolish the feud is. Remarkably, Huck constantly pretends to be less intelligent or less capable than he really is. It is easy to forget that he is only a boy of fourteen when he and Jim are floating down the river together. But, when they meet other people, Huck's interactions are always at a lower, less mature level. For instance, he tells the slave-hunters he is too weak to drag the raft ashore by himself, when in reality he has handled the raft alone many times. When he and Buck are together, he shows far more maturity than Buck, evidenced by his restraint in matters concerning the feud. Tom Sawyer also comes across as a young child in comparison to Huck's common sense approach to life.

Huck's interaction with the Duke and the King is at first puzzling and later annoying. He and Jim both are quite aware that the two men are con artists, forcing the reader to question why they put up with them. In fact, Huck is afraid of the consequences of crossing either man. He compares the men to Pap and remarks, "I learnt that the best way to get along with his kind of people is to let them have their own way." Thus, Huck and Jim realise that rather then stir up trouble with either of the men, it is best to play along and pretend they have been duped. Jim is unhappy with the situation, commenting at the end of Chapter 20 that he would prefer it if no more kings arrived during the trip. Huck seems to be considering a way out of the situation, but is unable to come up with a good plan. Partially, Huck enjoys watching the two men at work, since their actions create more of an adventure for him.

Summary and Analysis of Chapter 21 to Chapter 25

Summary: Chapter 21

The King and Duke turn their attention to performing scenes from Shakespeare. The King learns the lines for Juliet and practices sword-fighting with the Duke in order to perform part of Richard III. The Duke decides that a great encore would be for the King to perform Hamlet's soliloquy. Unfortunately, without the text at hand, the Duke must piece the famous lines together from memory. The end result is quite different from the true soliloquy, but still contains some elements of drama.

The men stop in a nearby town and decide to set up their show. They rent the courthouse for a night and print up bills proclaiming how wonderful the performance will be. Unfortunately, a circus is also in town, but they hope people will still attend their dramatic performances.

During the day of the show a man named Boggs rides into town. He is a drunk who comes in each month and threatens to kill a man, but never actually harms anyone. This time, he is after a Colonel Sherburn, the wealthiest man in town and a storeowner. Boggs stands outside the store and screams insults at the Colonel. The Colonel comes out of his store and tells Boggs that he will put up with the insults until one o'clock and after that he will kill him if Boggs utters even one word. Boggs continues relentlessly, and at exactly 1pm, the Colonel appears and kills Boggs on the spot. At that exact moment, Boggs's daughter approaches, hoping to save her father, but she is too late. After Boggs is laid to rest, the crowd turns into a mob and concludes that Sherburn should be lynched for the killing.

Chapter 22

The crowd travels to Sherburn's store and rips down the front fence. They halt when Sherburn emerges with a shotgun and calmly stands in front of them. He lectures the mob on how pathetic they are, tells them they are being led by half of a man, Buck Harkness, and calls them all cowards. When he finishes his speech, he cocks his gun and the crowd runs off in every direction. Huck leaves and goes to the circus which is in town until late that night, and after which the Duke and King plan to perform their show. He sneaks in and watches all the fun activities, such as the clown and showgirls. Huck then remarks that it is the best circus he has ever witnessed and the most fun. That night, the Shakespearean show is a disaster, with only twelve people showing up and none of them staying until the end. In response, the Duke prints up some new handbills touting a show titled the Royal Nonesuch. He then cleverly adds the line, "Ladies and Children Not Admitted" and comments that if such a line does not bring an audience, then he does not know Arkansas.

Chapter 23

The Royal Nonesuch opens to a house packed with men. The Duke greets them and hypes up the audience for the King. The King emerges completely naked, covered in paint, and crawling on all fours. The audience laughs their heads off, and he is called back to do it twice more. Then the Duke thanks them all and wishes them a good night.

The men are furious that the show is so short and realise they have been "sold," or cheated. But, before they can rush the stage in protest, one man stands up and tells them that they will be the laughingstocks of the town if it ever is revealed how badly they were cheated. They all agree to leave and tout the show for being wonderful so the rest of the town can be cheated as well. As a result, the next night's performance is also full, and the audience leaves just as angry. The third night, all the men show up, carrying rotten eggs, dead cats, and other foul items with them. The Duke pays a man to mind the door and he and Huck rush away to the raft. They immediately push out onto the river and the King emerges from the wigwam where he and Jim have been hiding all along. Together, the two con-artists made four hundred sixty-five dollars.

That night, Jim grieves over no longer being able to see his wife and children. Huck remarks that Jim cares almost as much about his family as a white person would. Jim then tells

Huck a story about when he was with his daughter, Elizabeth, one day. Jim told her to shut the door and she just stood there smiling at him. Jim got mad that she did not obey and yelled at her until he finally whacked her on the side of the head for not listening to him. Ten minutes later Jim returned and his daughter still had not closed the door. She was standing in the same place, crying. At that moment, a strong wind slammed the door behind her, causing Jim to jump. However, his daughter never moved an inch. Jim realized his poor daughter had lost her hearing. Jim tells Huck that he burst out crying upon making this realization and grabbed his daughter to give her a hug. Ever since, he has felt terrible about how he treated her.

Chapter 24

To avoid tying Jim up in ropes during the day (since he has been pretending to be a runaway slave), the Duke figures out a better solution. He paints Jim in blue and makes him wear a costume. Then, he writes a sign that reads, "Sick Arab - but harmless when not out of his head." Jim is happy that he can now move around.

The King and Huck cross the river and meet a young fool waiting for the ferry to Orleans. He proceeds to tell them all about how a Peter Wilks has died, leaving his whole estate to his daughters and brothers. The two brothers have not yet arrived from England, which greatly saddened the man before he died. The King takes a keen interest in the story and gathers every detail he can. Once he has all the details, the King gets the Duke and tells him the entire story. The two men agree to pretend to be Peter Wilks's brothers from Sheffield, England. Together, with Huck acting as a servant, they get a steamboat to take them to the town and drop them off. Their ploy works perfectly and when they hear that Peter is dead, both men put up a huge cry and lament. Huck remarks that, "It was enough to make a body ashamed of the human race."

Chapter 25

The two con artists are taken by the crowd that greeted

them upon arrival to visit the family, which consists of three orphaned girls: Mary Jane, Susan, and Joanna. Everyone exchanges hugs and cries, and then the King and Duke go to view the coffin. The two men burst out crying again, and finally the King makes a speech about how sad the whole situation is. They finish off by kissing all the women on the forehead and acting heartbroken. Huck comments that the whole scene is "disgusting."

The King and Duke discover they have received the bulk of the estate holdings as well as three thousand dollars cash. The three girls have also received three thousand dollars and the house they live in. Wilks's will tells them where in the cellar to find the cash, and the two men go downstairs and find it. The King and Duke count the money and come up four hundred and fifteen dollars short. To alleviate any suspicion, they add the money they made from the Royal Nonesuch to the pile. Then, to permanently win the town over to their side, they graciously give their share of the money to the three girls, knowing they can steal it back at anytime.

The King gives a speech and foolishly digresses. A Doctor Robinson enters the crowd, hears the King and laughs heartily, calling the King a fraud because his British accent is such a bad imitation. The townspeople rally around the King, who has been so generous, and defend him. The Doctor warns Mary Jane directly, but in response, she hands the bag of money to the King and tells him to invest it for her. The doctor warns them one final time of the mistakes they are making, and then departs.

Analysis

In these chapters, Twain again provides commentary on human nature and presents a scathing portrayal of society. Twain's 'version' of Shakespeare, Boggs's death, Jim's feelings about his family, and the Royal Nonesuch all seek to provoke the reader into analyzing the foolish ways of society. Huck assists in this encouragement by adding commentary that brings Twain's critiques into sharper focus.

The use of Shakespeare is at once funny and tragic. In

describing the butchered Hamlet's soliloquy, it is immediately obvious that the Duke has muddled the lines. Moreover, the vision of the King, with his white hair and whiskers, playing fair Juliet makes even more of a mockery of the plays. Boggs's death focuses the reader's attention on a much more serious aspect of the society. Boggs is shot to death in front of a crowd of people, including his daughter. The disrespect Boggs showed to Colonel Sherburn hardly justifies murder. Twain further derides the society for is cowardly actions, as the mob ready to lynch Sherburn is easily manipulated and succumbs to cowardice. Twain also makes several pointed comments about the general attitude towards blacks when Jim discusses his family. Huck comments that he is surprised to find that Jim is almost as concerned about his family as a white person. This prevailing attitude, often invoked to justify breaking up slave families, is something Huck is beginning to overcome. Jim's touching story about his daughter Elizabeth, in which he hits her for not obeying him, is a powerful indication to Huck that Jim is in fact more concerned about his children than Huck's father ever was about him.

The Royal Nonesuch is perhaps Twain's most brilliant philosophical creation, a show in which the audience sees exactly what it pays for: nothing. Not only does the title accurately describe the show, but Twain cleverly has the Duke and King add the line, "Ladies and Children Not Admitted." Thus the show comments on human nature, namely that we cannot imagine a show being about nothing, even when the very title states it. The men are further fooled into thinking the Nonesuch must be some great, sexual thing, since their wives are excluded. Moreover, to avoid embarrassment, the duped men then talk up the show to their friends. Again, Twain gives a scathing review of his fellow citizens by demonstrating how fragile human egos are. The final showing, which truly is non-existent since the Duke and King run off before it starts, is a coup for the two conmen, who once again give the citizens exactly what they pay for. One wonders whether it is possible to hold them guilty of a crime, considering that in reality, they were honest about the content of the show. However, the conmen's next adventure proves them highly despicable individuals. The Duke and King sink even lower in their abuse of human gullibility and nature by pretending to be the uncles of three orphaned girls in order to steal their inheritance. Huck's views on this scheme are clear, as he calls the King and Duke "disgusting" and remarks that he is "ashamed of the human race."

These chapters offer us a great deal of new insight into Huck Finn. He is obviously maturing in his views, as evidenced by his belief that black and white people are not so different. He is also changing from a boy who lacks firm morals to a man with a commitment to values. Thus, his commentary is no longer merely descriptive, but increasingly evaluative. It is becoming obvious that Huck will soon not be content to stand aside and let things slide past, as the metaphor of gliding down the river suggests. Instead, Huck will take a stand and assert himself as an individual. Huck's attitudes will eventually bear fruit in his actions, marking the final step in his journey towards maturity.

Summary and Analysis of Chapter 26 to Chapter 30

Summary: Chapter 26

The night of the doctor's warning, Joanna and Huck eat together, since they are the youngest two people present. She asks him all about England, and Huck lies to her in order to sound knowledgeable. She catches him in several of the lies, and Huck keeps pretending to choke on a chicken bone in order to think of a way out. Mary Jane overhears Joanna telling Huck that she does not believe him and makes Joanna apologize to Huck for being so rude. Huck decides he cannot let the King and Duke steal the money from these extremely kind girls.

Huck goes to the King's room and hides when he hears the Duke and King approaching. The conmen debate whether they should leave now that suspicion has been raised or wait until the rest of the property is sold off. They choose to stay and hide their money in the straw tick mattress. Huck steals the money immediately and waits until it is safe to slip downstairs to hide it.

Chapter 27

Huck is afraid he will be caught with the stolen money, so he hides it inside Peter Wilks's coffin. That day, the funeral service is held, and is interrupted by loud barking from a dog locked in the cellar. The undertaker goes to silence the dog, returns, and tells the audience the dog caught a rat. Huck remarks that the service was long and tiresome, but is relieved when Peter Wilks and the money are finally buried.

The King and Duke immediately begin selling everything they can, including the slave family owned by the household. To sell the slaves faster, they break up the family. The girls are extremely upset by this insensitivity. Many of the townspeople also expressed disapproval, but the men are not swayed. On the day of the auction, the King realizes the money is gone. He questions Huck, who cleverly blames the slaves who were sold. Both the Duke and King feel extremely foolish for selling the slaves at such low prices considering all their money is now lost.

Chapter 28

Later that morning, Huck sees Mary Jane sitting on her floor, crying while packing to go to England with her uncles. Mary Jane explains that she is upset about the slaves being so mistreated, and Huck blurts out that they will be together again in two weeks at the most, knowing the Duke and King will abandon the town. When he realizes he has slipped, he decides to tell her everything. She becomes furious as he relates the story, and when Huck finishes, she calls the King a "brute."

Huck makes Mary Jane leave the house and stay with a friend across the river. Before she leaves, he writes down where the money is located so she will be able to find it later on. Huck is afraid that if Mary Jane stays at the house, her face will give away Huck's indiscretion.

Huck tells her sisters that she is across the river trying to stir up interest in buying the house. After telling this part of the story to the reader, Huck remarks that he has never forgotten Mary Jane and still thinks she is one of the most beautiful girls he has ever met.

The auction occurs that afternoon and the King works hard to sell every last thing. In the middle of the auction, a steamboat lands, and two men claiming to be the real heirs to the Wilks's fortune disembark. As they approach the crowd, Huck notices that the elder man is speaking, and that the younger man's right arm is in a sling.

Chapter 29

The new heirs claim to have lost their baggage and are therefore unable to prove their identity. The King and Duke continue pretending to be the real heirs. Both groups are taken to the tavern where Levi Bell and Dr. Robinson grill them for information.

The first information revealed is that the Wilks money has been stolen, which looks bad for the King and Duke. However, they blame it on the slaves and continue pretending. The lawyer, Levi Bell, manages to get all three men to write a line for him. He pulls out some old letters and examines the handwriting, only to discover that none of three men had written the letters to Peter Wilks. The real Harvey Wilks explains that his brother had transcribed all his letters because his handwriting is so poor. Unfortunately, since his brother has a broken arm, he cannot write and therefore they cannot prove their case.

Harvey Wilks then remembers that his deceased brother had his initials tattooed on his chest and challenges the King to tell him what was on Peter's chest, assuming that the men who had laid his brother out would have seen the mark and will be able to determine who is lying. Refusing to give up, the King continues pretending and tells them Peter had a blue arrow tattooed on his chest. The men who laid out Peter Wilks cannot remember seeing anything, and thus they are forced to exhume the body.

The entire town travels to the gravesite. When they finally unearth and open the casket, they discover the gold Huck has hidden there. Immediately, the men holding the King and Duke let go to get a look at the money. At this opportunity, Huck, the King, and the Duke run to the river as fast as they can. Huck gets to the raft and takes off down the river, hoping to escape the two men. When the Duke and King catch up to him in a little skiff, he almost starts to cry.

Chapter 30

After the King boards the raft, he grabs Huck, shakes him, and yells at him for trying to get away and for escaping without waiting. The Duke finally intervenes and calls the King an "old idiot," asking, "Did you enquire for him when you got loose?"

Next, the King and Duke get into an argument about the money and start accusing each other of stealing the cash and hiding it, especially since they had added the proceeds of the Royal Nonesuch to the pot. The Duke finally physically attacks the King and forces him say that he took the money. Next, both men get drunk, but Huck notices the King never again admits to taking the money and rather denies it at every opportunity.

Analysis

These chapters mark Huck's first moments of maturity. Up until this point, he followed the authority of those around him, such as Pap, the Widow, Miss Watson, Judge Thatcher, and the King and Duke. The moment Huck decides to steal the money, he breaks free of this authority. For the first time, Huck acts on his convictions and morals to help other people, rather than simply acting on his personal desires.

Huck's interaction with Mary Jane also highlights an emerging aspect of his growth, namely an interest in women. In The Adventures of Tom Sawyer, Huck viewed girls as nothing more than an annoyance and did not believe they were to be taken seriously. Here, in contrast, Huck calls Mary Jane beautiful, and comments that when he saw her light a candle in the window, his "heart swelled up sudden, like to burst."

In addition, it is notable that Huck is desperate to escape

the King and the Duke by the end of the Wilks ordeal. Huck is not simply scared of them (when he first meets them he compares them to his Pap), but is truly attempting to break free from the authority and control that they hold over him.

Interestingly, Jim is not a part of these scenes. However, we do meet a slave family torn apart by the King and Duke. Twain places this scene directly after Jim's emotionally charged story of his daughter's hearing loss and their subsequent separation, a very purposeful choice. Twain was vehemently opposed to slavery, and abhorred this aspect of the institution. Thus, Twain is trying to subconsciously influence his reader every step of the way by directing their emotions towards sympathy for the slaves. In observing the fate of this slave family, the reader begins to more powerfully grasp Jim's reasons for running away.

Summary and Analysis of Chapter 31 to Chapter 35

Summary: Chapter 31

The Duke and King spend a few days plotting how to recover their fortunes. Soon, they reach a village named Pikesville. The King leaves and tells the Duke and Huck to follow him if he does not return by midday. After he fails to reappear, they go to find him, leaving Jim with the raft. Huck and the Duke search for quite some time, and finally find the King in a tavern. Soon, both the Duke and King are drunk.

Huck sees his chance and runs straight back to the raft, but when he arrives Jim is gone. A young man on the road tells him Jim, a runaway slave, was just captured and sold to the Phelps family, down the road. Huck realizes that in an effort to make some money, the King had snuck back to the raft while he and the Duke had been searching for him, took Jim, sold him for forty dollars, and returned to the town to drink.

Huck sits down and contemplates his next move. He is torn between his friendship for Jim and his belief that helping a runaway slave is a sin. Huck finally writes a letter to Miss Watson explaining where Jim is. Not quite satisfied, he thinks about it some more, and, in one of the most dramatic scenes in the novel, rips apart the letter saying, "All right, then, I'll go to hell!"

Huck starts walking to the Phelps's farm, but encounters the Duke along the way. The Duke is posting advertisements for the Royal Nonesuch, which the two men are planning to perform again. When he sees Huck, the Duke gets extremely nasty and is afraid Huck will warn the townspeople. Next, he lies to Huck and tells him Jim was sold to a farm several days away and threatens Huck in order to keep him silent. Huck promises not to say a word, and hopes he will never have to deal with men such as the Duke and King ever again.

Chapter 32

Huck decides to trust his luck, and walks directly up to the front door of the Phelps's farm. He is quickly surrounded by about fifteen hound dogs, which scatter when a large black woman chases them away. Aunt Sally emerges and hugs Huck, saying "It's you, at last! - ain't it?" Entirely surprised, Huck merely mutters "yes'm."

Aunt Sally drags Huck into the house and starts to ask him why he is so late. Not sure how to respond, Huck says the steamboat blew a cylinder. The woman asks if anyone was hurt, to which Huck replies, "No'm, killed a nigger." Before he has a chance to answer any more questions, Silas Phelps returns home after picking up his nephew at the wharf. Aunt Sally hides Huck, pretends he is not there, then drags him out and surprises Silas. Silas does not recognize Huck until Aunt Sally announces, "It's Tom Sawyer!" Huck nearly faints from joy when he hears his friend's name and realizes Aunt Sally is Tom's aunt.

Over the next two hours, Huck tells the family all about the Sawyer's and entertains them with stories. Soon, he hears a steamboat coming down the river, and realizes Tom is probably on the boat, since the family was expecting him. Eager to meet his friend and keep himself safe, Huck tells Aunt Sally and Silas that he must return to town to fetch his baggage, quickly explaining they need not accompany him.

Chapter 33

Huck meets Tom Sawyer on the road and stops his carriage. Tom is frightened, thinking Huck is a ghost, but Huck reassures him and they settle down to catch up. Huck tells Tom what has happened at the Phelps's, and Tom thinks about how they should proceed. He tells Huck to return to the farm with his suitcase, while Tom returns to town and begins his trip to the Phelps's again.

Huck arrives back at the Phelps house, and soon thereafter, Tom arrives. The family is excited because they do not get very many visitors, so they make Tom welcome. Tom makes up a story about his hometown and then suddenly and impudently kisses Aunt Sally right on the mouth. Shocked at his behaviour, she nearly hits him over the head with her spinning stick, until Tom reveals that he is Sid Sawyer, Tom's brother. Next, Silas tells the family that their new slave Jim warned him about the Royal Nonesuch, and that he took it upon himself to inform the rest of the town. Silas figures the two cheats Jim spoke of will be ridden out of town that night. In a last minute attempt to warn the Duke and King, Huck and Tom climb out of their windows, but they are too late. They see the two men being paraded through the street covered in tar and feathers. Observing the scene, Huck remarks that human beings can be awfully cruel to one another.

Chapter 34

Tom and Huck brainstorm ways to break Jim out of his prison. Huck plans to get the raft, steal the key to the padlock, unlock the door and then float down the river some more. Tom claims that plan is too simple and would work too well. Tom's plan is much more elaborate and stylish, and takes a great deal longer to implement. The boys go to the hut where Jim is being kept and search around. Finally, Tom decides that the best way, or at least the way that will take the longest, is to dig a hole for Jim to climb out of. The next day, he and Huck follow the black man who is delivering Jim's food. Jim recognizes Huck and Tom and calls them by name, but both boys pretend not to hear. When he has a chance, Tom tells Jim that they are going to dig him out. Jim is so happy he grabs Tom's hand and shakes it.

Chapter 35

To create as fantastical a story and game as possible, Tom tries to determine how to make Jim into a real prisoner before his daring escape. He decides that he and Huck will have to saw off the leg of Jim's bed in order to free the chain, send him a knotted ladder made of sheets, give him a shirt to keep a journal on, and get him some tin plates to write messages on and throw out the window. To top it off, Tom tells Huck that they will use case-knives to dig Jim out, rather than the much quicker and more appropriate picks and shovels.

Analysis

This section of the novel dramatically forces Huck to finally decide what he believes about slavery, and, as such, solidify his own morality. The most powerful scene occurs when Huck writes a letter to Miss Watson explaining where Jim is, only to tear it up, accept his fate no matter what the consequence of following his conscience, and set out to free Jim. Huck is willing to sacrifice his soul for Jim's freedom, showing a tremendous amount of personal growth. This scene indicates how his relationship with Jim has changed over the course of the journey downriver, from companion, to respected friend, to the only family Huck will acknowledge. Huck decides to free Jim after remembering all the times Jim protected and cared for him, something which no one else has ever done for Huck.

Therefore, there is bitter irony in Huck's story about the steamship cylinder exploding. Huck concocts the tale as an excuse for arriving in town so much later than expected, and when asked if anyone was hurt, he replies "No'm, killed a nigger." Aunt Sally is relieved to hear that no white people where hurt or killed, and does not care that a black person died. In the beginning of the book, the reader could easily attribute racist attitudes to the culture and time, forgiving the speaker for his or her ignorance, but after being introduced to Jim, the reader is unable to maintain that distance. Thus, it is surprising to hear Huck make such a racist and hypocritical off handed comment, but perhaps he is simply speaking in a way he thinks Aunt Sally would relate.

In this section, Twain's writing style also returns to that of The Adventures of Tom Sawyer. Tom's return signifies that logical thinking will disappear, and an excessive sense of adventure and fantasy will take over. Huck quickly takes a backseat when Tom's unlimited creativity is released upon the Phelps home. Tom's willingness to steal a slave is surprising to Huck. It is somewhat of a surprise to the reader too, considering the long moral journey Huck experience to decide he would risk hell for his friend. Thus, Huck questions Tom's motives, and finally concludes it is simply Tom's juvenile love for adventure that is spurring him on. The reader must recognize this as a false assumption. Tom has never committed a true crime with serious moral repercussions, and is thus unlikely to do so now. As the reader discovers in later chapters, Tom knows that Jim is already free, although Jim is unaware. Therefore, Tom knows he and Huck aren't breaking the law, but keeps this information from Huck so he will continue to play the prisoner game.

Summary and Analysis of Chapter 36 to Chapter 40

Summary: Chapter 36

The next night, Tom and Huck sneak out and start digging with their case knives. They tire soon and their hands quickly develop blisters, but it seems they haven't accomplished anything. Tom finally sighs and agrees to use a pick and shovel, but only as long as they pretend to be using case knives. Huck agrees and tells Tom his head is getting "leveler" all the time. The next day, they steal some tin plates and a brass candlestick for Jim to write with. They also finish digging the hole and make it possible for Jim to crawl out. Jim wants to escape immediately, but Tom then tells Jim all about the little things he needs to do first, including writing in blood, throwing the tin plates out of the hut, etc. Jim thinks all of these ideas are a little crazy, but agrees to do it. Tom then convinces the man who brings Jim his food that Jim is bewitched and offers to heal him by baking a pie, in which he plans to conceal the sheet ladder.

Chapter 37

Aunt Sally notices that she has lost a sheet, a shirt, six candles, a spoon and a brass candlestick. Very confused by the strange disappearances, she becomes absolutely livid. Aunt Sally yells at poor Silas, who eventually discovers the missing spoon in his pocket, where Tom had placed it. He looks ashamed and promises her he has no idea how the spoon got into his pocket. Aunt Sally then yells at everyone to get away from her and let her get some peace and quiet. Tom decides that the only way to steal back the spoon is to confuse his poor Aunt Sally even further. Tom has Huck hide one of spoons while Aunt Sally counts them, and then Huck puts it back when Aunt Sally counts again. By the time she has finished counting, Aunt Sally has no idea exactly how many spoons she has, and Tom is able to take one without any more trouble. Tom then does the same thing with the sheet, by stealing one out of her closet and putting it on the clothesline, only to remove it the next day. The boys bake Jim a witches pie, in which they hide the rope. It takes them several hours to get it right because the pie is so large, but they finally succeed. The man who normally takes Jim his food takes the pie in to him, and Jim happily removes the rope.

Chapter 38

Tom designs a coat-of-arms for Jim to inscribe on the walls so as to permanently leave his mark on the prison cell. Next, Tom works out three mournful inscriptions and tells Jim he must carve them into a rock. Huck and Tom go to fetch an old grindstone for Jim to use as his rock, but it is too heavy for them to carry, so they are forced to allow Jim to leave his "prison" and come help them. Jim rolls the rock into the hut and sets to work on the inscriptions. Tom decides that Jim needs some cell companions, such as snakes and spiders. He tells Jim that he and Huck will find some for him, but Jim is vehemently opposed to the idea. Tom then tries to convince Jim to get a flower so he can water it with his tears. Jim replies that the flower would not last very long. Tom finally gets frustrated, and gives up for the night.

Chapter 39

Huck and Tom spend the next day catching creatures to live with Jim in his cell. They first gather about fifteen rats, but Aunt Sally's son frees them by accident and both Tom and Huck receive beatings for bringing rats into her house. Determined, the boys catch another fifteen rats, along with some spiders, caterpillars, frogs, and bugs. At the end of the day they gather some garter snakes and put them in a bag, but after dinner they discover all the snakes escaped in the house as well. Huck remarks that there was no shortage of snakes in the house for quite a while after that. Uncle Silas decides to start advertising Jim as a runaway slave in some of the local newspapers because he has failed to receive a reply to his earlier letters. Since the plantation to which he wrote never existed, it makes sense that he never received a reply. Tom figures out how to stop Silas, by planting anonymous letters that warn him off this plan of action. Tom and Huck first plant a letter reading, "Beware. Trouble is brewing. Keep a sharp lookout." The next night the boys tack up a letter containing a skull and crossbones, which they follow with a picture of a coffin. Tom plans a final coup by drafting a longer letter. Pretending to be a member of a gang of robbers who are planning to steal Jim from the family, he warns them that the gang will be coming late at night from the north to get Jim. The family is terribly frightened and does not know what to do.

Chapter 40

The letter has a strong effect, and over fifteen armed farmers are sitting in the house waiting for the robbers to come during the night of the escape. Huck is frightened for their safety when he slips out the window and tells Tom they must leave immediately or they will be shot. Tom gets very excited when he hears about how many people came to catch them. As Tom, Huck and Jim start to move away from the hut, Tom gets caught on the fence and his britches rip quite loudly. All three start to run, and the farmers shoot after them. When they get to a dark area, Huck, Jim, and Tom hide behind a bush and let the whole pack of farmers and dogs run past them.

Once safe, they proceed to where the raft is hidden and Tom tells Jim he is a free man again, and that he will always be a free man from now on. Jim thanks him and tells him it was a great escape plan. Tom then shows them where he got a bullet in the leg, but Jim is worried for Tom's health. Jim rips up one of the Duke's old shirts and ties up the leg with it.

Jim tells Tom that he is not going to move until they get a doctor there and make sure he is safe. Tom gets mad at both of them and yells, but Huck ignores him and gets the canoe ready to go to town. Tom makes him promise to blindfold the doctor before bringing him back to their hiding place.

Analysis

Most of the action in these chapters mirror Tom's humorous adventures in The Adventures of Tom Sawyer. There is a serious anti-slavery undercurrent, as Jim and Huck are concerned only with breaking Jim out of slavery, and don't understand that for Tom, this is all just a game.

In truth, these chapters provide a conclusion to Huck and Jim's journey downriver. Huck is reunited with Tom, and it is becoming clear that there will be happy ending for all. We have now departed from Huck's story and reentered the story of Tom and Huck, which is where the novel began. Once again, Tom is making the decisions, while Huck merely plays along, and Jim simply accepts. Interestingly, Tom is still the same boy he was when the reader last saw him in the earliest chapters of the novel. However, Huck has developed into a more mature, morally sound individual. Huck always thought Tom's make believe adventures were not worth the time or effort Tom put into them. But, here, he believes they are truly setting Jim free, and releasing him from the bonds of slavery. For Huck, this is one of the most serious and risky actions he has ever undertaken, but for Tom, it is all just a game.

Summary and Analysis of Chapter 41 to Chapter 43

Summary: Chapter 41

Huck returns to town and finds a doctor. Instead of allowing Huck to come along, the doctor makes Huck tell him where the raft is and takes the canoe out alone to find Tom and Jim. Huck falls asleep on a woodpile while waiting for him to return. When he wakes up, he is told the doctor has not yet returned.

Huck soon sees Silas, who is very glad Huck is not hurt. Together, they go to the post office, and Silas asks where Sid is. Huck makes up a story about Sid taking off to gather news about the events of the night. When they return home, Aunt Sally makes a fuss over Huck, but is glad he has returned. A large gathering is held at the house, and the women discuss how they think Jim must have been crazy due to Jim's grindstone inscriptions and the tools found in his hut, all of which Huck and Tom actually crafted. Aunt Sally is worried about Sid's whereabouts. Huck tells her the same tale he told Uncle Silas, but it does not set her mind at ease. During the night, Huck sneaks out several times and each time sees her sitting with a lit candle on the front porch, waiting for Sid's return. Huck feels very sorry for her and wishes he could tell her everything.

Chapter 42

The next day, the doctor appears, bringing Tom on a stretcher and Jim in chains. Tom is comatose due to a fever from the bullet wound, but is still alive. Aunt Sally takes him inside and immediately starts to care for him. Tom improves rapidly and is almost completely better by the next day. Huck goes into the bedroom to sit with Tom and see how he is doing. Aunt Sally walks in as well and while both of them are sitting there, Tom wakes up. He immediately starts to tell Aunt Sally about everything the two of them did and how they managed to help Jim escape. Aunt Sally cannot believe they were creating all of the trouble around her house. When Tom hears that Jim has been recaptured he shouts at them that they cannot chain Jim up anymore. He tells them that Jim has been free ever since Miss Watson died and freed him in her will. Apparently Miss Watson was so ashamed about planning to sell Jim that she felt it best to set him free.

At that moment Aunt Polly, Aunt Sally's sister, appears. Aunt Sally is so surprised that she rushes over to her sister to give her a hug. Aunt Polly proceeds to tell Aunt Sally that the boys masquerading as Tom and Sid are actually Huck and Tom. Embarrassed, the boys look quite sheepish. Aunt Polly only gets angry when she discovers that Tom has been stealing and hiding her letters. She also explains to Aunt Sally that in regards to Jim, Tom is correct. Miss Watson freed Jim in her will.

Chapter 43

Tom tells Huck he had planned for them to run all the way to the mouth of the Mississippi if they had managed to escape unharmed. Jim gets a positive reception in the house because of how well he cared for Tom when he was sick. Tom, feeling slightly guilty, gives Jim forty dollars for putting up with them the entire time and for being such a good prisoner. Jim turns to Huck and tells him he was right about being a rich man one day. Huck asks about his six thousand dollars, assuming Pap managed to take it all. However, Tom explains that Pap was never seen again after Huck disappeared. Finally, Jim reveals that the man he and Huck found dead in the floating house was in fact Pap, but Jim had not wanted Huck to see him. Huck ends the novel by announcing that Aunt Sally wants to adopt him now, so he needs to start planning on heading west since he tried to be civilized once before, and did not like it.

Analysis

There are several key facts revealed in the final chapters

that influence how the reader views each character. Tom announces that Jim is free, which reveals why Tom was willing to help Huck in what Huck thought was a true crime. Since Jim was already a free man, Tom was not breaking any laws and therefore thought the entire ordeal was a great adventure.

The second major revelation is that Pap is dead. Jim has known this for most of the journey, in fact since leaving Jackson's Island. However, Jim's motivation for hiding this secret from Huck is unclear. Perhaps Jim felt sorry for Huck and wanted to care for him since he was now an orphan. Or, perhaps Jim knew that if Huck found out Pap was dead, he would simply have returned to town and ended his runaway journey. Without Huck, Jim would have had a far more difficult journey downriver as a lone black man and runaway slave. Having developed a strong understanding of Jim's character, it seems most likely that Jim was motivated by kindness, but a selfish desire for Huck's companionship might also have played a role.

The ending appears to leave Huck almost exactly where he started. However, Huck has changed significantly during the course of his travels. Huck's comment that he needs to head west before they try to civilize is significant, because we know that Huck can act civilized when he needs to, as he survived well in his many extended stays at Southern family estates. In the beginning of the novel, Huck is a poor, simple, uneducated boy. However, by the conclusion of novel, Huck is a crafty, intelligent, wealthy young man who simply does not care to be a part of a boring middle-class lifestyle. Huck changes profoundly in the course of this novel, struggles with powerful moral issues, risks his life for those he cares about, and thrives in the process.

In addition, the depiction of black slaves changes dramatically in the course of the novel. At first, slaves are merely background characters, carrying out chores while white characters monopolize the plot. However, this changes with the introduction of Jim, and continues to develop even when Jim leaves the plot for brief periods. Thus, the King's forced break-up of the Wilks's slave family powerfully impacts the reader, whereas before getting to know Jim, it might not have been perceived as so significant. In addition to being a story about Huck's growth and maturation, and resulting freedom from his Pap, The Adeventures of Huckleberry Finn is also a story about Jim's journey towards freedom. By ending the novel with Jim becoming a free man, with money to his name, Twain provides a clear social commentary about the immorality of slavery.

The Adventures of Huckleberry Finn is Twain's literary masterpiece. To create this novel he first overcame the difficulty of writing in the first person from a young boy's perspective. The novel is also a testament to the various dialects and characteristics of the southern regions. Lastly, The Adventures of Huckleberry Finn is a story about freedom, as it deals with physical freedom for the slaves and spiritual freedom for both Jim and Huck. Few novels have approached the success of The Adventures of Huckleberry Finn in combining such serious issues with Twain's characteristically delightful humour.

Chapter 11

Irony in The Adventures of Huckleberry Finn

Dramatic

Chapter 9

"When we was ready to shove off we was a quarter of a mile below the island, and it was pretty broad day; so I made Jim lay down in the canoe and cover up with a quilt, because if he set up people could tell he was a nigger a good ways off."

Here, Huck incorrectly assumes that people can distinguish a black person from a white person from a significant distance. At this point, he still holds the belief that blacks are essentially different from whites.

Chapter 10

"His foot swelled up pretty big, and so did his leg; but by and by the drunk begun to come, and so I judged he was all right; but I'd druther been bit with a snake than pap's whisky."

Huck is inadvertently demonstrating how little he cares for his Pap, by saying he'd rather be bitten by a snake than be drunk off Pap's whisky.

Chapter 14

"...he judged it was all up with him anyway it could be fixed; for if he didn't get saved he would get drownded; and if he did get saved, whoever saved him would send him back home so as to get the reward, and then Miss Watson would sell him South, sure. Well, he was right; he was most always right; he had an uncommon level head for a nigger." -Pg. 81

Raised in Southern slave owning society, Huck joins in the common belief that blacks are less intelligent than whites. Therefore, he seems astonished that Jim has such a "level head".

Chapter 17

'I bet you can't spell my name,' says I.

'I bet you what you dare I can', says he.

'All right,' says I, 'go ahead.'

'G-e-o-r-g-e J-a-x-o-n-there now,' he says.

'Well,' says I, 'you done it, but I didn't think you could.

It ain't no slouch of a name to spell-right off without studying.'

I set down, private, because somebody might want me to spell it next, and so I wanted to be handy with it and rattle it off like I was used to it." -Pg. 103

Ironically, Buck misspells Huck's pseudonym, and Huck memorizes the misspelling in case someone asks him about it.

Chapter 18

"Each person had their own nigger to wait on them-Buck too. My nigger had a monstrous easy time, because I warn't used to having anybody do anything for me, but Buck's was on the jump most of the time." -Pg. 109

Most people in Huck's place would have loved having a personal servant, but Huck is uncomfortable, and refuses to take advantage of the man assigned to him. Although he does adhere to aspects of racism ingrained in him due to his upbringing, he has more respect for blacks than most Southerners of the time.

Chapter 19

..."we was always naked, day and night, whenever the mosquitoes would let us-the new clothes Buck's folks made for me was too good to be comfortable, and besides I didn't go much on clothes, nohow." -Pg. 121

Again, Huck is offered the chance to assimilate with mainstream society, but eschews it in favour of comfortable, free living.

Chapter 22

"The minute he was on, the horse begun to rip and tear and jump and cavort around...It warn't funny to me, though; I was all of a tremble to see his danger." Huck is the only person in the crowd with the sense to worry about the safety of the drunkard on the horse. Even though he's a runaway, Huck is morally superior and more aware than the common people who surround him in this scene.

Chapter 24

"He said it was a sight better than lying tied a couple of years every day, and trembling all over every time there was a sound." Jim is wearing clothes for which he is ridiculed as a freak, but to him, ridicule is far better than being tied up and left alone.

Chapter 25

"...every woman, nearly, went up to the girls, without saying a word, and kissed them, solemn, on the forehead, and then put their hand on their head, and looked up towards the sky, with the tears running down, and then busted out and went off sobbing and swabbing, and give the next woman a show. I never see anything so disgusting."

Huck seriously dislikes fake and contrived people, and the act these women are putting on frustrates him to no end. Although they are weeping, Huck is actually a more sensitive and honest person.

Chapter 28

"I says to myself, I reckon a body that ups and tells the truth when he is in a tight place is taking considerable many resks, though I ain't had no experience, and can't say for certain; but it looks so to me, anyway..."

Here, Huck is honest about his dishonesty.

Situational

Chapter 11

"'Some think old Finn done it himself... But before night they changed around and judged it was done by a runaway nigger named Jim.'" -Pg. 83

In this quote, Twain demonstrates that when crimes occurred, blacks were immediately blamed before whites.

Chapter 15

"We could sell the raft and get on a steamboat and go way up the Ohio amongst the free states, and then be out of trouble." Huck believes his and Jim's lives will be perfect if they are able to get down the river, but in reality, there's no way of knowing whether they might end up worse off than when they started.

Chapter 16

"There warn't nothing to do now but to look out sharp for the town, and not pass it without seeing it. He said he'd be mighty sure to see it, because he'd be a free man the minute he seen it, but if he missed it he'd be in a slave country again and no more show for freedom." -Pp. 91-92

Jim believes he will be free only if they land in Cairo, but in fact, he will still be oppressed by whites. Jim bases his self-worth on the dollar, and it seems that "freedom" is not a state of mind, but rather a state of the Union.

Verbal

Chapter 12

"'See? He'll be drownded, and won't have nobody to blame for it but his own self. I reckon that's a considerable sight better'n killin' of him. I'm unfavorable to killin' a man as long as you can git aroun' it; it ain't good sense, it ain't good morals. Ain't I right?'" This misguided man judges it a lesser crime to let a man drown than to kill him outright. Here, Twain satirizes the idiocy and cruelty of human society.

Chapter 20

"They asked us considerable many questions; wanted to know what we covered up the raft that way for, and laid by in the daytime instead of running-was Jim a runaway nigger? Says I: 'Goodness sakes, would a runaway nigger run south?'

No, they allowed he wouldn't."

Huck uses his own mistake to cover up their scheme. He wasn't intentionally going south; but had made a wrong turn.

Chapter 21

"This is the speech-I learned it, easy enough, while he was learning it to the king:

To be or not to be; that is the bare bodkin
That makes calamity of so long life;
For who would fardels bear..."

Huck, while being impressed to no end with the actors, has gotten the soliloquy entirely wrong, yet another demonstration of his inability to become a member of "civilized" society.

"Then at the bottom was the biggest line of all, which said: LADIES AND CHILDREN NOT ADMITTED 'There,' says he, 'if that line don't fetch them, I don't know Arkansaw!'

The duke recognizes and profits from the locals' ignorance and attraction to crass humour.

Chapter 23

"'But Huck, dese kings o' ourn is reglar rapscallions; dat's jist what dey is; dey's reglar rapscallions.'

'Well, that's what I'm a-saying; all kings is mostly rapscallions as fur as I can make out.'

'Is dat so?'

'You read about them once-you'll see. Look at Henry the Eight; this 'n' 's a Sunday-school Superintendent to him.'"

Huck is under the impression that all kings, or authority figures, for that matter, are corrupt and cruel because of a few examples that have supported this theory. Therefore, their "king's" actions seem minor in comparison to the massive corruption Huck expects.

Chapter 26

"'How is servants treated in England? Do they treat 'em better 'n we treat our niggers?'

'No! A servant ain't nobody there. They treat them worse than dogs.'"

At this point in America history, slaves were often treated worse than dogs. Throughout the novel, Huck is the only person to acknowledge this unfairness.

Chapter 29

"'Set down, my boy; I wouldn't strain myself if I was you. I reckon you ain't used to lying, it don't seem to come handy; what you want is practice. You do it pretty awkward.'" Throughout the novel, Huck has survived through lies and dishonesty. Here, he is in the middle of telling one lie when caught in another.

Chapter 30

"'But answer me only jest this one more-now don't get mad; didn't you have it in your mind to hook the money and hide it?' The duke never said nothing for a little bit; then he says: 'Well, I don't care if I did, I didn't do it, anyway. But you not only had it in mind to do it, but you done it.'"

The duke seems guilty about even wanting to commit the crime, while the king, who committed the act, is accusatory.

Themes, Motifs and Symbols

Themes

Themes are the fundamental and often universal ideas explored in a literary work.

Racism and Slavery

Although Twain wrote Huckleberry Finn two decades after the Emancipation Proclamation and the end of the Civil War, America—and especially the South—was still struggling with racism and the aftereffects of slavery. By the early 1880s, Reconstruction, the plan to put the United States back together after the war and integrate freed slaves into society, had hit shaky ground, although it had not yet failed outright. As Twain worked on his novel, race relations, which seemed to be on a positive path in the years following the Civil War, once again became strained. The imposition of Jim Crow laws, designed to limit the power of blacks in the South in a variety of indirect ways, brought the beginning of a new, insidious effort to oppress. The new racism of the South, less institutionalized and monolithic, was also more difficult to combat. Slavery could be outlawed, but when white Southerners enacted racist laws or policies under a professed motive of self-defence against newly freed blacks, far fewer people, Northern or Southern, saw the act as immoral and rushed to combat it.

Although Twain wrote the novel after slavery was abolished, he set it several decades earlier, when slavery was still a fact of life. But even by Twain's time, things had not necessarily gotten much better for blacks in the South. In this light, we might read Twain's depiction of slavery as an allegorical representation of the condition of blacks in the United States even after the abolition of slavery. Just as slavery places the noble and moral Jim under the control of white society, no matter how degraded that white society may be, so too did the insidious racism that arose near the end of Reconstruction oppress black men for illogical and hypocritical reasons. In Huckleberry Finn, Twain, by exposing the hypocrisy of slavery, demonstrates how racism distorts the oppressors as much as it does those who are oppressed. The result is a world of moral confusion, in which seemingly "good" white people such as Miss Watson and Sally Phelps express no concern about the injustice of slavery or the cruelty of separating Jim from his family.

Intellectual and Moral Education

By focusing on Huck's education, Huckleberry Finn fits into the tradition of the bildungsroman: a novel depicting an individual's maturation and development. As a poor, uneducated boy, for all intents and purposes an orphan, Huck distrusts the morals and precepts of the society that treats him as an outcast and fails to protect him from abuse. This apprehension about society, and his growing relationship with Jim, lead Huck to question many of the teachings that he has received, especially regarding race and slavery. More than once, we see Huck choose to "go to hell" rather than go along with the rules and follow what he has been taught. Huck bases these decisions on his experiences, his own sense of logic, and what his developing conscience tells him. On the raft, away from civilization, Huck is especially free from society's rules, able to make his own decisions without restriction. Through deep introspection, he comes to his own conclusions, unaffected by the accepted—and often hypocritical—rules and values of Southern culture. By the novel's end, Huck has learned to "read" the world around him, to distinguish good, bad, right, wrong, menace, friend, and so on. His moral development is sharply contrasted to the character of Tom Sawyer, who is influenced by a bizarre mix of adventure novels and Sunday-school teachings, which he combines to justify his outrageous and potentially harmful escapades.

The Hypocrisy of "Civilized" Society: When Huck plans to head west at the end of the novel in order to escape further "sivilizing," he is trying to avoid more than regular baths and mandatory school attendance. Throughout the novel, Twain depicts the society that surrounds Huck as little more than a collection of degraded rules and precepts that defy logic. This faulty logic appears early in the novel, when the new judge in town allows Pap to keep custody of Huck. The judge privileges Pap's "rights" to his son as his natural father over Huck's welfare. At the same time, this decision comments on a system that puts a white man's rights to his "property"—his slaves—over the welfare and freedom of a black man. In implicitly comparing the plight of slaves to the plight of Huck at the hands of Pap, Twain implies that it is impossible for a society that owns slaves to be just, no matter how "civilized" that society believes and proclaims itself to be.

Again and again, Huck encounters individuals who seem good—Sally Phelps, for example—but who Twain takes care to show are prejudiced slave-owners. This shaky sense of justice that Huck repeatedly encounters lies at the heart of society's problems: terrible acts go unpunished, yet frivolous crimes, such as drunkenly shouting insults, lead to executions. Sherburn's speech to the mob that has come to lynch him accurately summarizes the view of society Twain gives in Huckleberry Finn: rather than maintain collective welfare, society instead is marked by cowardice, a lack of logic, and profound selfishness.

Motifs

Motifs are recurring structures, contrasts, or literary devices that can help to develop and inform the text's major themes.

Childhood: Huck's youth is an important factor in his moral education over the course of the novel, for we sense that only a child is open-minded enough to undergo the kind of development that Huck does. Since Huck and Tom are young, their age lends a sense of play to their actions, which excuses them in certain ways and also deepens the novel's commentary on slavery and society. Ironically, Huck often knows better than the adults around him, even though he has lacked the guidance that a proper family and community should have offered him. Twain also frequently draws links between Huck's youth and Jim's status as a black man: both are vulnerable, yet Huck, because he is white, has power over Jim. And on a different level, the silliness, pure joy, and naïveté of childhood give Huckleberry Finn a sense of fun and humour. Though its themes are quite weighty, the novel itself feels light in tone and is an enjoyable read because of this rambunctious childhood excitement that enlivens the story.

Lies and Cons: Huckleberry Finn is full of malicious lies and scams, many of them coming from the duke and the dauphin. It is clear that these con men's lies are bad, for they hurt a number of innocent people. Yet Huck himself tells a number of lies and even cons a few people, most notably the slave-hunters, to whom he makes up a story about a smallpox outbreak in order to protect Jim. As Huck realizes, it seems that telling a lie can actually be a good thing, depending on its purpose. This insight is part of Huck's learning process, as he finds that some of the rules he has been taught contradict what seems to be "right." At other points, the lines between a con, legitimate entertainment, and approved social structures like religion are fine indeed. In this light, lies and cons provide an effective way for Twain to highlight the moral ambiguity that runs through the novel.

Superstitions and Folk Beliefs: From the time Huck meets him on Jackson's Island until the end of the novel, Jim spouts a wide range of superstitions and folktales. Whereas Jim initially appears foolish to believe so unwaveringly in these kinds of signs and omens, it turns out, curiously, that many of his beliefs do indeed have some basis in reality or presage events to come.

Much as we do, Huck at first dismisses most of Jim's superstitions as silly, but ultimately he comes to appreciate Jim's deep knowledge of the world. In this sense, Jim's superstition serves as an alternative to accepted social teachings and assumptions and provides a reminder that mainstream conventions are not always right.

Parodies of Popular Romance Novels: Huckleberry Finn is full of people who base their lives on romantic literary models and stereotypes of various kinds. Tom Sawyer, the most obvious example, bases his life and actions on adventure novels. The deceased Emmeline Grangerford painted weepy maidens and wrote poems about dead children in the romantic style. The Shepherdson and Grangerford families kill one another out of a bizarre, overexcited conception of family honour. These characters' proclivities toward the romantic allow Twain a few opportunities to indulge in some fun, and indeed, the episodes that deal with this subject are among the funniest in the novel. However, there is a more substantive message beneath: that popular literature is highly stylized and therefore rarely reflects the reality of a society. Twain shows how a strict adherence to these romantic ideals is ultimately dangerous: Tom is shot, Emmeline dies, and the Shepherdsons and Grangerfords end up in a deadly clash.

Symbols

Symbols are objects, characters, figures, or colors used to represent abstract ideas or concepts.

The Mississippi River

For Huck and Jim, the Mississippi River is the ultimate symbol of freedom. Alone on their raft, they do not have to answer to anyone. The river carries them toward freedom: for Jim, toward the free states; for Huck, away from his abusive father and the restrictive "sivilizing" of St. Petersburg. Much like the river itself, Huck and Jim are in flux, willing to change their attitudes about each other with little prompting. Despite their freedom, however, they soon find that they are not completely free from the evils and influences of the towns on the river's banks. Even early on, the real world intrudes on the paradise of the raft: the river floods, bringing Huck and Jim into contact with criminals, wrecks, and stolen goods. Then, a thick fog causes them to miss the mouth of the Ohio River, which was to be their route to freedom.

As the novel progresses, then, the river becomes something other than the inherently benevolent place Huck originally thought it was. As Huck and Jim move further south, the duke and the dauphin invade the raft, and Huck and Jim must spend more time ashore. Though the river continues to offer a refuge from trouble, it often merely effects the exchange of one bad situation for another. Each escape exists in the larger context of a continual drift southward, toward the Deep South and entrenched slavery. In this transition from idyllic retreat to source of peril, the river mirrors the complicated state of the South. As Huck and Jim's journey progresses, the river, which once seemed a paradise and a source of freedom, becomes merely a short-term means of escape that nonetheless pushes Huck and Jim ever further toward danger and destruction.

Chapter 12

Important Quotations Explained

The Widow Douglas she took me for her son, and allowed she would sivilize me; but it was rough living in the house all the time, considering how dismal regular and decent the widow was in all her ways; and so when I couldn't stand it no longer I lit out. I got into my old rags and my sugar-hogshead again, and was free and satisfied. But Tom Sawyer he hunted me up and said he was going to start a band of robbers, and I might join if I would go back to the widow and be respectable. So I went back.

In these lines, which appear on the first page of the novel, Huck discusses events that have occurred since the end of The Adventures of Tom Sawyer, the novel in which he made his first appearance. Here Huck, establishes his opposition to "sivilizing," which seems natural for a thirteen-year-old boy rebelling against his parents and other authorities. Our initial inclination may be to laugh and dismiss Huck's urges for freedom. At the same time, however, we see that Huck's problems with civilized society are based on some rather mature observations about the worth of that society. Huck goes on to associate civilization and respectability with a childish game—Tom's band of robbers, in which the participants are to pretend to be criminals. Under the influence of his friend, Huck gives in and returns to the Widow's, but as the novel progresses, his dislike for society reappears and influences the important decisions he makes.

I hadn't had a bite to eat since yesterday, so Jim he got out some corn-dodgers and buttermilk, and pork and cabbage and greens—there ain't nothing in the world so good when it's cooked right—and whilst I eat my supper we talked and had a good time.... We said there warn't no home like a raft, after all. Other places do seem so cramped up and smothery, but a raft don't. You feel mighty free and easy and comfortable on a raft.

At this point in Chapter XVIII, Huck has just escaped from the Grangerford-Shepherdson feud and is thoroughly sickened by society. Compared to the outrageous incidents onshore, the raft represents a retreat from the outside world, the site of simple pleasures and good companionship. Even the simple food Jim offers Huck is delicious in this atmosphere of freedom and comfort. Huck and Jim do not have to answer to anyone on the raft, and it represents a kind of utopian life for them. They try to maintain this idyllic separation from society and its problems, but as the raft makes its way southward, unsavory influences from onshore repeatedly invade the world of the raft. In a sense, Twain's portrayal of life on the raft and the river is a romantic one, but tempered by the realistic knowledge that the evils and problems of the world are inescapable.

It was a close place. I took... up [the letter I'd written to Miss Watson], and held it in my hand. I was a-trembling, because I'd got to decide, forever, betwixt two things, and I knowed it. I studied a minute, sort of holding my breath, and then says to myself: "All right then, I'll go to hell"—and tore it up. It was awful thoughts and awful words, but they was said. And I let them stay said; and never thought no more about reforming.

These lines from Chapter XXXI describe the moral climax of the novel. The duke and the dauphin have sold Jim, who is being held in the Phelpses' shed pending his return to his rightful owner. Thinking that life at home in St. Petersburg—even if it means Jim will still be a slave and Huck will be a captive of the Widow— would be better than his current state of peril far from home, Huck composes a letter to Miss Watson, telling her where Jim is. When Huck thinks of his friendship with Jim, however, and realizes that Jim will be sold down the river anyway, he decides to tear up the letter. The logical consequences of Huck's action, rather than the lessons society has taught him, drive Huck. He decides that going to "hell," if it means following his gut and not society's hypocritical and cruel principles, is a better option than going to everyone else's heaven. This moment of decision represents Huck's true break with the world around him. At this point, Huck decides to help Jim escape slavery once and for all. Huck also realizes that he does not want to reenter the "sivilized" world: after all his experiences and moral development on the river, he wants to move on to the freedom of the West instead.

Tom told me what his plan was, and I see in a minute it was worth fifteen of mine for style, and would make Jim just as free a man as mine would, and maybe get us all killed besides. So I was satisfied, and said we would waltz in on it.

In this quotation from Chapter XXXIV, we see Huck once again swayed by his friend Tom. Although in practical terms it would be quite simple to break Jim out of the shed, Tom insists on a more complicated plan with "style." Dependent on Tom not to blow his cover—at this point, Huck is pretending, for the benefit of the Phelpses, to be Tom, while Tom is pretending to be his brother Sid—Huck has to go along. Indeed, as we see, Tom's return in the final chapters of the novel temporarily stops or reverses Huck's development: Huck, in many ways, reverts to the status of Tom's follower that he occupied at the beginning of the novel. Nonetheless, Huck maintains his characteristic realistic outlook on the world, and his prediction that Tom's plan could get them killed is more accurate than he knows.

But I reckon I got to light out for the territory ahead of the rest, because Aunt Sally she's going to adopt me and sivilize me, and I can't stand it. I been there before.

These lines are the last in the novel. By the final chapter, most everything has been resolved: Jim is free, Tom is on his way to recovering from a bullet wound, and Aunt Sally has offered to adopt Huck. Although Huck has come to like Sally and Silas, he knows they are still a part of the society he has come to distrust and fear. Aunt Sally's intentions for Huck cnetre around the upbringing that society thinks every boy should have: religion, clean clothes, education, and an indoctrination in right and wrong. Huck, however, has come to realise that the first two are useless and that, in reference to the third, he can provide a much better version for himself than can society. The "territories," the relatively unsettled western United States, will offer Huck an opportunity to be himself, in a world not yet "sivilized" and thus brimming with promise. Weary of his old life, Huck contemplates ways to continue living with the same freedom he felt on the raft. Huck's break from society is complete, and before the dust from his adventures is fully settled, he is already scheming to detach himself again.

Chapter 13

Key Facts

Full title

The Adventures of Huckleberry Finn

Author

Mark Twain (pseudonym for Samuel Clemens)

Type of work

Novel

Genre Picaresque novel (episodic, colorful story often in the form of a quest or journey); satire of popular adventure and romance novels; bildungsroman (novel of education or moral development)

Language

English; frequently makes use of Southern and black dialects of the time

Time and place written

1876–1883; Hartford, Connecticut, and Elmira, New York

Date of first publication

1884

Publisher

Charles L. Webster and Co.
narrator · Huckleberry Finn

Point of view: Huck's point of view, although Twain occasionally indulges in digressions in which he shows off his own ironic wit

Tone: Frequently ironic or mocking, particularly concerning adventure -novels and romances; also contemplative, as Huck seeks to decipher the world around him; sometimes boyish and exuberant

Tense: Immediate past

Setting (time): Before the Civil War; roughly 1835–1845; Twain said the novel was set forty to fifty years before the time of its publication

Setting (place): The Mississippi River town of St. Petersburg, Missouri; various locations along the river through Arkansas

Protagonist: Huck Finn

Major conflict: At the beginning of the novel, Huck struggles against society and its attempts to civilize him, represented by the Widow Douglas, Miss Watson, and other adults. Later, this conflict gains greater focus in Huck's dealings with Jim, as Huck must decide whether to turn Jim in, as society demands, or to protect and help his friend instead.

Rising action: Miss Watson and the Widow Douglas attempt to civilize Huck until Pap reappears in town, demands Huck's money, and kidnaps Huck. Huck escapes society by faking his own death and retreating to Jackson's Island, where he meets Jim and sets out on the river with him. Huck gradually begins to question the rules society has taught him, as when, in order to protect Jim, he lies and makes up a story to scare off some men searching for escaped slaves. Although Huck and Jim live a relatively peaceful life on the raft, they are ultimately unable to escape the evils and hypocrisies of the outside world. The most notable representatives of these outside evils are the con men the duke and the dauphin, who engage in a series of increasingly serious scams that culminate in their sale of Jim, who ends up at the Phelps farm.

Climax: Huck considers but then decides against writing Miss Watson to tell her the Phelps family is holding Jim, following his conscience rather than the prevailing morality of the day. Instead, Tom and Huck try to free Jim, and Tom is shot in the leg during the attempt.

Falling action: When Aunt Polly arrives at the Phelps farm and correctly identifies Tom and Huck, Tom reveals that Miss Watson died two months earlier and freed Jim in her will. Afterward, Tom recovers from his wound, while Huck decides he is done with civilized society and makes plans to travel to the West.

Themes: Racism and slavery; intellectual and moral education; the hypocrisy of "civilized" society

Motifs: Childhood; lies and cons; superstitions and folk beliefs; parodies of popular romance novels

Symbols: The Mississippi River; floods; shipwrecks; the natural world

Foreshadowing: Twain uses parallels and juxtapositions more so than explicit foreshadowing, especially in his frequent comparisons between Huck's plight and eventual escape and Jim's plight and eventual escape.

Chapter 14

Study Questions and Answers

Q. Significance of Father Figure in Huckleberry Finn.

Or

Q. Huck Finn, Finn is a young boy with many problems going on in life and was in need of a father figure more then any thing else in life. Discuss

Mark Twain, the author of Huckleberry Finn, has written a story that all will enjoy. Huck is a young boy with not much love in his life, his mother died when he was very young, and he had drunk for a father. Huck lives with the widow and she tried to raise him right. While at the widow's, Huck went to school and learned to read and write. The widow also tried to civilize him. She would buy him nice clothes, and make him do his homework.

The main character in this story is Huck Finn, Finn is a young boy with many problems going on in life. Huck was in need of a father figure more then any thing else in life. He needed someone to talk to about anything. Huck's Pap was never there for him except maybe to give him a tanning. Huck's Pap thought that he was trying to out do him, because he went to school. "You've put on considerable many frills since I been away. I'll take you down a peg before I get done with you. You think you're better'n your father, now don't you, because he can't? I'll take it out of you. Who told you you might meddle with such hifalut'n foolishness, hey?-who told you you could" Pap scolded . Huck didn't like having to wear nice clothes, or even going to school, but the he had to go. "Starchy clothes-very. You think you're a good deal of a big-bug, don't you" Pap asked ?

Huck would try and be a rebel because he had no male to tell him right from wrong. If Huck needed help the only real person that he could talk to would be Tom Sawyer, a very good friend also a thief, a rebel, and he lived on his own. Tom was not that great of a role model, for a young boy like Huck. His father was always away, and never there for him, and when he was around he was always drunk. It is hard enough to talk to a drunk man let alone when you have a problem and need advice. The childhood of a young boy is very crucial in what he will be like in his own life.

Huckleberry Finn was written to show young males that there are ways of finding someone. Mark Twain has a very unique perspective on the whole subject. He found a way to find love in a place where the reader would never imagine.

Huck's pap came and took him away from the widow and Huck thought that everything would be so much better, but no. The only good thing that came out of it was that he didn't have to go to school. His Pap locked him in the cabin whenever he went away, an if ever did anything wrong he would get a tanning (otherwise known as being spanked).

When a young boy is growing up being locked up all the time does not help a young boy to develop into a man. Young boys need a role model to look up to, and if the only role model around is a drunk then you will become a drunk. Huck would see his Pap so drunk and yell at him all the time.

Huck went to school just to spite the old man, but when his Pap found him, Huck sure did get a tanning. Huck would have to get money for his Pap just so that he wouldn't get a tanning. The influence of being abused and being around a drunk person is never the way to grow up. Huck couldn't take the abuse anymore, from being tanned, to being locked in a cabin for days. So he ran away, and planned to never return. Huck figured out a way to get away from his Pap, the widow and everyone else. Huck was gonna learn to raise himself and become his own role model.

Huck had a raft, supplies and his freedom. He felt as if his life could get a whole lot better if he got away from all the abuse. Huck traveled during the night and slept during the day. That's how he found the runaway black man from Miss Watson's. Huck was resting during the day, and he found a camp fire that was freshly put out.

Then while Huck was trying to sleep he heard a noise and out popped Jim. "Hello Jim," I said . Huck was so glad that Jim was now there with him.

Jim was a very good man that was just never understood, but Huck learned all about him on their voyages down the river. Huck and Jim were inseparable. They would talk about everything. The only thing that they really did that was a little bad was smoking tobacco. Jim understood why Huck ran away, because of his Pap always beating him. Jim knew what that was like, being a black person and all. This is the first time that Huck had ever had a male adult to talk to this way. With having a person of Jims intelligence Huck could learn a lot. Huck had someone to look up to, to learn from.

Jim and Huck got into some trouble when they thought that they were in Cairo and got separated. By this time Miss Watson had a two-hundred dollar reward out for him. Jim got captured and Huck was alone, again. Huck found out where Jim was and realized who lived there, and it was Tom Sawyer's aunt. This was the best news that he heard because Tom was suppose to being coming out for a visit and so Huck became Tom, and Tom became Sid. Together Huck and Tom rescued Jim. Huck was so afraid that he was going to lose Jim, but when Huck was just a black man. Huck actually had an adult that liked him and wanted to help.

Huckleberry Finn is a classic story. It shows that Huck can find someone that he can depend on since his father never helped him. Jim became Huck's father in more then one way. Jim was a very good friend that Huck could talk to about anything. Jim cared so much about Huck, that when Jim was left behind he would miss him so. When Jim was being held captive Huck would do anything to get him freed. Jim and Huck had a very special bond. They could never be separated ever again. Huck was in need of a father figure and Twain was the author who brought it all to together. Twain used characterization to bring the elements of the literature to life.

From Jim being black, and Huck thinking that his father could ever be there for him. Twain gives Huck chances to have Tom Sawyer to be his father figure, but Huck chose Jim. Huck didn't seem to care that Jim was black he still cared about him still the same way as if he were white. Jim would look out for Huck, and Huck would look out for Jim. If Huck had not cared about Jim he would be back in slavery, and would never have found someone to be his father figure.

Q. Huckleberry Finn–Complex Character

Or

Q. Huckleberry Finn is a complex character. Discuss

Huckleberry Finn is a complex character. As this book progresses, so does Huck. Huck is about thirteen years old, from the low end of the white middle class. His father is a ruffian who disappears for months on end. This book starts off with Huck being 'reformed' by the widow Douglas and therefore remains a marginalized member of society. He has not been brought up with the same social values as an average middle-class boy might be, but this helps to create Huck's unique personality. The way he has been brought up affects his traits, values, and relationships throughout the book.

Although Huck's character progresses in this story his traits that he portrays at the end are very similar to those at the beginning. His ingenuity, morality, and intelligence are consistent throughout the story. Huck's ingenuity is shown throughout his clever actions. His decision to make his escape on the canoe look like a murder to hide his tracks is just one example, "And they'll follow that meal track to the lake and go browsing down the creek that leads out of it to find the robbers that killed me and took the things.

They won't ever hunt the river for anything but my dead carcass. They'll soon get tired of that, and won't bother no more about me." This idea continues as he decides to dress up as a girl to gain information. Although this idea doesn't fully succeed because he is found out, it is an excellent plan, which also reviles his ingenuity. Another time we see this unique cleverness is when he pretends to be `George Jackson' to live with the Wilkes family.

Also throughout this story, Huck develops his own morality, however it has a different turn from the accepted norm for that society at that time. An example of his morality coming through is how he didn't tell on Jim when he ran away. Although the society would see this as wrong, Huck took Jim's point of view and concluded to help him. Huck also showed his morality when he tried to return the stolen money to the girls and escape from the Duke and King after the burial. This is another trait that continues to show throughout the book.

Another repeating trait that Huck shows is his intelligence. When Huck is compared to an average boy at his age, like Tom, in the school education view he is a bit behind. School is not that important to Huck, "At first I hated the school, but by and by I got so I could stand it. Whenever I got uncommon tired I played hookey, and the hiding I got next day done me good and cheered me up. So the longer I went to school the easier it got to be." Also in comparison to Tom, Huck is less intelligent in the reading aspect; Tom has read much more books than Huck will ever want to read. However, when they are compared in a worldly view, he is much more intelligent and mature. Huck has been beaten, out-casted, and alone at the age of thirteen more that most people are their whole lives. His intelligence, although not exactly what people at that time were looking for, is much more advanced than other children at thirteen years of age. Huck's different traits that are shown throughout the story all contribute to his very unique character.

Another major independent character note on Huck are his views on situations and society. Huck sees situations from a much different point of view that most people would for his age and time. "I was most ready to cry; but all at once I thought of a way, and so I offered them Miss Watson-they could kill her." At the beginning of this novel he shares his first thoughts about his family situation or lack there of. In society's view he should be sad and upset because he is alone; but in the reality of Huck's view he is upset because he has no one to kill. This is the first time Huck shares his views about being out-casted. On the other hand, where is Huck is wishing for a family at the beginning (although it is only to kill them) at the end Aunt Sally offers to adopt him, however, he sees this as a negative situation and plans to go out on his own.

Huck's view on society is a unique quality about him. Another different view that Huck has are his views on society. There are many people that Huck run into that cause him to act differently because of his views. An example of this is when he finds out that the King and Duke are liars. He knows that what they are doing is wrong; but he views them as a part of society and lets it go, "If I never learnt nothing else out of pap, I learnt that the best way to get along with his kind of people is to let them have their own way." Huck is constantly patronizing different members of society and creates a `You see it your way; I'll see it mine point of view.' He doesn't really care how they see things and has no desire to find out. Huck also shows at more than one event his little suppositions, this adds some fun to Huck's character, "One morning I happened to turn over the salt-cellar at breakfast. I reached for some of it as quick as I could to throw over my left shoulder and keep off the bad luck, but Miss Watson was in ahead of me, and crossed me off." Huck's views are very different from every other character in this novel.

The character that Huck portrays is greatly affected by the relationships he is in. His three main relationships in this book are with Pap, Tom, and Jim. Huck's relationships with Pap although short is very intense. Pap looks downward towards Huck with jealousy and frustration. Huck has gotten away from his destructive father at the beginning but not fully, although living with Miss Watson; Pap still comes around when he is drunk, needs money, or is frustrated with Huck for one reason or another. Ironically through all this Huck still speaks favorably about his father. He puts him down very little and doesn't describe him as a bad father. While Hick describes the situation of Miss Watson trying to get sole custody, he never chooses a side, of which he would rather live with. Huck has an understanding of his father and has adjusted his living to work with and at times around his father.

Another important relationship that affects Huck's

Character is with Tom Sawyer. Huck and Tom have the classic best friend relationship in many ways. In their friendship Tom is the leader and Huck tries to stay out of his way and just does what he is told. This is evident in the beginning when Tom comes to get Huck as they sneak out of the house. Huck lets Tom steal the candle even though money is left to pay for them. As they pass Jim and Tom plays the trick on him, Huck knows that it's mean to play a trick on Jim but he does nothing to stop it. In Huck's mind, Tom is better than him, more knowledgeable and creative. This friendship remains the same when we get to the end of the novel. When Tom comes and pretends to be Sid, their old friendship picks back up. The two of them plan to help Jim escape, or in their minds to set him free, and through all the planning of how to get Jim out instead of doing it the easy way like Huck wants to at first, Huck lets Tom convince him that it has to be done the 'right way.' What is even more ironic than Huck letting Tom have control is that Tom knows all along that Jim is really already free, "Old Miss Watson died two months ago, and she was ashamed she ever was going to sell him down the river, and SAID so; and she set him free in her will." Huck has been traveling down the river with Jim, on their own without anyone to depend on, they have faced liars, murders, and scammers; and Huck just lets Tom stroll back into his life going back to the same type of relationship they had in the beginning. Huck is more of Tom's lackey than friend.

Another major relationship in this novel is Huck's relationship with Jim. As it starts out Huck has some respect for Jim and all the slaves. When Huck encounters Jim on the island he faces a moral dilemma. He decides to help Jim get to freedom and this starts their adventure and friendship. Through their journey Jim and Huck become very close. Jim needs to depend on someone, that is how he has lived all his life with someone telling him what to do, where to go, and what to say. Luckily for Jim, Huck can be this person and still be his friend. Huck has a respect for Jim and treats him as an equal whenever he can. Uniquely with their friendship through their adventures Jim plays the surragate father role to Huck,

"It's a dead man. Yes, indeedy; naked, too. He's ben shot in de back. I reck'n he's ben dead two er three days. Come in, Huck, but doan' look at his face — it's too gashly." Protecting him when he can, scolding him at times and teaching him some of life's little lessons. As they travel the path towards `freedom' and continue on their adventure they become closer and closer. Then their relationship takes a backward step. As soon as Tom is back in the picture, Huck completely abandons Jim and their relationship in Huck's point-of-view is back to square one. Huck treats him as a slave having him do whatever Tom says, not questioning Tom and how he is treating his friend. Jim still depends on Huck because there is no one else to depend upon. He does everything Huck says and soon doesn't question what Tom says either because Huck doesn't. Their relationship is rare and unique their relationship is continually growing through the novel and then goes back as though they had never traveled down the Mississippi River together. Huck's different relationships throughout this novel help to shape Huck's character.

Huck is a very unique character shaped by his traits, values, and relationships. Huck is a character different from every other one in this novel. He is alone, no one around him has had the same experiences he has and none of them view things the way he does. Huck must have lived a hard life being all alone and envying those who weren't. Although he portrayed a strong character he at times was also very weak. He was very independent and at times would leave everyone to just be by himself. Huck's character is not a straightforward one. There are a ton of different things throughout this book that affect and show different parts of his character. However, this character is the hero of our story making us smile to ourselves as we follow along on his incredible journey.

Q. Huckleberry Finn–Does His Character Represent Racism?

Or

Q. Racism means "the belief that race accounts for differences in human character or ability and the belief of one specific race's superiority". This word plays a

major role in history and in the Adventures of Huckleberry Finn. Discuss

Racism means "the belief that race accounts for differences in human character or ability and the belief of one specific race's superiority". This word plays a major role in history and in this novel. Many people and many facts lead you to believe Huckleberry Finn represents racism. I, on the other hand, believe Huckleberry Finn does not represent racism.

Throughout history critics have criticized Mark Twain about Huckleberry Finn being a racist novel and Twain himself being a racist. Mark Twain, through his writings in Huckleberry Finn make it clear he does not support racism in any way. For example, Mark Twain portrayed Pap Finn, a racist, as an uneducated, alcoholic that beats his kid. On the other hand, he portrays Jim, a slave, as a caring, loving father and a trustworthy companion to Huck.

"... the reader is presented with a very caring and father-like Jim who becomes very worried when he loses his best friend Huck in a deep fog.

Mark Twain is pointing out the connection which has been made between Huck and Jim. A connection which does not exist between a man and his property."

The story takes place when black people were not considered equal to white people. Back then the word "nigger" referred to black people. Mark Twain did not write the word to degrade black people or to be racist, he wrote it to be historically accurate of the times. " To say that Twain is racist because of his desire for historical accuracy is absurd."

"...search through all of Twain's writings, not just the thirty-plus volumes of novels, stories, essays, and letters, but also his private correspondence, his posthumous autobiography and his intimate journals, and you'll be hard put to find a derogatory remark about the black race, and this at a time when crude racial stereotypes were the basic coin of popular fiction, stage comedy, and popular songs." If Mark Twain wrote the "politically correct" style of writing the critics talk about it would take away the deep undertone the novel contains and it would lose it's classic quality.

Throughout history, and even today, people's racist society upbringing blinded them from forming their own opinion. Mark Twain also knew how much society had on people's opinions; therefore, he gave Huck a choice to form a opinion on his own. Huck could either turn Jim in because of society's influence on him or he would not turn in Jim because of their friendship.

"When Huck first meets Jim on the island he makes a monumental decision, not to turn Jim in. He is confronted by two opposing forces, the force of society and the force of friendship. Many times throughout the novel Huck comes very close to rationalizing Jim's slavery. However, he is never able to see a reason why this man who has become one of his only friends, should be a slave. Through this internal struggle, Twain expresses his opinions of the absurdity of slavery and the importance of following one's personal conscience before the laws of society. By the end of the novel, Huck and the reader have come to understand that Jim is not

Someone's property and an inferior man, but an equal."

All the satire and symbolism Mark Twain wrote in his great novel led me to believe that Huckleberry Finn does not portray racism. Instead Huckleberry Finn portrays historical accuracy, satire about racists and how much society can influence someone's opinions. " Mark Twain a "racist"! Isn't it about time we put this ridiculous notion to rest?"

Lately, there has been increasing discussion of the outward racist ideas expressed by Mark Twain in Huckleberry Finn. In some cases the novel has even been banned by public school systems and censored by public libraries. All this controversy caused by one character Jim, a black slave. Jim is a black slave who runs away from Miss Watson. At several points in the novel, Jim's character is described to the reader, and some people have looked upon the characterization as racist. However, before one begins to censor a novel it is important to separate the ideas of the author from the ideas' of his characters. It is also important not to take a novel at face value and to read between the lines in order to capture the underlying themes of a novel. If one were to do this in relation to Huckleberry Finn, one would, without doubt, realise that it is not racist and is even anti-slavery.

At first, Huckleberry Finn might appear to be racist. The first time the reader meets Jim he is given a very negative description of Jim. The reader is told that Jim is illiterate, childlike, not very bright and extremely superstitious. However, it is important not to lose sight of who is giving this description and of who it is being given. Although Huck is not a racist kid, he has been raised by racist people who have put some feelings of racism into his mind. It is also important to remember that this description, although it is quite sad, was probably accurate. Jim and the millions of other slaves in the South were not permitted any formal education, were never allowed any independent thoughts and were constantly mistreated and abused. Twain is merely portraying by way of Jim, a slave raised in the South during that time period.

Despite the few times in which Jim's description might though as racist, there are many points in the novel where Twain through Huck, voices his extreme opposition to the slave trade and racism. In chapter six, Huck's father objects to the governments granting of suffrage to an educated black professor. Twain wants the reader to see the absurdity in this statement. Huck's father believes that he is superior to this black professor simply because of the colour of his skin. In Chapter 15 the reader is told of an incident which contradicts the original "childlike" description of Jim. In chapter 15 the reader is presented with a very caring and father-like Jim who becomes very worried when he loses his best friend Huck in a deep fog. Twain is pointing out the connection which has been made between Huck and Jim. A connection which does not exist between a man and his property.

When Huck first meets Jim on the Island he makes a massive decision, not to turn Jim in. He is confronted by two opposing forces, the force of society and the force of friendship. Many times throughout the novel Huck comes very close humanizing Jim's slavery. However, he is never able to see a reason why this man who has become one of his only friends, should be a slave. Through this struggle, Twain expresses his opinions of the silliness of slavery and the importance of following one's personal conscience before the laws of society. By the end of the novel, Huck and the reader have come to understand that Jim is not someone's property and less of a man, but an equal.

Throughout the novel society's voice is heard through Huck. Racism comes many times in Huck's journey to free a slave. But, it is critical for the reader to understand these are society's ideas and to recognize that Twain throughout the novel disagrees with these ideas. Twain brings out into the open the ugliness of society and causes the reader to challenge the original description of Jim. In a clever manner, twain creates a way to show that slavery is wrong while keeping his book controversial.

Q. Huckleberry Finn as a Racist

Or

Q. Mark Twain's novel The Adventures of Huckleberry Finn depicts how he is a racist.

Mark Twain's novel The Adventures of Huckleberry Finn depicts how he is a racist. He shows it in many ways in which his characters act. All of the people in the towns are slave owners, and treat black slaves with disrespect. In the time period of the novel slavery was not legal, but racism was. Many scenes in his novel make slaves look like fools. Mark Twain does this purposely to make colored people look and sound like fools, because he is a racist person.

Before even getting to chapter, one Mark Twain puts a notice on the book. "Persons attempting to find a motive in this narrative will be prosecuted; persons attempting to find a moral will be banished; persons attempting to find a plot in it will be shot" (Twain, 2). Twain uses this to show people how he is as a person. If you go against him, you may be prosecuted, banished or even shot. This most likely is because he was a racist and needed power. If slaves were to go against him, they will lose. Mark Twain uses these words to build himself up, and make himself sound like a more powerful person.

Mark Twain uses characters that are very similar to him as a person. Huck's father, Pap, is a person like Twain. Pap is a drunken man that is very temperamental. He tells Huck of all the things that Pap feels is nonsense. Pap is always trying to be a powerful figure in Huck's life. Mark Twain probably uses Pap in the book to show readers that he is the same type of person. Twain uses this book to show that he is racist person, and used Pap to show that he is a power thirsty person as well.

The Adventures of Huckleberry Finn is a book that was made to degrade the black population of America. Jim, a runaway slave, meets up with Huck after he runs away from Pap. When Jim and Huck see each other, Jim drops to his knees pleading Huck not to turn him in, or hurt him. Mark Twain does this to show that when a black slave and a white person meet the slave should drop to their knees before the white person. He must feel that when a colored person approaches him they should bow towards him, because he feels he is a better person.

Some of the words that Mark Twain uses are intended solely to offend colored people. He constantly is using the word "nigger." This word is a horrible word for a black person to hear. That is what they are called and to a white person like Twain, a nigger is lower than dirt. He uses this word as often as he can. This word hurt many of the slaves, and colored people years ago. Mark Twain was a very intelligent person, because he knew that if he used it during a racist period it would hurt the colored readers. It would also hurt colored readers many years later. This was probably his main reason for using the word as often as he could.

James S. Leonard, who wrote a criticism about Mark Twain's book, says "And though society's highest praise for his action is that he is a `good nigger,' Huck has his own formulation: Jim is `white inside.'" (Leonard, 146) He is saying that Mark Twain will only allow Jim, who is a good person, to be a good nigger. Huck sees Jim as a person with a colored covering. Twain doesn't want to write about people seeing Jim as a colored person with a white mans heart. He wants to see Jim as a slave who is just a good nigger. Twain thinks about everything that he can do to make black people sound horrible.

Mark Twain does not only try to harp on the African

American race, but he does the French as well. Huck and Jim wonder why Frenchmen talk funny. The reader knows it is their accent, but Twain does this to just put a little tease in against the French readers. Mark Twain, who is not French, decides that he is no a Frenchman so why not make fun of the way that they talk. If people are not like him then he is against them. The French people will be an easy target, because they bring along their French dialect to the English language. Twain wrote his novel to show all of the problems that other people have, and not to show his own.

As Huck and Jim are talking about the way Frenchmen talk, Huck says that it is natural and right for cats and cows to talk differently from each other. Natural and right can be thought of in many different ways. There is no real natural and right type of person in the real world. In Mark Twain's world there is. He is the natural and right person. He believes that everything he does the correct thing to do. Twain may also believe that racism is the correct thing to do as well. Racism was what Mark Twain was brought up into, wrote about, and lived by.

After arguing about the differences of cats and cows, Huck gives up. He says, "You can't learn a nigger to argue" (Twain, 77). Instead of arguing with Jim about how cats and cows speak Huck just gives up. Huck realizes that Jim thinks that English is the only language spoken. When Jim receives this new information about another language, he is overwhelmed. Instead of trying to understand, he just tells Huck that there is no possible way that there can be another language. Huck understands that Jim does not understand him, so Huck just gives up. Mark Twain uses this conversation to show how illiterate Jim really is. He shows the readers that Jim is so foolish that he doesn't even know there are other languages other than English. Twain uses Jim for this because he was a runaway slave. Since most of the slaves in that time were illiterate, Twain tries to use that against colored people in later years.

Later in The Adventure of Huckleberry Finn Huck and Jim meet up with two men who call themselves the Duke and the Dauphin. These two men stroll up and down the Mississippi River looking for towns that they can perform for and scam the people out of their money. The Duke and Dauphin recite lines from three of Shakespeare's plays. They combined parts of the plays together. They find a town that has a circus and it is there last show. The Duke and Dauphin decide to go into this town and scam the people with their play. They call their play the "Royal Nonesuch" (Twain, 133). The play is formed into three parts, Romeo and Juliet, King Richard's sword fight, and Hamlet's Immoral Soliloquy. The Duke and Dauphin just about ruin the play.

Mark Twain brings Shakespeare's plays into his book, because Shakespeare is another person that Twain can tease. Twain uses these plays because they are some of Shakespeare's most know. He gets the Duke and Dauphin to totally ruin the parts of the plays. The Duke and Dauphin are the only two characters in all three plays, so they would not have been very good in the first place. They only did a little piece of each play, because they were the only parts they knew. Mark Twain wrote his book like this to make William Shakespeare's plays look foolish. Twain does not understand Shakespeare's plays so he decides they do not make any sense. If things don't make sense to Mark Twain then they should be destroyed. Twain tried to destroy the plays, so he would look like a better person. If people read Twain's book and see that Shakespeare's plays can be teased that easily then they may think that Shakespeare isn't as good of a person as Mark Twain.

In chapter, thirty-two of The Adventures of Huckleberry Finn there is a boating accident. Huck's Aunt Sally asks if anyone was hurt. Huck then replied, "No'm. Killed a nigger" (Twain, 213). Aunt Sally then said, "Well, its lucky; because sometimes people do get hurt"(Twain, 213). All of the characters in The Adventures of Huckleberry Finn don't really seem to care about colored people. It doesn't matter what happens not a single person cares. Mark Twain really hits the slaves on this part. With putting this piece in Twain is just saying, no one cares about you. When people here someone died, they are worried, but when it is a black person, they could care less. Twain just does this to show that the only people that care about blacks is themselves. When Aunt Sally said its lucky no one got hurt it is like saying that blacks were not even people back then. Many of the people just saw blacks as animals and don't show the slightest bit of respect towards them. Mark Twain probably wrote this part, because he was a racist and he felt that blacks were animals. By writing this it made him feel better about himself because he was degrading the colored people.

Mark Twain uses the same part of the book to show another way that blacks were treated. Through most of the book, Huck and Jim seem to have been getting along. They seemed to have made a friendship during their time on the river. This friendship has not changed Huck's feelings towards blacks one bit.

When his Aunt Sally asked him if anyone got hurt and he replied, "No'm. Killed a nigger," it showed the readers that Huck has not gained any respect towards blacks. Jim and Huck have been together and Huck gets along fine with Jim. He seems to like him and respect him, but when it comes to another black, Huck still feels the same way he did when the book started.

This is in the book to show readers that even after a friendship with a black person, whites still feel that they are better then blacks. The book really shows how whites used blacks. Jim was used by Huck, because Huck did not care one bit about blacks, but he did when it was a benefit to him. Mark Twain thought he was better than all of the blacks, so he wasn't going to let Huck and Jim's relationship with each other change how is white characters feel about blacks.

Throughout the entire book, Jim's dialect has been very poor. Huck's is not the best, but it is much better than Jim's is. Whenever Jim speaks it is hard to understand, because Mark Twain wrote it to be so poorly that he can barely be understood. The reason behind this is to make Jim look like a fool. Twain wants the readers to see that he is illiterate, like most blacks were in this time. Huck has a Mississippi accent, and he is not the best speaker, but when Jim is speaking, it is all broken up and slang. Mark Twain shows people that blacks were never as smart as whites, by making his black characters look stupid. He has probably felt that his entire life, and would never understand that there are people better than he is, and may be black.

The Adventures of Huckleberry Finn was written to mainly show how life was in the southern states, and the purpose of life. Mark Twain got a little out of hand when he started to constantly try to build himself up. A very racist man who did everything he could to make other people seem foolish, Mark Twain wasn't only racist to blacks, but all types of groups.

It is a hard decision to make, if he is racist or if he just lacks self-esteem. Whatever it may be, Mark Twain wrote his book to show how he feels about racism. It could be that he just is a person that needs to be the best and feels that no one is a good as him, but Mark Twain's book The Adventures of Huckleberry Finn is one that shows how he really feels about blacks and other minorities.

Q. In the Style of Twain The Adventures of Huckleberry Finn, is said to be " the source from which all great American literature has stemmed. Discuss.

The Adventures of Huckleberry Finn, the main character finds himself living in a society that does not suit him. Everywhere he looks there are people who value things that he sees as meaningless. Huck Finn feels trapped and begins his journey down the river in an effort to find someone or some place that will bring him happiness. Almost immediatly he finds this person in the form a run away slave. In this story, Huck and Jim are against the entire world, and every person they come in contact with has the potential to destroy their plans of happiness and freedom. Under these circumstances Huck is forced to tell many lies, but the only one he regrets is the one that he tells Jim. The biggest and most harmful lie Huck tells is when he fakes his own murder in his fathers shack. He goes through a great deal of trouble to make sure that people believe that he is dead, and it is not until the end of the novel that it becomes known to the people of his home town that he is actually alive. He had been a likable young boy, and people in the town had thought highly of him. This is evident from his relationship with adults like the widow and the judge. Jim even tells him 'I'uz powerful sorry you's killed, Huck, but I ain't no mo, now'. Based on Huck's consistent concern for others, it is likely that he would have written home to inform them that he was still alive if it had not been for his situation with Jim. However, he does not want to risk doing anything that might get Jim captured, so he writes no letter. Huck finds himself working against the world. He is not an immature boy that tells lies just for the sake of doing so, but rather he tells them in order to protect himself and also Jim. In the instance where he dresses up like a girl and speaks with the farmer's wife in an effort to find out what is being said about their situation, the information that he gets ultimately saves them from the capture of a building search party.

Even though he is caught in the first lie and it is discovered that he is actually a young boy rather than a girl, Huck manages to convince the woman that he simply a run away. He quickly creates a new lie and better lie, and she has no idea about his true identity. In this instance of lies that Huck tells there is no victim.

Huck learns crucial information that he would have never gotten through honesty, and with this information he is able to continue on his journey with Jim. Another one of Huck's lies is one that he tells to the watchman on the on the steam ship. He knows that this man is the only person who can help the group of murders that were soon going to drown in the river. Under the circumstances, Huck could not tell the man the truth because he had stolen their boat to save Jim's and his own life, Jim would have been danger of being captured, and most lily the watchman would have not bothered to go save a band of murders. Since the truth was not an option, Huck creates an elaborate story of women in distress, and reward money.

After all is done, in reflection on his actions Huck says 'I was feeling ruther comfortable on accounts of taking all of the trouble for that gang, for not many would a done it.' He clearly believes here that he has done a good thing in telling that lie. He knows that he saved these men's lives, and he would not have been able to do so with the truth. The one lie that Huck clearly regrets telling is the one that he tells to Jim. After their accidental separation, Huck returns to the raft and acts as though he hasn't been gone. Huck goes on to claim that Jim imaged the entire thing. In response to Jim's delight in seeing Huck alive and well Huck says, 'What is the matter with you Jim' You been a drinking" Jim asks Huck to look him in the eye and say that he had not been gone anywhere, and Huck does as he asks. Jim soon realizes that Huck is not telling him the truth. Jim says to Huck 'en trash is what people is dat puts dirt on de head er dey fren's en makes 'em ashamed.' This makes Huck feel terrible and after apologizing to Jim he claims that he would have never had done it if he had known how it would have made him feel. The above are not the only lies that Huck tells in this story. He is actually quite good at telling lies and he continues to tell them up unitl the end of the story, but what the majority of Huck's lies have in common is that they protect both him and Jim from the society of southerners that he has turned his back on. Huck chooses to follow what he feels in his heart rather that what he has been taught by those around him.

The lies he tells are told so that he can continue in his search for happiness, truth, and freedom. For the most part Huck's lies are morally good which seems like a contradiction. Ironically, The Adventures of Huckleberry Finn ends with Huck's salutation of 'Yours Truly'. The fact is that Clemens uses Huck's morally sound lies as a reflectionon the true nature of American society during the time of slavery.

In the Style of Twain The Adventures of Huckleberry Finn, is said to be " the source from which all great American literature has stemmed". This is in part attributed to Mark Twain's ability to use humour and satire, as well as incorporating serious subject matter into his work. Throughout the novel Twain takes on the serious issue of Huck's moral dilemma.

One such issue which is particularly important in the novel is pointed out by Smith: He swears and smokes, but he has a set of ethics all his own. He believes that slaves belong to their rightful owners, yet in his honest gratitude toward his friend Jim, he helps him to escape the bonds of slavery: This is something that tears at Huck throughout the novel and helps Twain show how complex Huck's character really is. "The recognition of complexity in Huck's character enabled Twain to do full justice to the conflict of vernacular values and the dominant culture".

Throughout Huck and Jim's adventures Huck is constantly playing practical jokes on Jim who seems to take them all in stride. But unknown to the reader Twain uses this aspect as another notch in Huck's moral 2 growth. Critic Frank McGill points this out: Huck's humble apology for the prank he plays on Jim in the fog is striking evidence of growth in Huck's moral insight. It leads naturally to the next chapter in which Twain causes Huck to face up for the first time to the fact he is helping a slave escape.

Another serious issue addressed by Twain is the abuse that was given to Huck by his father. Huck was kidnaped from the Widow Douglas by his father who had heard of his inheritance. Huck's father then took him to a cabin far away in the woods where he kept the boy a prisoner, beating him and half starving him. Twain tells us how Huck felt about life with his father: Before long Huck began to wonder why he had even liked living with the widow. With his father he could smoke and swear all he wanted, and his life would have been quiet pleasant if it had not been for all of the constant beatings. Huck would soon after grow tired of the beatings and fakes his death to escape the cabin.

The humorous side of Twain is probably what he is most well known for. Humour is considered an art form by many writers. Jane Bernadette states the difference between humour and comical stories: The humorous story is strictly a work of art high and delicate and only an Curran 3 artist can tell it; but no art is necessary in telling the comic and the witty story; anybody can do it. The art of telling a humorous story-understand, I mean by word of mouth, not print-was created in America and has remained at home. Twain satirizes the south for its seriousness on certain matters. "I think one of the most notably southern traits of Mark Twain's humour is its power of seeing the fun of southern seriousness" . Twain also satirizes the society of the 'day' by describing the colonel Grangerford as "the symbol of southern aristocracy".

Twain also goes on to satirize the south's racism. One such instance is pointed out in the novel when Aunt Polly hears of a steamboat explosion. " Good gracious is anyone hurt?" "No", "it just killed a negro". Religious satire is another aspect that Twain uses. An easy illustration of this is the Widow's attempt to teach Huck religious principles while she persists on keeping slaves. "Huck's principles of morality make him more 'Christian' than the Widow even though he takes no interest in her lifeless principles".

Twain's humour has been mistaken by some to be racist or politically incorrect. "The humour of Mark Twain contains a sense of the incongruous which frontiersmen felt in a region where civilization and uncultivated nature come face to face". In conclusion I think that the style and structure of Mark Twain's work not only exemplifies him as a humorist but as a serious writer as well; a writer who cannot be Curran 4 categorized by any one aspect of his writing. "To remember him only as a creator of boyhood adventure or as a relic of an American frontier or the voice of idiosyncracy is to do him disservice".

Q. The Moral Vistory in Adventures of Huckleberry Finn

Or

Q. Mark Twain's novel The Adventures of Huckleberry Finn is a perfect example of how one's heart and morals can change in difficult situations. Discuss

Mark Twain's novel The Adventures of Huckleberry Finn is a perfect example of how one's heart and morals can change in difficult situations. Huck's journey down the Mississippi River tested him to his limits of being able to handle situations in the way which he had been raised. Huck shows that how one is raised is something that will impact them tremendously in the rest of their life and that it is hard to change from what you've been molded into. Early in the novel Huck shows how much of a rebellious and joking boy he truly is. "I put out the light and I scrambled out of the window...," says Huck. Huck, at a young age, began getting himself into many difficult situations, such as escaping from the cave in Tom Sawyer. Huck often has a hard time abiding by rules, keeping himself out of trouble, and comprehending the things he has been taught. However, he does learn one thing, that he is better than the Negroes. So, as young boys, Huck Finn and Tom Sawyer spend a good bit of their time playing tricks on Ms. Watson's slave, Jim.

"He slipped Jim's hat off his head and hung it on a limb right over him..," tricks like these which Huck is never punished for are part of what confirm the teaching that he is in fact better than blacks. This conditioning as a young child is what makes it difficult for him to deal with Jim as an equal later in life. Once on the river Huck has a much more difficult time as he not only has to deal with Jim but also the King and Duke who join them on their journey. The King and Duke's actions around Huck make him realise that he needs to change his morals. When Huck realizes that the King and Duke are impostors his learning experience begins. "It didn't take me long to make up my mind that these liars warn't no kings nor dukes at all, but just low-down humbugs and frauds."

This statement shows that Huck has feelings about the King and Duke that show that his morals are of the kind which will not selfishly go against other's trust. Once the King and Duke decide on cheating the Wilks family, Huck says, " It was enough to make a body ashamed of the human race." When he says this it shows that he is definitely changing for the better. Until the trip down the river Huck's life was something that he never took very seriously. He would play jokes on innocent people just to see what would happen, such as when he and Tom hung Jim's hat on the tree branch. As the river brings Huck and Jim together in a strong friendship, Huck sees that Jim is actually an equal who has feelings. So when it comes time for Huck to go against everything he has ever been taught, he does it, just to save Jim. "All right, then, I'll go to hell,", says Huck just as he decides that he'll go ahead and do all he can to get Jim out of his life as a "slave" once and for all. This action shows that his sound heart took precedence over everything that his mentors placed in his mind. This turn around shows that Huck is a very civilized human being with a conscience that changes from what he was taught to what he truly believes in. Huck breaks free of his mold and becomes his own person. As soon as Huck realizes that his morals are incorrect he immediately begins changing them. His change from a person who plays jokes on Negroes for the fun of it to a person who steals them from slavery is a transition for the better. Huck Finn most definitely demonstrates the victory of a sound heart over a deformed conscience.

Q. Morality in The Adventures of Huckleberry Finn

In every persons life at one point they will have to make a choice based on their moral beliefs. These decisions can show what a person believes in right from the start. In Mark Twains' The Adventures of Huckleberry Finn the main character Huck, makes two very important moral decisions. The first being how he treats Jim when he first meets him at Jackson's Island and the second is to tear up the letter to Miss Watson out of his love for Jim.

When Huck first runs away from Pap he goes to Jackson's Island and thinks that he is the only person there. He soon finds out that this is not true, and that "Miss Watsons Jim" is taking refuge there as well. Many people would hate to be alone on an island with a "nigger", but Huck is instead happy to have someone to converse with. At first Jim thinks he sees Hucks ghost and is petrified. Huck eases Jims feelings by changing the subject and saying "It's good daylight, le's get breakfast", showing that Huck is not only real but he does not mind that Jim is black. Jim feels that Huck might tell on him for running away, but he then decides that it will be okay to tell him why he ran away from Miss Watson.

Jim keeps asking Huck if he is going to tell anyone about his running away, and Huck replies "People would call me a low down abolitionist and despise me for keeping mum but that don't make no difference I aint gonna tell". Hucks response truly shows that his ignorance has no bearing over his moral kindness. When taken into consideration good morality is much more important in the long run than being the most intelligent person. After journeying with Jim for quite some time Huck begins to feel bad about harboring a runaway slave. He decides to write a letter to Miss Watson explaining the whole story, because Jim had been sold and he does not know where he is. Huck was indeed confused about what he should do so he dropped he dropped to his knees and began to pray. He felt by helping Jim he was committing a sin, but he later realized "you can't pray a lie".

Huck saying this shows that he feels what he has done for Jim is not wrong; instead what others had done to Jim is wrong. Still not sure of what to do about the whole situation Huck writes the letter to Miss Watson, thinking he will be "cleaned of sin" and not feel so bad about what he is doing. After writing this letter of confession to Miss Watson, Huck starts to reminisce about the times he had with Jim. As he is thinking he comes across the times Jim would be "standing my watch on top of his'n, stead of calling me so I could go on sleeping". Huck begins to realise that he would not be able to "strike no places to harden me against him", showing that he realizes that Jim has done nothing but good for him.

Huck looks at what he is doing and feels ashamed. He takes one final look at the letter before saying "all right then, I'll go to hell" and then rips up the letter of confession. The fact that Huck looked back at his times with Jim before deciding to tear up the letter shows that the decision was obviously made conscientiously through his morals. Hucks morality has a major effect on the way he treats Jim at Jackson's Island and in his decision to tear up the confession letter to Miss Watson. The manner that these decisions are made shows that Huck does indeed have a good set of morals, which he uses to make his decisions. A lack of these Morals could give one of the greatest adventure novels ever written a completely different ending.

Chapter 15

Critical Essays

Discuss the personality of Huck finn in The Adventures of Huckleberry Finn

In the novel, The Adventures of Huckleberry Finn, Huck Finn was the main character. The story was told through his eyes, and most of the events that took place happened around him. But some of these events would not have happened without other main characters as well, like Jim, Tom Sawyer, the King, or the Duke.

Huck's personality at the start of the novel had changed gradually throughout the novel and until the end. At first, Miss Watson tried to make him pray for things but Huck did not believe in praying because it brought him bad luck. Later in the novel, Huck tries to pray for forgiveness and wants to erase his sin for stealing a nigger. After he prays, he feels he can pray openly now and will not sin anymore (CH. 31). Huck was also superstitious and believed that everything that went wrong was because of certain things he did, like the snake in Jim's blanket. And everything was blamed on the bad luck Huck and Jim had. Huck also became kind, especially after the quarrel with his father, pap. He learned that in order to get along with people (like the king and duke), you have to let them have their way, and Huck did.

Jim, at first, was looked upon as just an ordinary nigger. But Huck and Tom soon realized that he was very smart and had helped Huck through most of his adventures. But as a nigger, Jim was looked up to as a hero to other niggers. For instance, Huck tells the reader when niggers from all over the country came to see Jim and hear of his heroic stories and every nigger wanted to be like Jim. Jim was also very superstitious, especially in chapter eight when Jim talks about all of his superstitions, like counting the things for dinner and telling the bees that their owner had just died. All of this supposedly brought bad luck.

Tom Sawyer was also a very influential character to the story. He was the one who came up with all the solutions for things, which eventually made more of a disaster. But that is because he followed stories too much. For instance, in chapter 35, Jim is captured and Tom tries the most original and hardest way to get him out, thus creating more of a catastrophe. Tom is also a big liar. He tries to tell Huck about rubbing a tin lamp and making a genie appear. He also lies about his identity to his aunt, but Huck was also a big liar in that situation as well. One of the biggest characteristics Tom had was that he was too egotistic and did not listen to anyone's ideas. For example, in trying to free Jim, Tom does not listen to any of Huck's ideas to get Jim out and just does it his own way.

Around the middle of the story, Huck was passing along a "crick" when he saw two men, of whom he would soon meet. One of the men looked to be around thirty years old and told Huck and Jim that he was the Duke of Bridgewater. However, not until about the end of the novel did Huck and Jim find out that this man was just a fraud, like everything else in his life. For instance, the duke, Huck, Jim, and the king (also the other man) had begun an adventure on a river to nearby towns to fraud people and earn of money. On of the first scams was a Shakespeare show in which the duke and king had presented. The crowd was outraged in the play's performance and disliked it very much, especially when Colonel Sherburn shot the man and the play was stopped. But since the duke was skilled in printing, he persuaded the crowd to not tell the town about the play so that other people could come and spend money to see the duke and king perform.

The king, also like the duke, was a big fraud and lied about almost everything. Out of the three nights that the Shakespeare performance was held, tne duke and king had made around

465 dollars. Despite the king's earnings and lying, he proved to be very pious and concerned, especially when he meets Mary Jane and grieves with her family about the death of Peter Wilks. However, half of the reason he was being so caring was because he saw an opportunity to receive a large amount of money, so he pretended to be a family member of Peter Wilks.

One of the first minor characters that had a big influence on Huck was his father, pap. Pap was one of the major reasons Huck had ran away, mainly because pap was very aggressive. As for his appearance, Huck described him as being unclean and dressed in rags. Pap was also an alcoholic and was very controlling over Huck, especially when money had come into place. The first encounter that Huck had with his fake identity was with a woman named Judith.

She caught on to Huck's lie very easily but knew he was a hurt little boy that needed some direction. So she was caring enough to help him on his travel and was generous in letting Huck stay there until he left for Goshen. In chapter 17, Huck finds a farm in "Arkansaw" and the family living there gladly accepted him. One of their children, Buck, had become Huck's new companion, although Buck was more interested in killing animals and his family's rivalry. Buck was also treated like an adult, although he was only thirteen years old, by smoking pipes and carrying a gun at all times. Probably the most important setting in the novel was the island. The island was three miles long and contained deep woods and many fruits. Huck had stayed there for three days and nights and this setting was the basis for his adventure. On this island, he had met Jim, soon to be his best companion, and learned many tricks of survival on different lands.

Another major setting was the farmhouse in "Arkansaw". This was the house with Buck and his family. Huck described it as being a nice house with a big fireplace and big brass dog irons and many other elegant features. It also contained many beautiful paintings and poetry, written by one of the daughters Emmeline. But it only served Huck for a couple nights until he left with Jim down the river again.

The last major setting, also probably the most influential

setting, was the house of Mary Ann and the two other sisters of Peter Wilks. Huck had to stay there with the king and duke in order for them to persuade the family into selling the house and giving a lot of money to the kind and duke. But this drew the line for Huck, and he soon changed his ways and had to stop the king's nonsense. So, he stopped lying and wanted to tell Mary Ann about the money in the coffin and how the king was not related to Peter Wilks.

One of the major themes of the novel is the separation of races. Over the course of the novel, Huck's opinion of Jim changes. In the beginning of their voyage, Huck feels he shouldn't be helping Jim to freedom and almost turns him in to slave catchers. Huck says, "I was paddling off, all in a sweat to tell on him; but when he says this (that Huck is his one and only friend) it seemed to take the tuck all out of me." Huck soon realizes that he enjoys Jim's company and when the duke and the king sell Jim, Huck breaks down and cries. When asking the duke where Jim was, Huck says, "'Sold him' I says, and begun to cry; 'why he was my nigger, and that was my money.

Where is he? — I want my nigger.'" Jim was important to Huck because he knew all kinds of signs about the future, people's personalities, and weather forecasting. Even more important, Huck feels a comfort with Jim that he has not felt with the other major characters in the novel. With Jim, Huck can enjoy the best aspects of his earlier influences. Jim allows Huck freedom, but he does it in a loving, rather than an uncaring, fashion. Thus, early in their relationship on Jackson's Island, Huck says to Jim, "This is nice. I wouldn't want to be nowhere else but here."

Before the novel begins, Huck Finn has led a life of absolute freedom. His drunken and often missing father never paid much attention to him; his mother was dead and when the novel began, Huck was not used to following any rules. The book's opening finds Huck living with the Widow Douglas and her sister, Miss Watson. Both women were fairly old and were really somewhat incapable of raising a rebellious boy like Huck Finn. Nevertheless, they attempt to make Huck into what they believed would be a better boy. As Huck said, they wanted to "sivilize" him. Huck, who had never followed many rules in his life, found the demands the women placed upon him constraining and the life lonely. As result, soon after he first moves in with them, he ran away. He soon came back, but even though he became somewhat comfortable with his new life as the months go by, Huck never really enjoys the life of manners, religion, and education that the Widow and her sister imposed upon him.

Then, Huck believes he will find some freedom with Tom Sawyer. Huck is eager to join Tom Sawyer's Gang because he feels that doing so will allow him to escape the boring life he leads with the Widow Douglas. Unfortunately, such an escape does not occur. Tom Sawyer promises robbing stages, murdering and ransoming people, kidnapping beautiful women, but none of this happens. Huck finds out too late that Tom's adventures are imaginary.

Another person who tries to get Huck to change is pap. Pap's appearance reflects his feelings, as he demands that Huck quit school, stops reading, and avoids church. Huck is able to stay away from pap for a while, but pap kidnaps Huck three or four months after Huck starts to live with the Widow and takes him to a lonely cabin deep in the Missouri woods. Here, Huck enjoys the freedom that he had prior to the beginning of the book. But Huck begins to become dissatisfied with this life and Huck soon realizes that he will have to escape from the cabin if he wishes to remain alive. As a result of his concern, Huck makes it appear as if he is killed in the cabin while pap is away, and leaves to go to a remote island in the Mississippi River, Jackson's Island.

Then, his adventure down the Mississippi begins. It is after he leaves his father's cabin that Huck joins yet another important influence in his life: Miss Watson's slave, Jim. Soon after joining Jim on Jackson's Island, Huck begins to realise that Jim has more talents and intelligence than Huck has been aware of. The first encounter they came upon was the island itself, in which they explored thoroughly. From there, they reached their first problem, which was trying to escape from

Huck's father and friends, and then travel to St. Petersburg. In St. Petersburg, Huck disguises himself as a woman in order to disguise his identity, but the woman he meets soon realizes he is just a man in trouble. From there, Huck and Jim lose the boat and travel down the river until they come upon a wreck and some fog, where Huck loses their raft once more.

The next big event was in "Arkansaw" when Huck and Jim encounter a farmhouse. Soon, Huck goes up to the house and enters it, only being greeted by a feudal family. Huck spends a few days their, experiencing the feud between two families and finally escapes one night to go back to Jim by the river. Now, the two drift down the river once more, only to find two men who were soon to be their new companions: the duke and the king. All four of them set out to different towns, conning the townspeople into seeing ridiculous plays. However, the duke and the king got away with it and earned a great deal of money. While going through one town, the town drunk, Boggs, came into the picture and was shot by Colonel Sherburn. This stirred up the town and the people confronted the Colonel at his house, only to be turned away.

Towards the end of the novel, the four meet up with a stranger who tells of a dead man, Peter Wilks. This gives the duke and the king a great idea to change their identity to a relative of Mr. Wilks and con his family for money. Mr. Wilks sister was persuaded and the king had the money in his possession, until Huck took it and hid it. Huck finally confessed to hiding the money and the townsmen went to try to recover it. While doing so, Huck escapes once more. Soon, Huck encounters Tom Sawyer's aunt, and Huck portrays to be Tom. However, this only creates more problems. Jim is captured and is held in a little hut, and Tom comes to help Huck free him. Jim gets free after days and days of hard work, but Tom gets shot and Jim finds a doctor for him. Eventually, Tom confesses to his aunt about the lie and Huck will soon live with Tom's aunt, whom he dislikes.

One of the main symbols in the novel was the Mississippi River. It was a symbol from the start of Huck's adventure until the end. What makes it a symbol is that it was an opening for

Huck's escape and gave him the opportunity to explore the country and be free. In other words, it was his course for self-discovery and the source of danger, delight, and meditation.

Another symbol in the novel was the fog in chapter fifteen. Since Huck and Jim had just begun their adventure, any obstacles that they encounter will be treacherous for them. Well, the fog was a symbol of one of these obstacles in which Huck and Jim had to pass in order to advance. However, it took patience and Huck really had to dig down inside himself and stay calm or else a disaster would have occurred. So this fog symbolized a warning and there would be many more warnings to come.

The third symbol in the novel was the feud between the two families in Arkansas: the Grangerfords and the Shepherdson. During the Civil War, the south was prominent for starting many feuds with the federates as well as other southerners. The south had often taken a feud from several years ago and kept the feud alive. The two families in this novel did the same. One family killed a member of the other family, so the other family killed a member of the first family in order to get pay back.

Eventually, the two went back and forth, creating a feud, which symbolizes how the Civil War had taken place. In The Adventures of Huckleberry Finn, the story was told through the eyes of Huck Finn, the main character in the novel. Thus, the point of view was the 1st person because Huck had narrated the story while being a character in the novel. Throughout the novel, I had read the word "I" at least a thousand times because that is all Huck talked about: himself and what is happening around him. But that is only normal because he cannot tell of other things unless he sees them or hears about them, so he can only say what happens in his own view. There are countless quotes I can use to prove my statement, but here are a couple that are said by Huck as he narrates the story:

> *"I don't know how long I was asleep, but all of a sudden there was an awful scream and I was up. There was pap looking wild, and skipping*

around every which way and yelling about snakes."
"They went off and I got aboard the raft, feeling
bad and low, because I knowed very well I had
done wrong, and I see it warn't no use for me to
try to learn to do right…"

The Adventures of Huckleberry Finn, is based on a young boy's coming of age in Missouri of the mid-1800s. This story depicts many serious issues that occur on the "dry land of civilization" better known as society. As these somber events following the Civil War are told through the young eyes of Huckleberry Finn, he unknowingly develops morally from both the conforming and non-conforming influences surrounding him on his journey to freedom. Huck's moral evolution begins before he ever sets foot on the raft down the Mississippi. His mother has died, and his father is constantly in a drunken state. Huck grows up following his own rules until he moves in with the Widow Douglas and her sister, Miss Watson. Together, the women attempt to civilize Huck by making him attend school, study religion, and act in a way the women find socially acceptable.

However, Huck's free-spirited soul keeps him from joining the constraining and lonely life the two women have in store for him. The freedom Huck seeks in Tom Sawyer's gang is nothing more than romantic child's-play. Raiding a caravan of Arabs really means terrorizing young children on a Sunday school picnic, and the stolen "joolry" is nothing more than turnips or rocks. Huck is disappointed that the adventures Tom promises are not real and so, along with the other members, he resigns from the gang. Still, he ignorantly assumes that Tom is superior to him because of his more suitable family background and fascination with Romantic literature (Twain). Pap and "the kidnapping" play another big role in Huck's moral development. Pap is completely antisocial and wishes to undo all of the civilizing effects that the Widow and Miss Watson have attempted to instill in him. However, Pap does not symbolize freedom; he promotes drunkenness, prejudice, and abuse. Huck escapes the cabin to search for the freedom he yearns for. It is after he escapes to Jackson Island that he meets the most influential character of the novel, Jim. After conversing, Huck learns things about the runaway slave that he had never been aware of. Jim has a family, dreams, and talents such as knowing "all kinds of signs about the future," people's personalities, and weather forecasting (Twain 69). However, Huck sees Jim as a gullible slave.

He plays tricks on him like the "rattlesnake event" that nearly gets Jim killed. At this point in the novel, Huck still holds the belief that blacks are essentially different from whites. In addition, his conscience reminds him that he's a "low-down and dirty abolitionist" for helping Jim run away from his owner. Huck does not see that Jim is looking for freedom just as he is (Master Plots). The first adventure Huck and Jim take part in while searching for freedom is the steamboat situation. Huck shows development of character in tricking the watchman into going back to the boat to save the criminals. Even though they are thieves, and plan to murder another man, Huck still feels that the forfeit of their lives would be too great a punishment.

Some may see Huck's reaction to the event as crooked but, unlike most of society, Huck Finn sees the good in people and attempts to help them with sincerity and compassion. Getting lost in the fog while floating down the Mississippi River leads to a major turning point in the development of Huck Finn's character. Up to this event, he has seen Jim as a lesser person than himself. After trying to deny the fog event to Jim, he says, "It was fifteen minutes before I could work myself up to go and humble myself to a slave; but I done it, and I warn't ever sorry for it afterward, neither (Twain 92)." He continues by explaining how he could never do such a thing again.

Huck has clearly gained respect for Jim here, which explains the risks he is willing to take for Jim later in the book. A short yet significant scene is when the men on shore want to check Huck's raft for runaway slaves. He escapes by tricking them into thinking that his dad is onboard with smallpox. This scene shows a negative view of human nature. The men had helped Huck until they realized that they were in danger themselves. They put their own safety above that of others, and while this is sometimes acceptable, it is by no means a noble trait (Gerber). On the other hand, Huck risks his own freedom to see that Jim finds his. The feud between the Grangerfords and the Shepardsons adds to Huck's distaste for society and it's teachings. In this adventure, Huck learns what a feud is and also witnesses the horrid aftermath the hostility brought upon the two families.

Another part of Huck's moral metamorphosis in this event is that he has come to miss the one man that has given him fatherly love throughout the excursion. The Duke and the King join Huck and Jim in the middle of the novel. The two con men use Huck and Jim to fulfill their greed and desires. Like the two men from the steamboat occurrence, Huck knows that their schemes are wrong. The con men's attempt to masquerade as the brothers of the late Peter Wilks is an important part of Huck's development. Later on the Duke and King try to take Peter's estate, however, Huck decides to return the money to Peter's three daughters. This action demonstrates further moral growth, as does his choice to abandon the two con men.

Huck also learns how conniving people can be while attending the funeral of Peter Wilks. Women would walk up to Peter's daughters and "kiss their foreheads, and then put their hand on their head, look up towards the sky with the tears running down, and bust out sobbing just to give the next woman a show" Huck has never seen anything "so disgusting." When he sees one of the daughters crying beside the coffin, it makes a deep impact on him (Twain 213). Not only did he experience his first bout with puppy love, he also feels compassion for an innocent victim. "All right then, I'll go to hell!" represents the highest point in Huck's moral development. He has decided to go against his conscience by freeing Jim, and in doing so, reject society.

While the society he has grown up in teaches that freeing slaves is wrong, Huck has evolved to a point where he can realise that what he feels is right, and that his own beliefs are superior to those of Southern civilization (Englewood 47). Jim has taught him what it is like to feel free while gliding down the Mississippi. When Huck would need safety from the dry land, Jim has always been his haven. However, the next situation Jim and Huck go through will bring another turning point—for the worst. When Tom Sawyer's relatives catch Jim, Huck decides he will get his friend back. He sees Uncle Silas as such a good man, but fails to see that he owns slaves like all the rest. Also, just as Jim looks up to Huck, Huck looks up to Tom Sawyer, and let's his useless rescue attempts jeopardize Jim's freedom. Jim does show compassion yet again when he attempts to save the Duke and King from being tarred and feathered, but there is an apparent stagnant period in Huck's development during the "rescue attempt."

Huck let's Tom Sawyer take the controls and sits quietly while Tom puts Jim through ordeal after ordeal (Twain 296). When it is made certain that Jim is a free man, Huck learns the truth about his father's death and who was in the floating house at the beginning of the journey. It is made evident to the reader that Huck thanks Jim for protecting him from the gruesome nature, and does not regret the adventures he and Jim had together. Huckleberry Finn was able to rise above the rest of society. As a young boy, he learned many things about the cruel world, and what freedom really means. Huck will never accept "civilization" and he will always go back to the safety net of the Mississippi River. Though there were times when he made the wrong decision, the reader must realise that growing up is a trial-and-error. Society has come a long way since the Civil War, and it is important to realise that people like the characters, Jim and Huckleberry Finn, have made freedom accessible to all that need a harbor from the dry limits of society soil (Englewood 53).

Although Huckleberry Finn seems to get into a lot of trouble, as he is dishonest at many times throughout the novel, his character seems to melt in the reader's hand once his fine moral nature begins to unfold. The game Huck plays drifts him into an occasion of rare moral crisis, where he must choose between violating the entire code of social, religious, conventional behaviour which the world has taught him, and betraying the person who needs and loves him most and whom he loves most. He writes a letter which tells Miss Watson that her slave, Jim, is in Mr. Phelp's possession. After writing the letter he says: "I felt good and all washed clean of sin for the first time I had ever so in my life, and I knowed I could pray now. But I didn't do it straight off but laid the paper down and set there thinking how good it was all this happened so, and how near I come to being lost and going to hell." After studying the letter he then said, "All right, then, I'll go to hell" and tore it up (Twain 216).

Another thing that affected Huck and may have contributed to his unhappiness that brought him over the edge to run away was lack of money. Early on Huck and his father sold his fortune to Judge Thatched for a dollar. This lack of money may have put an even bigger strain on the father, causing him drink his sorrows away and act irrationally towards Huck. This brought on the constant beatings that Huck was forced to endure until he gained the courage to fake his death, and leave his pitiful life back at the mouth of the river. Money also played a part concerning those two swindling crooks, the King and Duke. The king and Duke tried to pass themselves off as being distant relatives. Their new identity would put them at hand with a large amount of cash. Ultimately their cover was revealed. Huck is able to escape unscathed, but the King and Duke weren't as fortunate as tar and feathers awaited them (Twain 318). Drinking also plays a part in Huck's dilemmas as the story unravels drinking led Huck's father to beat him. Living in an unhappy situation such as this gave Huck reason to start out on his own adventure. Drinking also led to the Duke's easy admittance of hiding the money. In this situation, the drunkenness exhibited by both characters helped to put a hole in their cover up. While they were questioned and served a heavy punishment, it was really Huck who stole the money before all of their eyes (Master Plots). Throughout the novel Huck overcomes numerous obstacles and endures various negative repercussions to attain both emotional and physical freedom. Twain's implied lessons were expressed within Huckleberry's moral dilemmas.

The novel ends with a frustrated Huck stating; " Aunt

Sally she's gonna adopt me and civilize me and I can't stand it. I been there before." Although the novel ends leaving the reader with a sense that Huck is truly free, he will forever be followed by his moral dilemmas.

Huckleberry Finn: A Father Figure

Mark Twain, the author of Huckleberry Finn, has written a story that all will enjoy. Huck is a young boy with not much love in his life, his mother died when he was very young, and he had drunk for a father. Huck lives with the widow and she tried to raise him right. While at the widow's, Huck went to school and learned to read and write. The widow also tried to civilize him. She would buy him nice clothes, and make him do his homework.

The main character in this story is Huck Finn, Finn is a young boy with many problems going on in life. Huck was in need of a father figure more then any thing else in life. He needed someone to talk to about anything. Huck's Pap was never there for him except maybe to give him a tanning. Huck's Pap thought that he was trying to out do him, because he went to school. "You've put on considerable many frills since I been away. I'll take you down a peg before I get done with you. You think you're better'n your father, now don't you, because he can't? I'll take it out of you. Who told you you might meddle with such hifalut'n foolishness, hey?-who told you you could" Pap scolded . Huck didn't like having to wear nice clothes, or even going to school, but the he had to go. "Starchy clothes-very. You think you're a good deal of a big-bug, don't you" Pap asked ?

Huck would try and be a rebel because he had no male to tell him right from wrong. If Huck needed help the only real person that he could talk to would be Tom Sawyer, a very good friend also a thief, a rebel, and he lived on his own. Tom was not that great of a role model, for a young boy like Huck. His father was always away, and never there for him, and when he was around he was always drunk. It is hard enough to talk to a drunk man let alone when you have a problem and need advice. The childhood of a young boy is very crucial in what he will be like in his own life. Huckleberry Finn was written to show young males that there are ways of finding someone. Mark Twain has a very unique perspective on the whole subject. He found a way to find love in a place where the reader would never imagine. Huck's pap came and took him away from the widow and Huck thought that everything would be so much better, but no.

The only good thing that came out of it was that he didn't have to go to school. His Pap locked him in the cabin whenever he went away, an if ever did anything wrong he would get a tanning (otherwise known as being spanked). When a young boy is growing up being locked up all the time does not help a young boy to develop into a man. Young boys need a role model to look up to, and if the only role model around is a drunk then you will become a drunk. Huck would see his Pap so drunk and yell at him all the time.

Huck went to school just to spite the old man, but when his Pap found him, Huck sure did get a tanning. Huck would have to get money for his Pap just so that he wouldn't get a tanning. The influence of being abused and being around a drunk person is never the way to grow up. Huck couldn't take the abuse anymore, from being tanned, to being locked in a cabin for days. So he ran away, and planned to never return. Huck figured out a way to get away from his Pap, the widow and everyone else. Huck was gonna learn to raise himself and become his own role model.

Huck had a raft, supplies and his freedom. He felt as if his life could get a whole lot better if he got away from all the abuse. Huck traveled during the night and slept during the day. That's how he found the runaway black man from Miss Watson's. Huck was resting during the day, and he found a camp fire that was freshly put out.

Then while Huck was trying to sleep he heard a noise and out popped Jim. "Hello Jim," I said . Huck was so glad that Jim was now there with him.

Jim was a very good man that was just never understood, but Huck learned all about him on their voyages down the river. Huck and Jim were inseparable. They would talk about everything. The only thing that they really did that was a little bad was smoking tobacco. Jim understood why Huck ran away, because of his Pap always beating him. Jim knew what that was like, being a black person and all. This is the first time that Huck had ever had a male adult to talk to this way. With having a person of Jims intelligence Huck could learn a lot. Huck had someone to look up to, to learn from.

Jim and Huck got into some trouble when they thought that they were in Cairo and got separated. By this time Miss Watson had a two-hundred dollar reward out for him. Jim got captured and Huck was alone, again. Huck found out where Jim was and realized who lived there, and it was Tom Sawyer's aunt. This was the best news that he heard because Tom was suppose to being coming out for a visit and so Huck became Tom, and Tom became Sid. Together Huck and Tom rescued Jim. Huck was so afraid that he was going to lose Jim, but when Huck was just a black man. Huck actually had an adult that liked him and wanted to help.

Huckleberry Finn is a classic story. It shows that Huck can find someone that he can depend on since his father never helped him. Jim became Huck's father in more then one way. Jim was a very good friend that Huck could talk to about anything. Jim cared so much about Huck, that when Jim was left behind he would miss him so. When Jim was being held captive Huck would do anything to get him freed. Jim and Huck had a very special bond. They could never be separated ever again.

Huck was in need of a father figure and Twain was the author who brought it all to together. Twain used characterization to bring the elements of the literature to life. From Jim being black, and Huck thinking that his father could ever be there for him. Twain gives Huck chances to have Tom Sawyer to be his father figure, but Huck chose Jim. Huck didn't seem to care that Jim was black he still cared about him still the same way as if he were white. Jim would look out for Huck, and Huck would look out for Jim. If Huck had not cared about Jim he would be back in slavery, and would never have found someone to be his father figure.

Adventures of Huckleberry Finn: Racism

The twentieth century has come to an amazing finale. Racism, ethnic prejudice and hate are on the decline. Perhaps some of these changes can be attributed to the novel, The Adventures of Huckleberry Finn, in which Mark Twain addresses the issues of racism and slavery. He writes in a humorous, almost childish way, yet the themes are clear and poignant. Twain utilizes Huck Finn and Jim as the ideal characters because they are the ones at the end of the novel who realise slavery is wrong. Mark Twain establishes the ideals by portraying them through the protagonists, Huck and Jim and criticizes the failure to live up to them by portraying them through the antagonists, Miss Watson.

Prejudice can be observed throughout the novel by the way the other characters treat Huck. Twain portrays Huck as an average boy of his time, mischievous, adventurous and funny. The society Huck lives in labels him "uncivilized" because he has an abusive, drunk father. "By and by pap got too handy with his hick'ry and I couldn't stand it. I was all over with welts" (Twain page #). Here the reader can observe the ultimate failure of an uncivilized person. Pap is an alcoholic, a dead beat and a racist. Nevertheless, society also considered Huck "uncivilized" because he did not wear shoes did not always attend school and he smoked. Society criticized Huck as uncivilized due to physical appearance when really Huck turned out to be more civilized than any other character in the novel because he learns how to respect Jim. Through the ironic criticism of society trying to civilize Huck, Huck teaches us a lesson on being civilized.

In the novel, Jim runs away from his slave owner, Miss Watson. By doing a thing like that Jim could have been killed or beat. The people of Jim's society would not have even listened to him or even considered his reason. "Well, you see, it 'uz dis way. Ole missus-dat's Miss Watson- she pecks on me all de time, en treats me pooty rough, but she alwuz said she wouln' sell me down to Orleans.... but she could git eight hund'd dollars for me" (Twain page #). Twain wanted to show, through Jim, just how cruel people were and how those feelings were condoned by society. Twain also shows the ideal of freedom through Jim and the failure to live up to that freedom when Miss Watson sells him. Ultimately Twain tries to point that we can still make up for the injustices just as Miss Watson did when she set Jim free.

Twain's contemporary society did not react well to the messages in the novel, which is why the novel was banned and burned. The people of Twain's society did not like being told they were wrong and they made that fact known. Another ideal Twain emphasizes is the idea that one should recognize their own fault and learn from their mistakes. One way to solve this would by setting aside prejudice feelings and just move on. An example of someone in the novel doing this is Miss Watson, "Ole Miss Watson died two months ago, and she was ashamed she ever was going to sell him down the river, and said so; and she set him free in her will" (Twain page #). Like many people Miss Watson finally realized the wrong she did and put her "racist" views aside. Here Twain shows how that despite some people fail to live up to their ideals it is never to late to make up for those failure and make them ideals. Through his simple novel The Adventures of Huckleberry Finn Twain establishes the ideals of society through his main characters and shows what happens when these ideals fail. If Huck Finn can learn to see past the racism and hate of his day and love a black man then perhaps our society can learn from this and move forward not as whites, blacks, Hispanics, niggers, waps, micks or wetbacks but as human beings sharing this precious world.

The Adventures of Huckleberry Finn Ignorance

While there are many themes expressed in the novel, The Adventures of Huckleberry Finn one makes a stronger presence by its continued, if not redundant display of itself. Far too often in society people's lack of knowledge on a given subject causes their opinions and actions to rely strictly on stereotypes created by the masses. This affliction is commonly known as ignorance. This is curable but people have to become open-minded and leave their reliance on society's viewpoints behind them. In the novel, The Adventures of Huckleberry Finn by Mark Twain, the ignorance of society becomes extremely evident at many parts of the book. Society forms ideals for all walks of life and then lets them become like stone in their minds. Thus, once a person has been put into a group they will remain there forever. The ignorance of society is clearly seen when one looks at Huck Finn, Jim the Slave, Pap, and the senseless violence of the Grangerfords and the Shepardsons. Many people see Huckleberry Finn as a mischievous boy who is a bad influence to others. Society refuses to accept Huck as he is and isn't going to change its opinions about him until he is reformed and civilized. The Widow Douglas and Miss Watson try to "sivilize" Huck by making him stop all of his habits such as smoking, etc.

They try to reverse all of his teaching from the first twelve years of his life and force him to become their stereotypical good boy. The rest of the town also refused to view him as good and he was considered undesirable. The only time that the town's people are able to put away their views of Huck was when there was excitement to be found, like when they all crowded on the steamboat to see if the cannons can bring Huck's body to the surface. Everyone got interested in him and tried to show that they cared about him, but this is only after he is presumed dead.

They take on these views to follow society in its ignorance. Few of them would have cared about Huck before because they didn't know him and didn't want to know him, but since taking interest in mysteries was the popular thing to do, society did it. Although Huck is viewed in an ignorant light, he was also in accordance with this novel and very ignorant himself. Huck said "I thought it all out, and reckoned I would belong to the widow if he wanted me, though I couldn't make out how he was a-going to be any better off then than what he was before, seeing I was so ignorant, and so kind of low-down and ornery." Huck talks about Pap with some disgust and disregard. While Huck is not completely afraid of him in this quote as he later becomes, he still does not show respect for his father.

The following is a good representation of what Huck does and does not understand. "I studied a minute, sort of holding my breath, and then says to myself: 'All right, then, I'll go to hell'—and tore it up." Huck wrote a letter to Miss Watson but tore it up. He decided that he would go to hell for Jim. Another good example is when Huck was having problems with Jim wanting his children back. "...[Jim] would steal his children — children that belonged to a man... a man that hadn't ever done me no harm." This quote shows that Huck is still troubled by helping Jim and that he still does not yet understand that Jim is just as human as those people who own his children. This shows a stage in his growth in understanding about slavery and Jim. Society once again set the stereotypes in another section of the book by their feelings toward Jim and Pap. Society automatically sees a black person, and even further, slaves, as inferior. They never thought of slaves as human beings, only as property. A slave, such as Jim, could be the nicest, most caring person you have ever met, but since he is a slave he would be presumed incapable of such things. While society is doing this it will let a person whom is as evil as Pap go on without question. Society's ignorance shines radiantly once again. They have the knowledge that Jim is a slave but make no judgments on his personality. This is shown when they assume that Jim killed Huck just because he ran away near the time of Huck's death. They don't consider the motives of such an action, but just look at the surface facts that he might do this because he is savage, missing, and possibly in the area at the time. Pap is also suspected, but not as much as Jim even though he has a motive, and could have easily committed such an evil deed in one of his drunken stupors. Society, because of their lack of knowledge of the personality of Jim, automatically assumes that he is the one that committed the murder. Society makes superficial accusations because it doesn't know what has really happened or of the true feelings of the two suspects.

Again, society isn't the only ignorant party. Jim is awfully ignorant, and if you search for proof you need to look no further than any direct quote in which he is speaking. "What's de use er makin' up de camp fire to cook strawbries en sich truck? But you got a gun, hain't you? Den we kin git sumfn better den strawbries." (When I typed this out it drove my spell check crazy!) In another part of the novel the Twain illustrates the ignorance of society very well with the feud between the Grangerfords and the Shepardsons. When Buck Grangerford was questioned about why he shot at Harvey Shepardson he first exclaims in disbelief that Huck doesn't know what a feud was, and says "Why, nothing — only it's on account of the feud." Then, however, he doesn't know why the two families are feuding in the first place and hasn't made any effort to find out. It is remarkable that people will continue on an old grudge without knowing how it originated.

On top of that, they won't make any attempts to gain knowledge about the subject. Buck, in this fragment of the novel, represents how society often bases its actions on what it has been told by others without questioning the motives. When Buck was asked when the feud was started, he told Huck that he didn't know, but replied, "Oh, yes, pa knows, I reckon, and some of the other old people; but they don't know now what the row was about in the first place." Without true knowledge of why the feud is occurring one might wonder how people could continue on with the killing. It may seem bizarre, but so are many of the other actions of society. When a large group of people takes one viewpoint others are often forced into this mentality even if they are more enlightened. People can oppress others into conditions by forcing their incorrect views on them. They often will not allow people to rise through the ranks without blatant proof of improvement.

The oblivious members of society who only consider the surface instead of looking deep for true knowledge can falsely accuse people. Society constantly judges people based on stereotypes of a certain group and it often fails to consider the personality of an individual. Society takes action without being properly informed or will take up arms against opposing groups just because someone who it respects has blindly told them to. The ignorance of Society constantly causes people, issues, and views to be regarded in adverse ways.

Huck Finn's Moral Changes

In the book The Adventures of Huckleberry Finn, the main character Huck Finn undergoes many moral changes. In the beginning of the book, Huck is wild and carefree, playing jokes and tricks on people and believing them all to be hilarious. When Huck's adventures grow to involve more people and new moral questions never before raised, you can tell that he has started to change. By the time the book is almost over, people can see a drastic change in Huck's opinions, thoughts, and his views of "right and wrong".

Sometimes, serious events can affect a person's morals, opinions, and values. This is clearly shown in Huck as his adventures progress further into seriousness. Even through the seriousness, Mark Twain has still added a twist of humour to keep everything interesting, and that is what keeps readers interested in reading the book. Readers might even be affected by reading The Adventures of Huckleberry Finn their opinions prior to reading the book and opinions following the exposure to these ideas may differ.

Huck's views on theology, "right and wrong" opinions, views of slavery, and the tricks he plays all reflect the beliefs that Huck holds when he is introduced in the early part of the book. Hucks opinion of religion shows his lack of concern for serious things. When lectured on heaven and hell (by which he refers to by the "good" and "bad" place respectively), he quickly decides that he wants to go to the "bad" place because he finds no interest in singing and praying to god, while the bad place appeals to him as he hears that his friend Tom Sawyer is going to the bad place. His views of praying also reflect his lack of serious concerns. Instead of praying for help in finding faith, he prays for a fishing line.

This upsets him when he finds that there are no fishing hooks and takes prayer lightheartedly until faced with another moral problem later into the book. His carefree and wild ways are expressed with his superstitions as well. This is shown with his throwing salt over his shoulder and his other superstitions such as burning the spider, about the snakeskin, and talking about the dead . Another way Mark Twain expresses Huck's wildness and confused morals is that he never tells the truth. One of his bloated lies is the one about being a girl that he keeps bloating and bloating to cover up his old lies. His seriousness later changes as the book progresses. By the middle of the book, Huck has shown certain sines of improvement. He now realizes that Jim is more human than he was led to believe. Huck's view of "right and wrong" have changed. He still lies and plays jokes, but now he feels some guilt whenever he does this. An example of this is when he tricks Jim into believing he was dreaming about the fog. When Jim says "en trash is what people is dat puts dirt on de head er dey fren's en makes 'em feel ashamed", which in more correct spelling means "trash is what people are who put dirt on their friend's heads".

This makes Huck feel bad enough to apoligize and he finally realizes that tricking Jim is wrong and that he has feelings. He also before that, had lied to save Jim from getting caught by saying that Jim was white and had a disease so that people wouldn't look for Jim and probably catch him. His seriousness grows after he sees Buck die, and Buck had been somewhat of a friend to him Later, when they encounter the "King" and the "Duke" and even later when he finds out that the King and the Duke are frauds, he does not tell Jim, but for a good reason. This reason is so he does not make Jim feel ignorant or gullible. This shows an improvement in Huck, that he still keeps the truth away, but he does it for the good of others now. By the late part of the book (or of what we read), Huck shows more seriousness to religion and actually thinks of how religion and his morals are contradicting. He stops to think of which should overrule. Religion, as he understands it, tells him stealing is wrong, and combined with what he was taught, it makes helping a slave escape appear as stealing.

On the other hand, Huck see's Jim as a human and wants to help him. Jim is his friend, and Huck now holds staying with your friends as one of his values. So after thinking seriously about it and even writing a note to Miss Watson, he eventually decides that his values overrule religion (by then ripping up the note), even though religion is still a force that should be thought about. In his eyes, he is going to go to hell and suffer eternally because of helping Jim escape and not returning him back to his "owner". This later shows that Huck is an "all the way" kind of person (meaning if he does something wrong and is going to have to suffer consequences for it, he might as well enjoy doing it). When he figures out that the "King" has sold Jim, he goes out to find Jim . We can now see that Huck is caring over his friends now and that he sticks by his morals as much as he can, and Huck's morals have changed alot since the beginning.

He does not seem to enjoy lying to people anymore if it hurts others. His dislikes of hurting others with lies started from when he tricked Jim about the fog and felt bad, to when he decided he would tell the truth to Mary Jane in a note . The Adventures of Huckleberry Finn is an excellant example of how people can change over time and events. This is shown in the above reasons. Huck generally feels that "humans are good and trustworthy, but you always have to watch out for people that always want to make a benefit at others loss". He is shocked by the fact that people have a tendency to do incredibly kind things (like when he helps Jim) and the fact that people can do terrible things to hurt others emotionally (as shown by the King and the Duke's heartless ways to get money, which even include disrespect to the dead). Huck talks to his conscience in many of the previous statements. He talks with his conscience to find what choice is better, turn in Jim or help Jim, and when he decides to help Mary Jane. As a general whole, the human race is generally good and kind, but there are always some exceptions.

Twain's Pre-Civil War America

American authors tend to write about life in their times. Mark Twain lived in the 1800's and witnessed the Civil War era. At that time, our nation was divided over the issue of slavery. The inhumane treatment of slaves moved Twain to use his talent to criticize their treatment. In one of his most famous novels named The Adventures of Huckleberry Finn, Twain depicts the injustice of slavery in the South just before the Civil War.

To begin with, Mark Twain uses the plot of The Adventures of Huckleberry Finn to reveal the truths about life in the South during the 1800's. For starters, slavery proved to be one of the most predominant aspects of southern life at that time. The birth of Mark Twain occurred during this era of slavery, so racism surrounded Twain his whole life. Twain based his writings upon his own personal experiences. Critics agree that, "The book is a strong voice against racism, but at the same time some passages mirror the values of the racist society Mark was raised in" (Meltzer 89).

Secondly, The Adventures of Huckleberry Finn portrays the appalling truths regarding enslavement which pervaded the South. Twain utilizes his work as a means to reveal the factuality of racism. "Perfectly 'nice' people didn't consider the death of a black person worth their notice," claims literary analysts (Salwen). Additionally, Mark Twain illustrates life in the South through the actions of the main character Huckleberry Finn. Huck, as he is known for short, has never perceived slavery as anything but a natural part of life. "Because of his upbringing, the boy starts out believing that slavery is part of the natural order," Salwen exclaims to clarify Huck's ignorance).

In addition, most of the remaining Southerners possessed the same views of slavery as Huck. "The satire of a decadent slaveholding society gains immensely in force when Mark Twain demonstrates that even the outcast Huck has been in part perverted by it," Smith comments on the oblivious views of Southerners. Finally, Twain's realistic masterpiece satirizes slavery along with man's quest for freedom.

Since many African-Americans had been impriso Twainned as slaves, it seems only natural that one would occasionally escape to search for freedom. An obvious quest for freedom in The Adventures of Huckleberry Finn would be that of Jim, an escaped slave. Huck meets Jim and they grow to become exceptional friends. Salwen explains, "It's about a slave who breaks the law and risks his life to win his freedom and be reunited with his family"(1). Huck contributes much aid to Jim's mission for freedom, and thus learns many truths about society. Meltzer elaborates, "Huck helps Jim to escape from slavery, and in a famous scene Huck's spontaneous self is placed in opposition to his acquired conscience,to the prejudices and values of the society he was raised in".

In addition to Jim's pursuit of freedom, Huck hopes for his own independence. By escaping and traveling along the Mississippi River, Huck aspires to gain Freedom for both of them. Unger illustrates, "The next twenty chapters detail adventures on the river or beside the river, in a pattern of withdrawal and return, as Huck and Jim float with their raft toward what they hope will be freedom for both". Huck wishes to prove his independence through his notorious trip along the Mississippi River.

"Huckleberry Finn speaks out against stupid conformity and for the freedom and independence of the individual," states Meltzer. Naturally, with issues such as slavery and racism pervading his novels, Twain would receive a variety of responses to his works. The Adventures of Huckleberry Finn, like most other novels, has its share of various public responses. First of all, many people respond to the novel in a negative way. For example, some readers possess a feeling of anger towards issues discussed in the novel. One critic elaborates, "The novel's semiliterate narrator, vernacular dialogue,forthright depiction of the hypocrisy and brutality of American life, and unrefined frontier humour were sufficiently radical at the time of its publication to warrant the novel's banishment from numerous libraries as 'the veriest trash'"

Contrarily, some people do not possess enough knowledge of the issues to understand the novel's message. "It is a concretely liberating effect, and therefore different in kind from Whitman's vision of democracy, which can hardly be said to have been understood by or to have found a response among any considerable number of Americans," explains DeVoto. On the other hand, many readers have felt positively towards the novel. They believe that The Adventures of Huckleberry Finn has caused society to recognize the mistakes of the past. Hall emphasizes, "Initially a clowning humorist, Twain matured into the role of the seemingly naive wise Fool whose caustic sense of humour forced his audience to recognize humanity's foolishness and society's myriad injustices". Along with this recognition came the realization that the treatment of slaves was inhumane. "To its everlasting credit, American society in the postwar period gradually came to the conclusion...that the ancient pattern of discrimination against Negroes was morally and legally indefensible," states Lynn. Finally, not only does Twain possess a negative view of slavery, he also has a distaste for war. In conclusion, Mark Twain utilizes the plot in The Adventures of Huckleberry Finn to express the immorality of life in the South during the 1800's. He depicts the code of slavery in the South and the quest for independence of a slave and a young boy. Additionally, Twain's work produced a wide range of readers' responses. Finally,Twain's last major work Pudd'nhead Wilson also strongly spoke out against slavery

Satire in Adventures of Huck Finn

The dominant tone of this work is satire. Twain pokes fun at many of the aspects of Southern life in the 19th century (including slavery and feuds), and several characters as well. His fiery attitude about the ills of society shows itself from the first page of this book. I think that one of the main themes in this novel is the conflict between the society's "good" and "bad". Huck believed that a person was "good" if they were educated, well read, religiously trained, and had the ability to follow rules. This, of course, is not the true nature of "goodness", and a key element in Twain's satire. In fact, Huck, who is one of the only good characters in the novel, believes good is based on the elements of dangers which face him every day, and due to this dicotomy, does not believe he is "good". This becomes painfully evident when Huck meets the Gregfords. The Gregfords are an obvious simile for pure evil. Though they have a temporal glow to them, after all, they are rich and aristocratic. However their misdeeds flowcontrary to society's label of "good". He labels them as "good", though afterhe hears their story behind their feud, he realizes that they are not quite asgood as he had believed. This shows the tumultuous journey between the "good"and "evil" occuring in Huck's mind.

The most clear occasion of this is when Huck dresses as a girl tosteal things from the neighborhood store. On a metaphorical level, thisshows Twain's alternate sexual preference (Freud pointed this out in"The Human Mind, Second Edition")—he is living vicariously through hiscreations. Twain uses the visage of Huck as a girl to ameliorate it againstthe society's "evil" perspective, in an attempt to popularize these acts.The bifurcation between his personal "good" and society's "good" is a keypoint in the book, and a universal theme which is best observed in this scene. Another important scene which goes along with this same theme wasthe scene with Huck Finn and his gang in the cave in the end of the secondchapter. Huck pretends to be an expert at the operations of gangs ofthat nature, because he had read a lot of books on it, but it turns out thathe is actually a phony. Though Isaac Hayes speaks out against him, Tom Sawyerquickly silences him and greets the other gang members. This shows how Tomidolized Huck and acted as the broomstick which held up his iron curtain.This is another clear example of Twain's theme of "good" versus "evil".

This scene also applies to the theme of society's "good" versusevil in broad sense. Huck secretly detested Tom (the symbol of society's"good"), as Twain secretly detested society's norms and accepted "good"."As diverse as Twain's tastes were, Society's stingency was inverselyproportional" said Freud. Tom's gang trusted him merely because he hadread a lot of books and spoke persuasively, just as society trustedTwain because he was outspoken and fit (through their eyes, at least)their ideas of "good".

When, in the end of the book, Huck is stuck on the raft with his father, Twain's true feelings about his own father are revealed. As Huck plunges the dagger for the final time into his father's soggy chest, a heavyburden is lifted off Huck and Twain both. Twain's father was very abusive,beating heim and his little sister often. Twain would provoke his father sothat he would recieve the beatings, sparing his sister pain and suffering. Inthe same way, Huck covers for Jimmy the escaped slave with whom Huck lives andsails. He takes criticism and humiliation as well as a loss of freedom tokeep Jimmy from being captured. This selfless act of generosity parallelsTwain's personal feelings. This book truly captures the spirit of giving andgenerosity, while telling a humorous story in the process.

Jim in The Adventures of Huckleberry Finn

Jim runs away for his family, so his kids might have a brighterfuture not for himself but for his family. While not even liking Tom, Jimrisks the dream he had for his family by helping save Tom's life. Jim alsoshows love and goodwill as kind of representing a father figure to Huck.Jim has not been given all the freedom of the white man but he willunselfishly give to all with no prejudice. Jim represents love andsymbolizes true goodwill to all.

Jim is symbolic with love in the whole story. While Huck and Jimare traveling down river Jim tells Huck why he is running away. It is notall for his own freedom it is more for his wife and his children. In thisone instance Jim is risking his life to possibly find a better way forsomeone he loves. An act such as this is an unselfish act that couldpossibly be rewarded with death. Most characters wouldn't give unselfishlysuch as this. This is truly a charater that is trying to do good and makethe best of a bad situation, not for himself but for others.

Huckleberry Finn and Tom Sawyer were planning to free Niger Jim.He was owned by Tom Sawyer's aunt and uncle. Before Tom arrived to hisuncle's farm Huck was already there and he stopped Tom before the Phelpsessaw him. Tom hid until that night when they planned to break Jim out. Butbeing the one for excitement that Tom was he derived a plan that would forsure get them caught. He left a note on the Phelps's porch that somethingwas going to happen. As Huck and Tom freed Jim Mr. Phelps fired a shot andit hit Tom but Huck and Jim didn't realise it until they got to the boatand floated to the island. On the island, they decided to leave to leaveTom while Huck went to get a doctor and Jim got away. But when the doctorarrived Jim was watching Tom. Jim sacrificed his freedom to help someonewho he really didn't like. Jim symbolizes love throughout the story, notjust in this one instance.

Superstitions in The Adventures of Huckleberry Finn

In The Adventures of Huckleberry Finn Jim and Huck use and believein many superstitions. There are many examples from the book, that showthis in the characters. Most of the superstitions are very ridiculous, butsome actually make a little sense. Huck seen a spider was crawling on his shoulder and he flipped itoff and it landed in a lit candle. It shriveled up and died. Huck said itwould fetch him some awful bad luck. He got up and turned around threetimes and crossed his breast every time. Then he tied up a little lock ofhis hair with a thread to keep witches away.

He says that the ritual hedid was for losing a found horseshoe and did not know if it would work.These superstitions and remedies seem pretty far fetched and it is hard tosay where they originated, but I would have to say they originated downSouth. I think it originated down south because I am from up North and Ihave never heard any one speak of those superstitions. Huck believes inthese probably because he grew up with them and they were always taught tohim and he is so ignorant he does not know better.

One morning Huck turned over the salt-cellar at breakfast. He wentto throw the salt- cellar over his left shoulder to cancel the bad luck,but Miss Watson stopped him. All day he wondered when something would fallon him and what it would be. This all implies that Huck thinks somethingis going to fall on him, because of his accident. I have heard about badluck from spilling salt so I think this Superstition started in the Northor maybe it was just popular and spread quickly. I do not believe there ishardly any fact at all to this. Huck believes in this probably because ofthe way he grew up.

Jim said when young chickens flew a yard or two at a time andlighting it was a sign that it was going to rain. He thought if birds didit, it would be the same. Also Jim said if you caught one of them youwould die. He thought this because his dad caught one and got sick and hisgrandmother said he was going to die. His father did die. Thesesuperstitions do have a little credibility. I think they originatedbecause some birds do fly in patterns when it is going to rain or storm.The part about his father dying might have a little credibility, but it iskind of stretching it. Maybe his dad caught the bird and ate it withoutcooking it all the way, or maybe the bird was infected and killed Jim's dad.Jim probably believed in the bird story about his dad's death because heexperienced it first hand.

Jim also said you should not count the things you are going to cookfor dinner, because that would bring bad luck. The same if you shook thetable the table-cloth after sundown. He said if a man who owned a bee-hivedied, the bees must be told before sun-up of the next morning or the beeswill die. These superstitions are all nonsense and having nothing to dowith anything. I think Jim believes this because he does not know anybetter. He experienced some Superstitions first hand and that is probablywhy he believes in them. The previous superstitions probably originatedout of stories told wrong, exaggerated, or people kept jazzing up storiesto make them interesting,until they turned into nothing, but nonsense.

Jim says if you have hairy arms and a hairy chest then you aregoing to be rich. This originated probably from a few rich men who werehairy. They probably told people they were rich because of their hair andsince they had the money to endorse their ideas people believed them.Money can buy many things, it can also make normal people understand andbelieve things they usually would not of. Jim probably believed thisbecause maybe his former master or masters were rich and were hairy. Hewas also hairy and had money at one time. At the end of the bookhe became free and Tom gave him $40, which supported Jim's theory. Huck grabbed a rattle-snake skin which was the worst luck Jim andHuck ever encountered. This superstition has good size of fact to it to.It probably originated because people like Huck picked up their skins andkept them in their bags or played tricks on the friends, like Jim. Themates probably came and defended their mate, by attacking the victim whohad the rattle-sake skin. The superstition probably got stretched a littleout of proportion, but I think a good deal of it is real. Huck and Jimprobably believe in the bad luck caused from touching the snakes skinbecause they experienced it too. When Huck played that trick on Jim, I amsure Huck became a believer of the bad luck.

Jim also said he would rather look at a new moon over his leftshoulder a thousand times instead of touching a snake skin again. Thissuperstition might have originated from people looking over their shoulderand then they probably stumbled and fell or ran into something. Huck andJim probably believe in this because it makes a good deal of sense to.

Twain's Adventures of Huckleberry Finn The Grangerfords' World

Huckleberry Finn provides the narrative voice of Mark Twain's Adventures of Huckleberry Finn, and his honest voice combined with his personal vulnerabilities reveal the different levels of the Grangerfords' world.

Huck is without a family: neither the drunken attention of Pap nor the pious ministrations of Widow Douglas were desirable allegiance. He stumbles upon the Grangerfords in darkness, lost from Jim and the raft. The family, after some initial cross-examination, welcomes, feeds and rooms Huck with an amiable boy his age. With the light of the next morning, Huck estimates "it was a mighty nice family, and a mighty nice house, too". This is the first of many compliments Huck bestows on the Grangerfords and their possessions.

Huck is impressed by all of the Grangerfords' belongings and liberally offers compliments. The books are piled on the table "perfectly exact", the table had a cover made from "beautiful oilcloth", and a book was filled with "beautiful stuff and poetry". He even appraises the chairs, noting they are "nice split-bottom chairs, and perfectly sound, too—not bagged down in the middle and busted, like an old basket". It is apparent Huck is more familiar with busted chairs than sound ones, and he appreciates the distinction. Huck is also more familiar with flawed families than loving, virtuous ones, and he is happy to sing the praises of the people who took him in. Col. Grangerford "was a gentleman all over; and so was his family". The Colonel was kind, well-mannered, quiet and far from frivolish.

Everyone wanted to be around him, and he gave Huck confidence. Unlike the drunken Pap, the Colonel dressed well, was clean-shaven and his face had "not a sign of red in it anywheres". Huck admired how the Colonel gently ruled his family with hints of a submerged temper. The same temper exists in one of his daughters: "she had a look that would make you wilt in your tracks, like her father. She was beautiful".

Huck does not think negatively of the hints of iron in the people he is happy to care for and let care for him. He does not ask how three of the Colonels's sons died, or why the family brings guns to family picnics. He sees these as small facets of a family with "a handsome lot of quality". He thinks no more about Jim or the raft, but knows he has found a new home, one where he doesn't have to go to school, is surrounded by interior and exterior beauty, and most importantly, where he feels safe. Huck "liked that family, dead ones and all, and warn't going to let anything come between us".

Huck is a very personable narrator. He tells his story in plain language, whether describing the Grangerford's clock or his hunting expedition with Buck. It is through his precise, trusting eyes that the reader sees the world of the novel. Because Huck is so literal, and does not exaggerate experiences like Jim or see a grand, false version of reality like Tom Sawyer, the reader gains an understanding of the world Mark Twain created, the reader is able to catch Twain's jokes and hear his skepticism. The Grangerford's furniture, much admired by Huck, is actually comicly tacky. You can almost hear Mark Twain laughing over the parrot-flanked clock and the curtains with cows and castles painted on them even as Huck oohs and ahhs. And Twain pokes fun at the young dead daughter Huck is so drawn to. Twain mocks Emmeline as an amateur writer: "She warn't particular, she could write about anything you choose to give her to write about, just so it was sadful". Yet Twain allows the images of Emmeline and the silly clock to deepen in meaning as the chapter progresses. Emmeline is realized as an early portent of the destruction of Huck's adopted family. The mantel clock was admired by Huck not only for its beauty, but because the Grangerfords properly valued beauty and "wouldn't took any money for her". Huck admired the Grangerfords' principles, and the stake they placed in good manners, delicious food, and attractive possessions. But Huck realizes in Chapter 18 that whereas the Grangerfords may value a hand-painted clock more than money, they put little value on human life.

The third view of the Grangerford's world is provided by Buck Grangerford. He is the same age as Huck; he has grown up in a world of feuding, family picnics, and Sunday sermon that are appreciated but rarely followed. Buck, from when he meets Huck until he is brutally murdered, never questions the ways of his family.. For the rest of the chapter, Buck provides a foil for Huck, showing the more mature Huck questioning and judging the world around him. In fact it seems Buck does not have the imagination to conceive of a different world. He is amazed Huck has never heard of a feud, and surprised by Huck's desire to hear the history and the rationale behind it.

In Buck Grangerford's rambling answers we hear Mark Twain's view of a southern feuding family, and after Buck finishes his answer, we watch Huck's reaction to the true nature of the Grangerfords. Buck details Twain's opinion that a feud is not started or continued by thought. The reasons for the feud have been forgotten, and the Grangerfords do not hate, but in fact respect, their sworn enemies. They live their lives by tradition, and the fact that the feud is a tradition justifies its needless, pointless violence. From the dignified Colonel with "a few buck-shot in him" to Buck, who is eager for the glory to be gained from shooting a Shepherdson in the back, the Grangerfords unquestioningly believe in de-valuing human life because it is a civilized tradition.

It is interesting that the only compliment Huck gives to a Grangerford after Buck shot at Harney Shepherdson was to Miss Sophia. He admits that the young women who denied part in any family feud is "powerful pretty". But the rosy sheen that had spurred Huck to use the word 'beautiful' six times previously in description of the Grangerfords has evaporated. He attends church with the family and notices all the Grangerfords keep their guns close by.

Huck thinks it "was pretty ornery preaching", but the feuding patriarchy praises the good values listed by the Preacher. The hypocritical mixture of guns and sermons, holy talk and bloodthirstiness make it "one of the roughest Sundays [Huck] had run across yet". He now questions the motives of everyone in the household, including Miss Sophia as she sends him to the church on an errand. By this point the cynical, sarcastic Twain and the disillusioned Huck are of one mind. Huck walks among a group of hogs who have sought the coolness of the church and notes "most folks don't go to church only when they've got to; but a hog is different".

The narration of Huck's final day with the Grangerfords is prefaced by: "I don't want to talk much about the next day". For Huck's easy-going fluid dialogue to become stilted and censored, the reader knows the young boy has been hurt. A senseless fatal feud is not the only tragedy depicted through the events of that day, also shown is the heartbreak of a young boy who loses every vestige of the hopeful trust he put in a father, brothers and sisters. Huck is shocked to hear the fatherless, brotherless Buck complain he hadn't managed to kill his sister's lover on an earlier occaison. And then from his perch in the tree, Huck hears Buck's murderers "singing out, 'Kill them, kill them!' It made [Huck] so sick [he] most fell out of the tree". He wishes he "hadn't come ashore that night, to see such things".

The end of chapter nineteen, when Huck returns to the raft and Jim, almost exactly mirrors the end of chapter eighteen. Both chapters conclude with Huck enjoying a good meal with good company in a cool, comfortable place. First it is with the Grangerfords in the cool, high-ceilinged area in the middle of their double house. "Nothing could be better", Huck thought. But only a few pages later the raft and Jim provide the same comforts. Nothing had ever sounded so good to him as Jim's voice, and Huck felt "mighty free and easy and comfortable on [the] raft".. Huck happily slides away from the bloody scene with the unorthodox father figure of a runaway slave. Huck has realized he does not need a traditional family to make him feel safe and happy. He must develop and live by his own integrity, not the past decisions of a father or grandfather. This is clearly Mark Twain's opinion also, and the reader, full of relief at Huck's escape, is aware that the author sent us all into the Grangerfords' world to prove just that point.

Adventures of Huck Finn And Moral Progress

The main character of Mark Twain's Huckleberry Finn undergoes a total moral transformation upon having to make life defining decisions throughout his journey for a new life. Huck emerges into the novel with an inferiority complex caused by living with a drunken and abusive father, and with the absence of any direction. It is at this point where Huck is first seen without any concept of morality. Fortunately, Huck is later assisted by the guidance of Jim, a runaway slave who joins him on his journey and helps Huck gain his own sense of morality. Throughout Huck's adventures, he is put into numerous situations where he must look within himself and use his own judgement to make fundamental decisions that will effect the morals of which Huck will carry with him throughout his life.

Preceding the start of the novel, Miss Watson and the widow have been granted custody of Huck, an uncivilized boy who possesses no morals. Huck looks up to a boy named Tom Sawyer who has decided he is going to start a gang. In order for one to become a member, they must consent to the murdering of their families if they break the rules of the gang. It was at this time that one of the boys realized that Huck did not have a real family. They talked it over, and they was going to rule me out, because they said every boy must have a family or something to kill, or else it wouldn't be fair and square for the others. Well, nobody could think of anything to do-everybody was stumped, and set still. I was most ready to cry;

but all at once I thought of a way, and so I offered them Miss Watson-they could kill her. At this moment, Huck is at the peak of his immorality. A person with morals would not willingly sacrifice the life of someone else just in order to be part of a gang. It is at this point where Huck can now begin his journey of moral progression.

Huck encounters his first major dilemma when he comes across the wrecked steamboat and three criminals. When Jim and Huck take the skiff for themselves, leaving the three robbers stranded, Huck realizes that he has left them to die. Now was the first time that I begun to worry about the men-I reckon I hadn't time to before. I begun to think how dreadful it was, even for murderers, to be in such a fix. I says to myself, there ain't no telling but I might come to be a murderer myself yet, and then how would I like it?. This is the first time that Huck questions the effects of what he has done on other people. After he realizes that he could now be considered a murderer, he makes a plan to get a captain to go investigate the wreck in order to save the men's lives. Even though the men he would be saving are murderers and robbers, he can not justify being responsible for their death, and makes it a point to correct what he has done wrong. This is the first major step in Huck's moral progression. At that point, he establishes a set of standards that considers leaving the men to die as immoral.

Throughout the book there is the recurring theme of Friend v. Society. This is a main moral decision that Huck is forced to make a few times in his journey. Upon arriving at Cairo, Huck must decide if he should go along with society and turn Jim in as a runaway slave, or keep his promise to his friend, and see him through to freedom. Huck feels guilty not turning Jim in when he hears him talking about hiring an abolitionist to steal his family. He does not think it is right to help take away slaves from people that he doesn't even know. To turn Jim in for these reasons would be the influence of society on Huck. Huck's decision on this matter marks another major step in Huck's moral progression, because he decides not to turn in Jim on his own. This is the first time he makes a decision all on his own based on his own morality. Both this incident and the Wilkes Scheme represent Huck's ultimate realization and rejection of society.

To encapsulate Huck's total moral progression through his decision to help Jim, Huck states, "I'll go to hell" to see Jim into freedom. Huck's moral progression can be traced throughout the book beginning from his total lack of morals to being able to make the right decisions on his own. It is only with the help of Jim as a moral guide that Huck is able to undergo this moral transformation to use his own judgement and truly progress. The situation that Huck is encountered with about choosing friend over society is the main dilemma that pushes Huck to establish his own standards of morality, rather than accepting those that society has set forth.

"The Widow Douglas she took me for her son, and allowed she would sivilize me; but it was rough living in the house all the time.... so, when I couldn't stand it no longer I lit out into my rags and was free and satisfied, but she always took me back." Huck is having trouble adjusting to living with the widow. He is accustomed to living free in the woods, without worrying about possessions, language, or cleanliness. "Pretty soon I wanted to smoke and asked the widow to let me, but she wouldn't."

This is just another example of Huck losing his freedom, as on his own he would have done what he wanted to. "And then I put out the light and scrambled out of the window on to the shed." Huck is exercising his longing for freedom by going out at night with Tom. Tom and Huck encounter Jim whose freedom is taken away because he is a slave. Huck joins Tom's gang and they plan to take people's freedom away by holding them for ransom. "Well, I got a good going-over in the morning from old Miss Watson on account of my clothes." This in part why Huck wants his freedom, of doing what he likes, because they want to civilize him. At first I hated school, but by and by I got so I could stand it. Whenever I got uncommonly tired I played hooky..." Huck doesn't like being caged in school, but begins to like it because when he gets tired of it he can take a break anyway.Huck confronts his father who spends some time with the judge and stops drinking, but begins again. So, as his freedom isn't taken."So he watched out for me one day and catched me and took me up over the river." Hucks father once again takes his freedom away, but he gets it back by living the good life in the woods, for a while. Huck escapes from his father by making it look like he was murdered; he now has total freedom. "I was powerful lazy and comfortable-didn't want to get up and cook breakfast."

Huck enjoys this total freedom. He also confronts Jim in this chapter and discovers Jim is now free too as he ran off from Mrs. Watson. Jim and Huck enjoy the good life being free. "I wanted to talk about the dead man, but Jim didn't wanna." Jim didn't want to talk of the dead man who had gained or lost his freedom by dying. Huck and Jim are still on their journey to be free, but when Huck finds another human in need of freedom he was prepared t tell a white-lie to a perfect stranger to help. Not only are they still in trouble, but they also are hating the fact they are still not completely free. Jim didn't want to go to the wreck at all, but Huck made him. And Huck has to send him ahead and catch up with him later. Huck is starting to wonder why he never thought about turning Jim in.

Then he realizes that Jim is his friend, and he will not take Jim's freedom into his own hands. Huck is now in paradise with the Grangerfords. He loves everything about this place; except for that there is no place for Jim here. He also knows that he still doesn't have total freedom.Huck is still enjoying life with the Grangerfords, until a seemingly meaningless fight begins and Huck realizes he is still not free from ignorance or death. This is just like it was with his father. So, he and Jim flee down the Mississippi. Huck enjoys the freedom he has once again gained by leaving the Grangerfords. They once again run into the problem of Jim being a runaway slave. Boggs freedom is taken into Col. Sherburns hands, when he is shot and killed. They again run into the problem of the runaway slave, Jim. They say he is a sick Arab and keep him confined to the raft. Huck begins to feel trapped by the King and the Duke. He feels he is losing his freedom.

Huck still feels he isn't totally free, because the King and the Duke still have control over him. So, he thinks of a way to take it back, by stealing the money.The King and the Duke sell Mary Jane and her sisters slaves and splits the mother and the kids up. This is another example of how slaves freedom was taken advantage of. Huck doesn't like this, so he continues with his plan."Not now; have it for breakfast, have it for breakfast! Cut loose and let her slide." Huck and Jim are happy to be by themselves again. They are free once again, but then Huck sees the King and the Duke coming in a skiff and he starts and gives up. Huck and Jim are now more or less enslaved by the King and the Duke again. "Set her loose, Jim; we're all right now!" The King and the Duke get in a fight and they are so preoccupied with themselves that Huck makes a run for it. Only Jim isn't there, he has been taken by Silas Phelps for the reward on him.

All right, then, I'll go to hell-" Huck thinks about writing a letter to Mrs. Watson telling her where Jim is because he thinks he'll go the hell if he doesn't. He decides not to and will take the consequences for friend. Huck is on the Phelps farm and assumes the identity of Tom Sawyer. Jim is still enslaved by Silas Phelps.The King and the Duke finally get caught. Their freedom is taken away when they are tarred and feathered. Tom and Huck find out where Jim is being kept. Jim is very happy about Huck finding him and hopes they will free him immediately. Jim is still locked up, but Huck is trying to free him. Tom and Huck dig a hole into Jim's cabin to try and free him, but Tom comes up with this ridiculous plan and drags it out.

The Adventures of Huckleberry Finn: Man as Coward

Throughout the novel, The Adventures of Huckleberry Finn, the author expresses a plain and poignant point of view. One of Mark Twain's main purposes in producing this work seems clear: he wishes to bring to attention some of man's often-concealed shortcomings. His point of view is that of a cynic; he looks upon civilized man as a merciless, cowardly, hypocritical savage.

While the examples of Mark Twain's cynic commentaries

on human nature can be found in great frequency all through the novel, several examples seem to lend themselves well to a discussion of this sarcastic view. In the beginning of the novel, it would seem that both Huck Finn and Jim are trapped in some way and wishing to escape. For Huck, it is the violence and tyranny of his drunken father. Kept in a veritable prison, Huck wishes desperately to escape. Jim feels the need to escape after hearing that his owner, Miss Watson, wishes to sell him down the river-a change in owners that could only be for the worse. As they escape separately and rejoin by chance at an island along the river, they find themselves drawn to get as far as possible from their home.

Their journey down the river sets the stage for most of Mark Twain's comments about man and society. It is when they stop off at various towns along the river that various human character flaws always seem to come out. Examples of this would include the happenings after the appearance of the Duke and King. These two con artists would execute the most preposterous of schemes to relieve unsuspecting townspeople of their cash. The game of the King pretending to be a reformed marauder-turned-missionary at the tent meeting showed that people are gullible and often easily led, particularly when in groups and subjected to peer pressure.

The execution of the Royal Nonesuch showed another instance of people in society being subject to manipulation. The fact that, after being taken by a poor show they sent rave reviews of it to their friends to avoid admitting they had been conned showed that people in groups are ever afraid of losing status, and will do nearly anything to protect such. Both the King and the Duke, also, showed such a ridiculous degree of corruptness that it is difficult to believe that all humans aren't at least somewhat evil. Another point made by the author is that of most men being basically cowards. A good example of this was when Col. Sherburn shot the drunk Boggs and the townsfolk came after Sherburn to lynch him. After Sherburn, one man with only a shotgun, held off the immense mob and made them disperse, it was obvious that no individual really had the courage to go through with the lynching.

The idea that people are basically savages, confined for the moment by society, is shown in more than one instance. For example, when the group was preparing to hang Huck and the King over their plot to defraud the daughters, or, more obvious, in the war between the Shephardsons and the Grangerfords.

The aspect of people being basically hypocrites is seen at the beginning when Miss Watson displays a degree of hypocrisy on insisting that Huck follow the Widow and become civilized, while at the same time deciding to sell Jim into a hard life down the river.

A final point seems to be that Man is continually fleeing from something. At the end, Jim and Huck found themselves at the end of their journey, neither having anything left to run from as Huck's father was dead and Jim was a free man. It would seem then that Huck and Jim had run a thousand miles down the river and ended up where they had begun.

From the above examples taken from The Adventures of Huckleberry Finn, it is apparent that Mark Twain wishes society to realise its shortcomings and the limitations imposed by human nature. He realizes that people will not change, but feels that they should be aware of who they are, of what comes with this thing we call humanity.

From Conformity to Manhood

In The Adventures of Huckleberry Finn, Huck is the narrator. The character of Huck Finn was very different than the society that he was born into. Mr. Twain uses Huck's open mindedness as a window to let humour and the book's points and morals shine through. Huck always takes things very literally. This not only adds to the humour of the book, but it also lets some of the books deeper messages come through. The Adventures of Huckleberry Finn, traces the story of a young man, Huck Finn, from conformity to the Southern way of thinking, to his own ideas about religion, wealth and slavery.

In the first scenes of the book Huck is struggling to understand the concepts of Miss Watson's heaven and hell.

He finds her harp strumming view of heaven boring and he wants to be in an exciting place. When Miss Watson tells Huck that he will get anything he prays for, he takes it very literally and decides to pray for fishing line, which he gets. But praying for fishing hooks didn't seem to work, when he asks her to pray for him to get some fishing hooks she calls him an idiot. These are both gentle pokes at southern religion. Christianity practiced a people so very pious, like Miss Watson, who can still treat their human slaves like property. This is an ongoing theme in the book. Twain points out some of the absurd incongruences between Christianity and the lifestyle of most of the south. Huck has not conformed to societies general way of thinking. When he is with the widow and Miss Watson, he begins to change, but Pap steals him away and he reverts back to a much more practical lifestyle.

Huck places very little value on the large sum of money that he has in the bank, while he finds smaller sums more important. Six thousand dollars was a fortune in the time that the book was written, but Huck, unlike the rest of his society wasn't impressed by it. This is again because of his literal mindedness. What could he use six thousand dollars for? He could use ten cents to buy some food, or five cents to buy some fishing line, but he had no use for huge sums of money. Society put value on wealth and property and book learning. Huck placed his value on free living. He saw no reason for any of the things society valued when you could float down the grand Mississippi with a friend.

The isolation on the Mississippi River affords a place for Huck to be Jim's equal. On the plantation Jim was just a slave, and even though Huck liked Jim back then, they could never have been friends because Jim was a black slave and Huck was white. At first Huck had grave misgivings about helping Jim escape, but he gradually decided that what he had observed of Jim was the basis on which he would judge him. Jim loved Huck and wouldn't bother to wake Huck up at night to take the watch. Jim always looked out for Huck and talked with him. He showed Huck that he loved his family just like a white man loved his family. Society had impressed upon Huck the concept that slavery was acceptable. However, as the story unfolds he comes to know Jim as a human and not a piece of property, he wrestles with his conscience, and when the crucial moment arises, he decides he will be damned to the flames of hell rather than betray his black friend. If Huck had been a member of society, he wouldn't have even thought of looking for a person inside of Jim. But because of his open mindedness in taking things at face value he gradually became aware that Jim was a beautiful person. He forms new ideas about himself and the world around him.

At the end of the book we find how right Huck is about Jim. We find that southern culture hasn't corrupted Huck's common sense. Huck has broken through all the pettiness and superficiality of that culture to form new ideas and values of his own. Mr. Twain showed us the power of an open mind in a beautiful story of Huck Finn's journey from ignorance to manhood -by simply using his common sense.

Adventures Of Huckleberry Finn And Society

"All modern American literature comes from one book by Mark Twain called Huckleberry Finn," according to Ernest Hemingway. Along with Ernest, many others believe that Huckleberry Finn is a great book, but is the novel subversive? Since this question is frequently asked, people have begun to look deeper into the question to see if this novel is acceptable for students in schools to read. First off subversive means something is trying to overthrow or destroy something established or to corrupt (as in morals). According to Lionel Trilling, " No one who reads thoughtfully the dialectic of Huck's great moral crisis will ever again be wholly able to accept without some question and some irony the assumptions of the respectable morality by which he lives, or will ever again be certain that what he considers the clear dictates of moral reason are not merely the engrained customary beliefs of his time and place." Trilling feels that Huck Finn is such a subversive character that this will not make people believe in something totally again, because they will fear being wrong like the society in Huckleberry Finn was.

I believe this and I think the subversion in the novel is established when Mark Twain begins to question the acceptable morality of society. Twain uses humour and effective writing to make Huckleberry Finn a subversive novel about society in the 19th century. Huck Finn, a boy referred to as "white trash," is a boy that has grown up believing totally what society as taught him. This passage shows an example of how society teaches him. "...And keep them till they're ransomed." "Ransomed? What's that?" "I don't know. But that's what they do. I've seen it in the books, and so of course that's what we've got to do." "Well how can we do it if we don't know what it is?" "Why, blame it all, we've got to do it. Don't I tell you it's in the books?

Do you want to go to doing different from what's in the books, and get things all muddled up?" This is a conversation between Tom Sawyer and his gang of robbers. This shows how the boys are influenced by society and believe they most follow exactly what is in the books, because that is the right way to do things. In today's society, ransoming someone is a huge crime and is totally unacceptable. In this book, Twain makes ransoming a humorous issue. In fact, throughout the novel Twain makes violence a humorous issue and does not act upon it as a serious issue. This goes with the whole theme of the novel that there is no moral.

The way Huck has been raised, he has no clue that what Tom's gang wants to do is ludacrist, and should be totally unacceptable. Twain uses this conversation also to show the beginning of questioning throughout the novel. This will show a pattern of how Huck questions things to learn. Whatever Hucks hears, he believes is the right and acceptable answer. Tom's Gang of Robbers was a part of humorous violence in the novel, but Huck would run into real violence as well. Huck faked his death, and headed down the river, and he decides to go ashore and stays with a stranger family named the Grangerfords. The Grangerfords who were a very nice family, but a family that was obsessed with death.

The Grangerfords and another family called the Sheperdson's have had a feud going on for 30 years, but no one knows why. "What's a feud?" "Why, where was you raised? Don't you know what a feud is?" "Never heard of it before-tell me about it." "Well," says Buck, "a feud is this way: A man has a quarrel with another man, and kills him; and then that other man's brother kills him; then the other brothers, on both sides, goes for one another; then the cousins chip in-and by and by everybody's killed off, and there ain't no more feud. But's it's kind of slow, and takes a long time." "Has this one been going on long Buck?" "Well I should reckon! It started thirty year ago, or som'ers along there. There was trouble 'bout something and then a lawsuit to settle it; and the suit went agin one of the men, so he up and shot the man that won the suit-which he would naturally do of course.

Anybody would." This conversation is a very important role in determining if this novel is subversive or not. The Sheperdsons and Grangerfords never question the principle of a feud. They are not even sure why they are having a feud in the first place. They are not positive on how it started, or who started it. The irony in this, would be that both families are totally fine with this, and continue with the killing of each other. Twain uses this scene to portray the real violence that also occurs in the novel. The killing of each other being acceptable is an example of subversive writing, and another is when Huck sees Jim as an equal person as himself.

As the novel goes on, and while Huck and Jim continue their voyage down the Mississippi, Huck begins to realise many things. In fact, the climax of the novel occurs when Huck is trying to decide to turn Jim in to Miss Watson, or not to. "...And I got to thinking over our trip down the river; and I see Jim before me all the time: in the day and in the night-time, sometimes moonlight, sometimes storms, and we a-floating along, talking and singing and laughing. But somehow I couldn't seem to strike no places harden against me, but only the other kind. I'd see him standing my watch on top of his'n, 'stead of calling me, so I could go on sleeping; and see him how glad he was when I come back out of the fog; and when I come to him again in the swamp, and would always call me honey, and pet me, and do everything he could think of for me, and how good he always was;.....and said I was the best friend old Jim ever had in the world, and the only one he's got now; and then I happened to look around and see the paper.....All right, then, I'll go to hell"-and tore it up.

Huck Finn's conscience is what he has learned, or what society has taught him, and it is telling him that it is not right to keep Jim with him. Huck's real conscience, or his heart, is telling him the right thing to do. Huck Finn has a sound heart and a deformed conscience. Huck thinks that he is doing something very evil, but the reader knows that he is not. This is important because it shows that Huck believes him and Jim are equal. The effect Jim has had on him as caused him to believe that a black man is not inferior to the white man. Now that Huck has realized this, him and Jim must re-enter society, because that is the only place they have to go. When Twain reaches this point in the novel, the only thing that he can do is try to bring Huck and Jim back into society.

The conversation between Tom Sawyer and Huck Finn where they were talking about "The Great Evasion" plays a significant role in this. "Well, by the end of three weeks everything was in pretty good shape. The shirt was sent in early, in a pie, and every time a rat bit Jim he would get up and write a line in his journal whilst the ink was fresh; the pens was made, the inscriptions and so on was all carved on the grindstone; the bed-leg sawed in two, and we had et up the sawdust, and it give us the most amazing stomach-ache. We reckoned we was all going to die, but didn't." This occurs when the boys finally have all their plans done to free the Jim out of captivity. Huck had a plan in the beginning that was much easier then the one Tom had planned, but Tom insisted they do his. It was so important to Tom to use his because, it was what they did in the books, just like with his band of robbers. Little does Huck know, that this was a cruel joke played on Jim. They could have freed Jim much easier, but Tom wanted to play this joke on Jim.

In the end, Jim was freed from his "dungeon" and Twain now must bring him and Huck back into the "real" world. Jim's escape led to Huck and him being discovered by Aunt

Polly and brought back into society. Jim finds out all along he was a free man, and Aunt Sally decides to adopt Huck and "sivilize" him, which Huck can't stand, cuz he'd been there. Mark Twain clearly has written a subversive novel in Huckleberry Finn. In the society that Huck and Jim lived in blacks were inferior to the whites, but that is not the way Twain portrays them in this novel. The fact that killing people is humorous is another way that Twain shows subversion in the novel. He is trying to prove that sometimes what is accepted is not always the correct way. This causes Twain's novel to be portrayed as a very subversive novel. After all, Mark Twain has put together a very interesting and entertaining, but subversive novel named Huckleb.

Realism and The Adventures of Huckleberry Finn

The Adventures of Huckleberry Finn, by Mark Twain, is an immensely realistic novel, revealing how a child's morals and actions clash with those of the society around him. Twain shows realism in almost every aspect of his writing; the description of the setting, that of the characters, and even the way characters speak. Twain also satirizes many of the foundations of that society. Showing the hypocrisy of people involved in education, religion, and romanticism through absurd, yet very real examples. Most importantly, Twain shows the way Huckleberry's moral beliefs form amidst a time of uncertainty in his life.

Realism is a literary style in which the author describes people, their actions, their emotions and surroundings as close to the reality as possible. The characters are not perfectly good or completely evil; they exhibit strengths and weaknesses, just as real people. The characters often commit crimes or do immoral things, and are not always just good or just evil. In a realistic novel, aspects of the time period or location are also taken into consideration. Characters dress in clothes that befit them, and speak with local dialects. Most importantly, characters are not sugar coated or exaggerated. The characters do things as they would normally do them, and are not worse or better then their real life counterparts.

Using his experiences as a steamboat engineer, Mark Twain creates a realistic novel through meticulous detail in the descriptions of the setting, diction, and characters. The setting is described with much detail and imagery, so as to make it as close as possible to the actual surroundings. Twain uses a page just to describe the sunrise over the river.

The first thing to see, looking away over the water, was a kind of dull line - that was the woods on t'other side; you couldn't make nothing else out; then a pale place in the sky; then more paleness spreading around; then the river softened up away off, and warn't black any more, but gray; you could see little dark spots drifting along ever so far away-trading-scows, and such things; and long black streaks-rafts... and by and by you could see a streak on the water which you know by the look of the streak that there's a snag there in a swift current which breaks on it and makes that streak look that way; and you see the mist curl up off of the water, and the east reddens up. This complex and almost photographic description of a simple dawn is an example of Twain's painstaking attempt to stay as close to reality as possible, placing him into the genre of realism.

The Adventures of Huckleberry Finn also displays realistic qualities in the way characters and their speech is written. Twain explains this in a preface: "In this book a number of dialects are used... The shadings have not been done in a haphazard fashion, or by guesswork; but painstakingly, and with the trustworthy guidance and support of personal familiarity with these several forms of speech" (EXPLANATORY). The dialects are not only realistic in grammar and word choice, but in the characters that display them. Characters who are less educated, such as Jim the slave, speak using slang, shortened words, or improper grammar; "Say, who is you? Whar is you? Dog my cats ef I didn' hear sumf'n. Well, I know what I's gwyne to do: I's gwyne to set down here and listen tell I hears it ag'in"(5). Characters who are more educated, such as Miss Watson, speak properly and do not use colloquial terms. The diction in general matches that of the south with such popular expressions as "dog my cats" and "by and by". The use of proper diction that fits the characters, time period, and location is another way in which The Adventures of Huckleberry Finn becomes a realistic novel.

In unmasking the identities of characters, Twain satirizes the falseness and hypocrisy of certain educators, religious leaders, and romantics. Twain shows how the characters act in front of others, and then reveals their true emotions and mannerisms. The Duke and the Dauphin, for example, are two characters whom Huckleberry meets while traveling with Jim. The two act sophisticated and well read, but are actually common crooks. At first, the two pass themselves off as royalty, but even Huckleberry realizes that they are simply conmen. "It didn't take me long to make up my mind that these liars warn't no kings nor dukes at all, but just low-down humbugs and frauds."

Claiming to also be a celebrated actor, the Duke recite and teaches the Dauphin excerpts from Shakespeare, whom he speaks of as "The historic muse is the darling. Have you ever trod the boards, Royalty?" Although at first the Duke seems like an educated gentleman, when he actually acts out Shakespearean plays it is evident that he knows very little; mixing scenes and lines from completely different plays. His recital of Hamlet's soliloquy contains lines from MacBeth, and perverts the actual lines from Shakespeare

To be, or not to be; that is the bare bodkin
That makes calamity of so long life;
For who would fardels bear, till Birnam Wood do come to Dunsinane.

In this way, Twain satirizes those who act educated and well-bred, but actually know very little.

Twain also satirizes religion, and the way people seem to be pious when in public, but completely disregard religious values when they are not beneficial to them. The Grangerfords and the Shepherdsons, two rivaling families whom Huckleberry stays with briefly, are an example of this type of religious hypocrisy. When the two families go to church, "the men took their guns along, and kept them between their knees or stood them handy against the wall. The Shepherdsons done the same". Even when in church, the two families still do not trust each other. More importantly, after agreeing that the sermon on brotherly love was a good one, the two families go out and continue fighting each other. Again, the families attend to church and act devoted, but do not actually apply what they have learned to their own life.

The most evident and humorous of Twain's satires is that of Tom Sawyer and romanticism. Tom Sawyer enjoys such romantic books as The Count of Montecristo, and makes all of his plans based on what he feels will be the most romantic, and oftentimes the least logical path. When rescuing Jim, Tom devises a complicated plan that is so difficult to accomplish that even he eventually gives up on certain parts, and just pretends that he is doing them. Even more outlandish is the fact that Jim eventually gets out of the prison to go and help Tom make the preparations for his escape. Instead of escaping quickly and painlessly, Jim must wait for weeks and finally run away under fire from the locals.

Just as certain people exhibited false or hypocritical traits, the society also displayed selfish and egotistical. People felt that it was normal to hurt or even kill another person if that was beneficial. Slaves and Negro's faced even more conflict; considered inferior to whites, they were often mistreated and regarded with suspicion. Huckleberry holds many of these morals to be correct, and often strives to uphold them, even when he really knows that he shouldn't. Originally, Huckleberry feels that Jim is inferior because he is a slave and describes him as such. He and Tom play tricks on him and abuse his superstitious beliefs. Huckleberry, for instance, places a snakeskin in Jim's bed, because he knows that Jim does not like it. Huckleberry also feels that Jim should be returned and does not deserve to be free. He even goes as far as writing a letter to Miss Watson that explains where Jim is being held. Huckleberry also feels that conning people is normal and expected. He allows the Duke and the Dauphin to put on fake plays and charity events in several cities, and does not feel that it is wrong for them to steal. Although Huckleberry upholds these morals at first, because they have been taught to him throughout his life, eventually he realizes that this type of behaviour is not right.

Ultimately, Huckleberry's character changes, and he denounces the morals of society, and does what he himself feels is morally correct. Huckleberry first revolts against the popularly held belief that school and education is not important. Although he starts of cutting school, he eventually begins to attend regularly, and even receives an award for good studies. Eventually Huckleberry runs away due to the mistreatment that he receives from his father and encounters other characters whose morals are tolerated by society. When Huckleberry meets up with the Duke and the Dauphin, he also begins rebelling against the "dog eat dog" mentality of only caring for oneself. Ultimately, when the Duke and the Dauphin try to scam two sisters by posing as relatives collecting money from a will, Huckleberry goes as far as revealing to one of the girls where the money is hidden and how she can get it, even though he could have easily taken it and left.

Huckleberry does this because, unlike the Duke and the Dauphin, Huckleberry does not feel that stealing is acceptable, even if one can get away with it. Huckleberry's most profound action is the rebellion against the belief that Negroes are inferior. He grows fond of Jim, and changes from thinking of him as a stereotypical uneducated Negro, to a real human being who is caring and compassionate. Huckleberry stops playing tricks on Jim, and treats him with more respect. Most importantly, when Huckleberry feels that he must return Jim, he eventually decides against it, even though he thinks that he is defying God: "All right, then, I'll go to hell". Through this, Huckleberry shows that he is willing to defy God to do what he feels is right. Huckleberry transforms from a delinquent, hoping to be like Tom Sawyer, who is the epitome of the thinking of the time, to a boy who can think for himself, and understands what is right and what is wrong, even if it might bring him pain.

Through The Adventures of Huckleberry Finn, Mark Twain tries to show the wrongdoings of society at the time and the ignorance and hypocrisy of the people. He does this through painstaking realism and almost factual description. Twain tries to show the wrongness in slavery and the view that slaves are simply mindless farm animals which is accepted by society. Twain tries to convey this from the point of view of a relatively innocent child, who has not been conditioned by society, and has had time to make his own opinions about life. Twain uses realism to show that this is not a fairy tale land, from one of Tom Sawyer's books, but that these are real people and real sentiments. Twain also uses realism to convey the fact that Jim is not an extraordinary or special salve, but that he is just like any other slave. By giving a real slave compassion and emotions, Twain shows slaves are just like any other people. Twain communicates a powerful and controversial message through what, at first, seems like a simple children's adventure book.

Huckleberry Finn–Freedom

Freedom is not a reward or a decoration that is celebrated with champagne...Oh no! It's a...long distance race, quite solitary and very exhausting." -Albert Camus. The dictionary defines freedom as the condition of being free from restraints. Freedom is not just a word one can say without meaning. It is a privilege, a privilege not everyone is granted. Freedom gives the liberty to choose what should is done and how.

Freedom is the capacity to exercise choice and free will. In the novel The Adventures of Huckleberry Finn, the narrator, Huck, seeks freedom from society. Huck, a thirteen year-old boy, lives with Widow Douglass and her sister Miss Watson. He lives with them because before this he had no home, only a drunken father, whom he rarely sees. Both of the ladies attempt to civilize Huck by sending him to school and teaching him good manners. "Pretty soon I wanted to smoke, and asked the widow to let me. But she wouldn't. She said it was a mean practice and wasn't clean, and I must try to not do it any more" In this passage from chapter one you can see that Huck enjoyed doing what he pleased when he choose. "I liked the old ways best, but I was getting so I liked the new ones, too, a little bit." This passage is from chapter four of the book spoken by Huck.

In it one can see that although Huck begins to like the civilized ways he still has a craving for his old ways, which seem uncivilized to all.

Freedom is not only having a choice but also having no restraints. The characters of the Duke and the Daphne, who were really two criminals running away, have an advantage of no restraints being given. In chapter 19 of the book, the two men introduce themselves to Huck and Jim. When they do this, they do not introduce themselves with their true identity. Because there were no restrictions, they could not only befriend Jim and Huck but also trick them. "He told them he was a pirate-been a pirate for thirty years out in the Indian Ocean-and his crew was thinned out considerable last spring in a fight, and he was home now to take out some fresh men, and thanks goodness he'd been robbed last night...and poor as he was. He was going to start right off and work his way back to the Indian Ocean...and though it would take him a long time to get there without money..." After the group hears this, they immediately start a collection.

The two men got away with almost 90 dollars. This passage, from chapter twenty of the novel, demonstrates that the Duke and the Daphne again have the freedom to fool people. They got away with stealing because no restraints existed. The river traveled by Jim and Huck symbolizes freedom. The Mississippi River is their escape route to freedom, Jim's to Cairo and Huck's away from his Pap, or father. Also the river puts out of sight the ideas of society. When out on the river, they have no one to answer to and no one to listen to. They have complete control over themselves and no restraints holding them back.

Freedom is not slavery. In The Adventures of Huckleberry Finn Jim, Ms. Watson's slave, runs away to escape being sold and having his family separated. Jim has no freedoms or choices. He is told to do something and must do it without any questions. Even when Jim escapes and meets Huck on the island, he is still required to hide and avoid all contact with anyone. Freedom is something Jim desires more than anything. Jim represents the slaves at that time; all required to struggle and risk their lives for freedom. To the slaves, freedom is a long fight that some never win.

The necessary components of freedom are liberty, free will, and independence. Without one, the other won't do. Freedom is an essential part of daily life. Without freedom, one might not be able to choose what breakfast he eats. Freedom gives a choice to all. Though freedom may be a tiring race in the end it is worth it.

Adventures of Huckleberry Finn Race Relations

Humans are fascinated with real life situations, tagged in with fictional story line. Mark Twain's novel, The Adventures of Huckleberry Finn, describes real life situations, in a fictional story line perfectly. Twain put the real life happenings of slavery, in a fun and fictional story. The novel is mainly about the racial relations between each human. Classes of society, loyalty/friendship, and rebellion shows how the novel evolves into a main theme of Race Relations.

Throughout the history of the world, people have been placed into categories based on their wealth, and all of the worldly possessions that we have. These classes of society can really make people talk, and act differently towards some people. In The Adventures of Huckleberry Finn, the novel shows these classes really well. In the beginning of the novel, we see a little bit of the black class, and how they were treated. "Miss. Watson's big nigger, named Jim, was setting in the kitchen door, we could see him pretty clear". Jim, Miss. Watson's run away slave in the story, is part of the black class. We see the sub ordinance that blacks were placed in America, because blacks were not allowed to be in the house, because they were uneducated, and had to be working in the fields.

Another example of the classes we put each other into is when Huck, the main character, and Jim were heading south. Jim and Huck are sitting on the banks of the Mississippi River, and Jim says "I owns myself en I's wuth eight hund'd dollars.". This shows the reader that blacks are so low, that the white people place prices on the blacks. As uneducated as the blacks are, they believe they are worth so much money, because that is all they hear from their owners. By doing such a thing to another human being, that degrades our country, and the black citizens themselves.

At the end, we see how these classes can effect one person, due to his social status. Like before, people say things to other people, to make themselves feel better, and they do not care what it does to the person they are talking about, because of their class in society. One example of this is when "They cussed Jim considerably, though, and give him a cuff or two upside the head". This shows how people can be when one group thinks that he is better than another group. These classes of society can show the relations between races. In this case, the whites thought they were better, and so, they would not allow blacks to be in the house, make them feel like objects, and not human beings and greatly persecuted and abused the blacks.

Another point that is with the main theme of race relations is loyalty/friendship. Huck shows this by being with Jim in the beginning, and shows some trust in Jim. The beginning of this friendship is seen when Huck goes to Jim with a problem with his Father coming back, and Jim says " sometimes he spec he'll go 'way, en den ag'in he spec he'll stay". That response from Jim really shows the reader that he cares about Huck, and he understands what Huck is saying. Like any relationship, it has to have an open, honest and submit caring feelings for one another. Jim proves that he cares by helping Huck, and telling the truth, even when it hurts.

Later on in the novel, Jim and Huck are going down the river, and Huck is continuously faced with the same problem. Huck does not know whether to turn Jim in or not. When a problem comes up, people can see how loyal or how much your friendship means to somebody when a problem occurs frequently. Huck says to himself "s'pose you'd a' done right and give Jim up? Would you felt better than what you do now? No, I'd feel bad-I'd feel just the same way I do now". With that decision by Huck, that shows two people the same thing. This shows both Jim and the reader that Jim is too good of a friend to be back stabbed. With that decision, Huck proves his loyalty to Jim, no matter if he is black or white.

Finally, at the end of the novel, we find out how much Huck appreciated Jim's good attitude through the whole adventure of going to New Orleans. When "Tom give Jim forty dollars for being prisoner for us so patient....", shows that Tom and Huck were very thankful for putting up with them, and their crazy ideas. The act of giving Jim the money proves Huck and Tom were very grateful for Jim's loyalty to do everything. The loyalty towards Huck was seen through the whole story. From being tied up, being painted or even being treated worse, Jim knew it was worth it. He was loyal and friendly towards the two children, because if it were not for them, he would still be a slave. Loyalty and friendship deals with race relations because even if somebody was black, or white, Huck showed that blacks were every bit as fun, caring and normal as the white people. Even if it meant rebelling against the law, loyalty and friendship was more important.

Speaking of rebelling, this is the final point for making this main theme race relations, the ultimate theme of the novel. Rebellion is another theme frequently seen through the whole novel. Huck rebels against his father, and the law. Huck's Father tells him to do one simple thing, but he rebels and does what he wants to any ways. The first thing is when his Father leaves him locked in the cabin. Huck obviously is supposed to stay inside, but he rebels and crawls out of the house. "He had wore the ground a good deal crawling out of the hole and dragging out so many things". This shows him rebelling against his Father by not doing what he was supposed to do. He then runs away, and meets Jim, where he really rebels. This will be the start of a stronger friendship between Huck and Jim. Speaking of Jim, he also rebels, but he rebels against the law. Jim made a big decision while there was a great deal of distraction with in the city.

When Jim and Huck first met, Jim says "Well, I b'lieve you, Huck. I-I run off". Jim tells Huck and Huck becomes very shocked and concerned for Jim. Huck tells Jim that he will help Jim escape, even if "People would call me a low-down Abolitionist". When Huck says that, he promises Jim he will help to the end, no matter what happens. That only shows the reader that Jim can really trust Huck with anything, improving their relationship.

Finally at the end of the novel, we really see the respect Jim deserves as a human being. Through the many escapades and adventures the two of them went through, Jim is first treated like garbage once again. When Tom, Huck's one and only friend, Huck and Jim arrive at Aunt Sally's, Tom's aunt, house, Aunt Sally becomes outraged that the two of them helped a slave run away. Once she finally realizes everything Jim had done for Tom and Huck, "Aunt Polly and Uncle Silas and Aunt Sally found out how good he helped the doctor nurse fix Tom, they made a fuss, and fixed him up prime, and gave him all he wanted to eat, and a good time and nothing to do". This is a big push for race relations and rebellion. Slaves are not supposed to eat and dress real nice and have nothing to do. Aunt Polly, Uncle Silas and Aunt Sally realized everything that Jim did, and, by being helpful, changed the minds of the three adults. They now viewed Jim as a person, and not a slave. By doing this, these few people strengthen the relationship between whites and blacks. They only did this because they looked inside, and found out what Jim really is about, and what he has to offer to the world.

Through history, blacks have been discriminated for being a different colour, or because of what they do not have, or how they act. Classes of society, loyalty/friendship, and rebellion shows how people can strengthen the race relations between whites and blacks. If the world only breaks free of our hateful chains, and isolated cages, we can see that each of us are no different from one another. We have to open our eyes, take each other for our qualities, not over our skin colour, or background.

Jim as Hero in The Adventures of Huck Finn

A hero is defined as a person noted for feats of courage ornobility of purpose. The character of Jim in Huckleberry Finn by MarkTwain certainly fits that description. He risked his life in order to freehimself from slavery, and in doing so, helps Huck to realise that he hasworth. Huck becomes aware of Jim's sense of love and humanity, his basicgoodness, and his desire to help others. There are many illustrations ofthis phenomenon in Huckleberry Finn.

The reader first becomes aware of Jim's sense of love and humanity when Jim discovers Pap's corpse on the houseboat:

But it didn't budge. So I hollered again, and then Jim says: "De manain't asleep — he's dead. You hold still— I'll go en see. "He went, andbent down and looked, and says: "It's a dead man. Yes, indeedy; naked, too.He's ben shot in de back. I reck'n he's ben dead two er three days. Come in,Huck, but doan' look at his face — it's too gashly."

This is an example of how Jim is a humane and loving person becausehe does not allow Huck to see his dead father's face once he sees andunderstands the position in wehich he is placed. Later, Huck wishes tospeak to Jim about the dead man, but Jim will not allow it since he doesnot want to reveal the truth about Pap to Huck. This is a second and moredirect approach that is used in the story in order to show this same point. Jim is also basically a good person. Although he is ignorant, heknows that it is a good thing for him to show Huck that he has worth sothat Huck can think of him as an equal. This is a tough idea for Huck torealize because at this point in time he still thinks of Jim in terms ofbeing a slave, and not on equal footing with him. This is shown by Jim'sstatement of his own self worth.

"Yes; en I's rich now, come to look at it. I owns mysef, en I's wuth eight hund'd dollars. I wisht I had de money, I wouldn' want no mo'."

This statement is one of the first that lead to the reversal of Huck's attitudes toward Jim while they navigate the river. Huck states that: "People would call me a low-down Abolitionist and despise me for keeping mum..."

Huck's statement shows that he cares significantly more for Jimthan he had in the past. This statement also paves the way for the feelingthat Huck has for "going to hell" for Jim because Huck cares for Jim somuch. Huck also shows about how much he cares for Jim when he escapes fromthe Wilks' graveyard scene. Huck explained the matter in this way:

"Out with you, Jim, and set her loose! Glory be to goodness, we're shut of them!"

Jim lit out, and was a-coming for me with both arms spread, he wasso full of joy; but when I glimpsed him in the lightning my heart shot upin my mouth and I went overboard backwards; for I forgot he was old KingLear and a drownded A-rab all in one, and it most scared the livers andlights out of me. But Jim fished me out, and was going to hug me and blessme...

This is another example of how much Huck loves Jim because all that Huck could think about was returning to Jim to continue their journey. Huck's colorful description of the incident only seems to compound the validity of this statement.

The third charictaristic that Jim exemplifies is a desire to help others. In Huckleberry Finn, Jim wishes to free himself from slavery. In doing so he enlists the help of Huck Finn. As they travel down the river, Jim sees that Huck will need some help understanding why he should be set free. Jim's objective is realized when he is sold back into slavery by the two frauds, the King and the Duke. Once Jim is sold back into slavery, Huck is left alone and begins to feel lonely without the presence of Jim. Huck speaks of his being alone in this way:

I see Jim before me all the time: in the day and in the night-time, sometimes moonlight, sometimes storms, and we a-floating along, talking and singing and laughing. But somehow I couldn't seem to strike no places to harden me against him, but only the other kind. I'd see him standing my watch on top of his'n, 'stead of calling me, so I could go on sleeping; and see him how glad he was when I come back out of the fog; and when I come to him again in the swamp, up there where the feud was; and such-like times... I was the best friend old Jim ever had in the world, and the ONLY one he's got now...

"All right, then, I'll GO to hell"

At this climactic point in the story, Huck not only sees that he and Jim are on equal ground and that he will do anything, including freeing Jim from slavery, which he accomplishes with the assistance of Tom Sawyer. The character of Jim in Huckleberry Finn is a hero because his sense of love and humanity, his basic goodness, and his desire to help others help Huckleberry Finn to realise why he should help to free Jim from slavery.

Huckleberry Finn–Loyalty and Trust

Huckleberry Finn does not address questions of law as directly as the other novels that we have read. Ostensibly, Huck is torn between disobeying the slavery laws and honoring his conscious. However, Huck shows a disregard for other laws throughout the story, so I think that his conflict stems not from a belief that one must obey the law because it is the law, or on a social contract theory.

Huck is never overly concerned with the truth or the norms of society, he adheres to the mores of society because of the consequences as opposed to any fundamental acceptance of them or authority. Unlike Billy Budd, however, Huck does not seem to be influenced by the fear of corporal punishment, as much as he is concerned with the social consequences that would result if his disobedience was discovered. The choice that Huck eventually makes is deeper than just choosing to accept the social consequences, he is willing to 'go to hell' for Jim, rather than betray the loyalty and trust that has grown between them.

I think that Mark Twain choose an excellent vehicle for the presentation of a sharp, social satire. By letting Huck tell the story, Twain was free to present the ignorance underscoring the mores that were passed onto to children. Huck interprets the world literally, which starkly contrasts with the romanticism of Tom Sawyer and spiritualism of the widows. Huck's literalism also allows him more leeway than a third-person narrator can have. Mark Twain could have presented his criticisms in an essay, or a more sensational, fictional novel; however, he has chosen the most powerful form because the realism of the scenes and Huck's literal perception of the world make the events seem truthful and their description seem unvarnished.

This does seem incongruous with Huck's casual disregard for the truth but as one gets to know him, the disregard seems more pragmatic than casual. He lies when he has to, but not for personal gain, or even for purposes of a game, for example, he saw no point in calling vegetables jewels so he quit the game. Moreover, he does not condone the lying of the duke and the King when it hurts the innocent daughters as opposed to licentious men in town and more importantly he makes efforts to remedy the perceived hurt. All of these factors lead the reader to trust Huck and his presentation of the story.

It seems to me that Huck learned a great deal along his journey and learned nothing at all. He was from the beginning an essentially good and earnest young man, the childish pranks were a result of his ignorance of their effects, not from any ill intent. He does not like to see people get hurt, and he tries to help whenever he can, even trying to warn the King and the Duke of their impending feathering despite their bad acts and betrayal. He is little like Billy Budd with experience, he is fundamentally good but society has taught him the wrong things, i.e., that slaves are not like him, and do not feel emotions.

From the first few days on the island until the very end, every time that he was confronted with Jim being in danger, his instinct was to protect him. As the trip went on, the choice became more deliberated and purposeful as Huck began first to see Jim as a human and then as a true companion, deserving of faith and loyalty. The climatic moment, to me at least, is not Huck's conscious decision to free Jim, which is arguably different from the prior decisions to protect him from discovery because it is actively rejecting society's mores and breaking the law. To me, the moment is Huck's genuine sorrow at having hurt Jim's feelings, and his willingness to apologize. While the subject of Jim's expertise is superstitions and that may seem to be an oxymoron, the larger point is Huck's first realization that Jim is even capable of having expertise. It is also clearer to the reader, that Jim bases some of expertise on common sense and awareness of his environment.

Actually, Jim seems one dimensional for a large part of the story. However, when one considers his earlier actions with the full knowledge of the book's later revelations, it seems that the character was three dimensional throughout and the reader got failed to see to it until Huck did. For example, shielding Huck from the sight of the dead man is fatherly and protective, but knowing that the dead man was Huck's father makes it even more poignant. I think that the beginning scenes where Jim explains his kidnapping by witches are more indicative of capitalizing on the situation (especially as the story grew in a positive correlation to the recognition he received) than ignorance.

Speaking of ignorance, I said that Huck learned nothing because he assented to Tom's escape plans despite the plainly apparent absurdity. He changed his personal perception about Jim, but he still accepts the authority and rightness of the society that misled him about the very humanness of slaves. He knows that Tom's way appears to be wrong, but defers because Tom is educated and there must be a reason for doing it that way even if he does not see it. This applies equally to Jim, I do not think that his acceptance of the scheme was a result of his confidence in Huck's loyalty, as much as it was acceptance Tom's way, without question and despite the indignities.

I think that given the time period, that this was Twain's larger point, physical freedom and/or recognition as humans, as opposed to property, is a veneer—that it alone, is not enough to remedy the wrongs because the underlying prejudices and ignorance runs so deeply. This point is driven home hard, by the revelation that the popular and beloved Tom Sawyer, could be so callous as to subject Jim to continued imprisonment and to intentionally create a dangerous situation. It is these unthinking, unintentional acts that so convincingly demonstrate the depth of the damage that ignorance and prejudice have instilled on the psyche of the young generation that will become 'society' during the Reconstruction era as well as the slaves themselves.

The dialect does much to contribute to the realism of the story and thus enhances its apparent authenticity. Huck does not have a motive to colour his portrayal of his environment, so even if he embellished some or understated his involvement, it is not important for Twain's purposes. The story is not really about Huck or Jim, its about exposing the ignorance that pervades the South at that time, and showing how deeply ingrained it is.

I think that Tom's actions are necessary to make readers fully comprehend the magnitude of the problem and so I forgive Twain for deviating from the realism of the storyline by utilizing a fantastic coincidence that seems more appropriate for the Romantic pieces so subtly satirized in this very work. He could have chosen another foil for Huck, but given the popularity of Tom at that time, and indeed today, no newly introduced character could provide it so unexpectedly, and thereby powerfully.

However, I do have an issue with how smoothly things end. Jim ran away and he tried to escape without knowing of his freedom, so he intended and attempted to break the law even if he was by good fortune not actually do so. I do not think that Twain had to answer the question of whether intent or actuality or both should be required for culpability or if they and/or after-the-fact-good deeds should excuse or mitigate it. I think could have explored the legal questions involving mistake more thoroughly and he should have raised them.

I find that Tom's assertion regarding the irrelevance because Jim was in fact free, to be somewhat contradictory to Tom's general character which places more value on appearance and form then reality. It seems more in line with Huck's literal outlook and interpretation of the world. It may well be that the novel is darker than it appears, because it is possible that Tom's disregard was not based on unintentional, ignorance but rather was intentional and selfish. I will have to re-read Tom Sawyer to consider that question, I remember that was my view the very first time I read the book because I did not read Tom Sawyer first.

I think I changed my mind upon learning that Tom was such a well-known and beloved character, I did not think the audience would accept it. However, today, I am not sure why I thought the audience's expected acceptance/rejection is indicative of the authors intent. Twain was very dark in his later years, and his use of the dialects, inclusion of the (arrogant, taunting?) notice/explanation (challenge?) and his biting satiric tone indicate that he would not feel constrained by the audiences expectations, and might seek to shock them.

Huckleberry Finn–Controversial

It seems like a never-ending question. When will we ever let it rest? You know the question I'm talking about; should the Adventures of Huckleberry Finn be banned from American Literature courses? It's been argued from so many different standpoints, but it has never been settled. Is Huckleberry Finn really a controversial book?

No, I do not agree with the banning of Huckleberry Finn. This book is considered to be a classic. It explores the depths of our past in many different ways. Those who think the book to be controversial probably have never ever read it before. Most likely, they're basing their judgments on the excessively used word, "nigger." For those who have read the book and still feel necessary to ban it are obviously missing the key points of this American classic.

If you understand Huckleberry Finn, then you'll realise it's not about slavery or racism. It's about being unprejudiced. In the book, Huck admits that Jim "had an uncommon level head for a nigger." If you were to take out the black and white scenario, you would see that this quote is clearly nothing but acceptance. Huck is accepting Jim, regardless of his ethnic background. If you looked deeper, you would also see, the book is about nothing less than freedom and the quest for freedom. It's about a slave who breaks the law and risks his life to win his freedom and be reunited with his family. He was lucky enough to have a friend who made him his best friend and helped him to escape. Truly this isn't controversial; it's real life.

Another controversial aspect of the book would be the use of the word "nigger" and its being in the book over 200 times creates constant scrutiny. I feel the word was not used to be racist and its usage in the book gives great representation of the way life was during the pre-civil war era. People need to grasp the concept that that's how black were treated then. In today's society, we would find quotes such as, "Good gracious! Was anybody hurt?" "No'm. Just a nigger," APPALING! But in fact, it was written in an earlier time setting when quotes like that were okay to say. I find it wrong to want to ban a book over racial slurs because it's like trying to cover up the past. We cannot hide the real truth of how whites treated blacks. Instead we have to let it surface and move on.

In today's society, the word "nigger" is still frequently used. Only more in rap songs and movies as opposed to everyday talk. If the word "nigger" is so unacceptable, then why do you still use it? And why aren't movies and songs being banned if great American classic books are? It just doesn't make sense to me.

Another thing, which causes controversy, is Jim and Huck's relationship. I think this is taken wrong by many people and assumed for the worse, when actually Jim is shown to be a positive role model for Huck. Even though Jim was shown to be somewhat lesser at first, Huck realizes that Jim is as much a human as any white person. Once again, this proves a point that Huckleberry Finn is not racist book.

All in all, The Adventures of Huckleberry Finn should no longer be considered a controversial book. It is nothing but the truth on how life used to be. For those who cannot understand that, then I feel bad for you. You need to learn how to look outside the box and see the bigger picture.

We cannot hide from the truth any longer. We can only learn from it.

Challenge to Slavery

Adventures of Huckleberry Finn In recent years, there has been increasing discussion of the seemingly racist ideas expressed by Mark Twain in Huckleberry Finn. In some extreme cases the novel has even been banned by public school systems and censored by public libraries. The basis for these censorship campaigns has been the depiction of one of the main characters in Huckleberry Finn, Jim, a black slave. Jim, is a "typical" black slave who runs away from his "owner,"

Miss Watson. At several points in the novel, Jim's character is described to the reader, and some people have looked upon the characterization as racist.

However, before one begins to censor a novel it is important to separate the ideas of the author from the ideas' of his characters. It is also important not to take a novel at face value and to "read between the lines" in order to capture the underlying themes of a novel. If one were to do this in relation to Huckleberry Finn, one would, without doubt, realise that it is not racist and is even anti-slavery. Through society, Huck's father and Huck, Mark Twain reveals a challenge to slavery.

On a superficial level Huckleberry Finn might appear to be racist. The first time the reader meets Jim he is given a very negative description of Jim. The reader is told that Jim is illiterate, childlike, not very bright and extremely superstitious. However, it is important not to lose sight of who is giving this description and of whom it is being given. Although Huck is not a racist child, he has been raised by extremely racist individuals who have, even if only subconsciously, ingrained some feelings of bigotry into his mind.

It is also important to remember that this description, although it is quite saddening, was probably accurate. Jim and the millions of other slaves in the South were not permitted any formal education, were never allowed any independent thought and were constantly mistreated and abused. Twain is merely portraying by way of Jim, a very realistic slave raised in the South during that time period. To say that Twain is racist because of his desire for historical accuracy is absurd.

Despite the few incidences in which Jim's description might be misconstrued as racist, there are many points in the novel where Twain through Huck, voices his extreme opposition to the slave trade and racism. In chapter six, Huck's father fervently objects to the government's granting of suffrage to an educated black professor. Twain wants the reader to see the absurdity in this statement. Huck's father believes that he is superior to this black professor simply because of the colour of his skin. In Chapter 15 the reader is presented with a very caring and father-like Jim who becomes very worried when he loses his best friend, Huck in a deep fog, contradicting the original "childlike" description of Jim. Twain is pointing out the connection that has been made between Huck and Jim - a connection that does not exist between a man and his property.

When Huck first meets Jim on the Island he makes a monumental decision, not to turn Jim in. Two opposing forces, the force of society and the force of his personal conscience confront him. Many times, throughout the novel, Huck comes very close to rationalizing Jim's slavery. However, he is never able to see a reason why this man, who has become one of his only friends, should be a slave. Through this internal struggle, Twain expresses his opinions of the absurdity of slavery and the importance of following one's personal conscience before the laws of society. By the end of the novel, Huck and the reader have come to understand that Jim is not someone's property and an inferior man, but an equal.

Throughout the novel society's voice is heard through Huck. The racist and hateful contempt, which existed at the time, is at many times present. But, it is vital for the reader to recognize these ideas as society's and to recognize that Twain throughout the novel disputes these ideas. Twain brings out into the open the ugliness of society and causes the reader to challenge the original description of Jim. In his subtle manner, he creates not an apology for slavery but a challenge to it.

We Should Not Ban the Adventures of Huckleberry Finn

There is a current debate that the description of Jim in the novel "Huckleberry Finn" is racist leading to some schools banning it from their libraries. Jim's character is described as an uneducated and simple sounding; illiterate slave and some people have looked upon this characterization as racist. Jim is depicted as a slave in the south during a period when slavery was common place and widely accepted as the way of life. Slaves of this time period were not provided any formal education; never allowed any independent thought and were constantly mistreated and abused.

The author in my opinion is merely describing how a slave

spoke in those days and was trying to give you the true feeling behind his thought, while writing this tale. Despite a few instances in which Jim's description might be misconstrued as being racist, such as the use of the word "nigger", the reader should be able to understand that this is a fictional portrayal of two boys, one white and one black, during a time when slavery was common place. There is an obvious contrast of the mind set depicted in Twain's novel compared to then and now. The use of the word "nigger" is most certainly a very slanderous slang term that is not socially acceptable in present times. The dialect in which Jim is speaking indicates how Jim spoke do to his lack of education and refinement that white people refused to provide to slaves.

This provision was not permitted as white slave owners viewed blacks as property and as being unable to learn proper grammar and structure of the English language. Some historians have stated that this was also so because it allowed the white's to maintain control over their slaves in order to "keep the upper hand", so to speak. We as a modern society should maintain an open mind when dealing with literary works such as Huckleberry Finn and bare in mind that novels such as these are written during socially diverse and sometimes opposite ways of thinking.

We should not ban a literary work such as Huckleberry Finn simply because it is not accepted by modern day standards. As we look further into the character's(Jim's) dialogue we find that Twain has written as accurately as possible the way that he would sound and also to make you stop and think and picture in your mind him speaking that way. Though difficult to interpret at times, it gives you an authentic feel of this character's persona. For those that are die-hard readers, that "lose themselves" in what they are reading, this approach is ideal.

Rejection of Civilization in The Adventures of Huckleberry Finn

In the book, The Adventures of Huckleberry Finn, Huck rejects "sivilized" life. He dreads the rules and conformities of society such as religion, school, and anything else that will eventually make him civilized. He feels cramped in his new surroundings at the Widow Douglas's house. He would rather be in his old rags and sugar-hogshead because he was free and satisfied. He felt out of place when he tried being "sivilized" because he grew up fending for himself and to him it felt really lonely. Huck Finn grew up living in the woods and pretty much raised himself because his pap was a drunk. He never had a civilized lifestyle and he believed that his way of living was good enough for him.

He was free to do what ever he liked and that is how he learned to live. He did not believe in school because all you need to know to live is not found in a book that you read at school. He believed that you learned by living out in the wild. Huck would rather be an individual than conform to society. Huck would rather follow his heart then his head and because of this Huck is ruled as a bad person because in society your suppose to use your head. Huck is being penalized for his beliefs and he does not want to be apart of a lifestyle that does not support his ways. For instance his choice not to turn in Jim shows that Huck understands why Jim is escaping. Huck sees Jim as a friend not as a slave and so he truly is able to see that society's way of treaty Jim is wrong. Huck is portrayed as a boy who sees life at face value and not by the set "standards" of the "sivilized" society. The rejection of the "sivilized" lifestyles shows that Huck does not agree with it rules. Because of this, he is able to see life from different perspectives. He can sympathize with all the class in society. He learns to figure out what is morally correct and wrong. Through out his journey down the river, Huck is able to learn more about himself and others. His adventures has taught him more than he will ever learn just by reading books. Huck is able to live a great life just by reacting to situations as they come along. Huck is better off not living a "sivilized" lifestyle because that is how he learns. Huck's rejection of a "sivilized" life can be seen as being rebellious, but as you read more and more about Huck's adventures, you come to the realization that this has helped Huck to become a well rounded person.

Huck is a practical and realistic person who grows more and more as he deals with every situation he is put in, but during his time, it was not right for a child to be on his own because they are too young to know anything and they need guidance through school and religion. Even though Huck is young, he has learned a lot by reading and by self-study. Huck believes in being free so he can able to adjust to situations rather than living a set life. Huck learns without the help of school and other forms that will eventually make him "sivilized"and he intends to keep it that way and therefore he runs away from the "sivilized" society. Huck learns from his actions and mistakes and not from others and that is how he grows mentally and physically.

The Adventures of Huckleberry Finn Should be in the Classroom

To teach or not to teach? This is the question that is presentlyon many administrators' minds about The Adventures of Huckleberry Finn byMark Twain. For those who read the book without grasping the importantconcepts that Mark Twain gets across "in between the lines", many problemsarise. A reader may come away with the impression that the novel is simplya negative view of the African-American race. Many scholars and educators,like Marylee Hengsetbeck who said, "If Huck Finn is used solely as a partof a unit on slavery or racism, we sell the book short." (Hengstebeck 32)feel that there is much to be learned about Blacks from this book and itshould not be banned from the classroom. This is only one of many themesand expressions that Mark Twain is describing in his work. Another centraltheme is how the depiction of race relations and slavery is used as insightinto the nature of blacks and whites as people in general. Overall, themost important thing to understand is that Mark Twain is illustrating hisvaluable ideas subtly and not pushing them upon the reader directly.

Primarily, Huck Finn teaches readers two important lessons aboutthe true nature of people. Throughout the book, one of these main lessonsis that Blacks can be just as caring as whites. The white characters oftenview the blacks as property rather than as individuals with feelings andaspirations of their own. Huck comes to realise that Jim is much more thana simple slave when he discusses a painful experience with his daughter.Jim describes how he once called her and she did not respond. He thentakes this as a sign of disobedience and beats her for it. Soon realizingthat she is indeed deaf, he comforts her and tries to make up for the actof beating. The feeling that Jim displays shows Huck that Jim has a veryhuman reaction and the fact Jim says, "Oh Huck, I bust out crying....'Ohthe po' little thing!" (Twain 151), only further proves to Huck that Jimis as caring as he is. Huck's realization allows him to see that Jim is nolonger the ordinary slave. The point where Huck completely changes hisattitudes towards blacks comes when he is faced with the dilemma of turningin Jim. Huck fights with his conscience and also reflects on the thingsthat Jim has done for him. "I'd see him standing my watch on top of his'n,stead of calling me, so I could go on sleeping; and see him how glad he waswhen I come back out of the fog; and when I come to him again in the swamp,up there where the feud was; and such likes the times: and would alwayscall me honey, and pet me and do everything he could think of for me, andhow good he always was..." (Twain) These two key scenes are among manythat illustrate the idea that Blacks can be as caring and emotional asWhites - one of the main lessons of the book.

The second main lesson that the book teaches is that the world isfull of hypocrites. Huck realizes that through his experiences with Jimthat he and Blacks like him are not what he has been told. People likeMiss Watson, who represent the established belief system of Huck's society,tells him that blacks were nothing but property and should be treated assuch. Huck now knowing that this is not the case sees that people, likeMiss Watson, made up these laws to suit themselves. Furthermore, Hucksees that Miss Watson would often make up a regulation for him but notabide by it herself. An example of this concerns the subject of snuff."And she took snuff too; of course that was alright, because she done itherself." (Twain) Huck noticed this double standard even more nowbecause he began to see that not everything Miss Watson told him was true.With this, Huck not only sees Jim in a new light, but begins to see thatthe people who supposedly know everything, didn't really know anything.Again other critiques of the novel state that as a whole the book is "amasterpiece of irony." (Kilpatrick) With this second main lesson, the bookdefends itself against being banned.

People who would ban "Huckleberry Finn" simply for the on thesurface racial content are no better than the character of Miss Watson.The idea of banning a book and not teaching it to others is selfish andsubjective in itself. Those who are seeking to ban it would often followtheir own agendas, like Miss Watson in only trying to get their own viewacross and not allowing the novel to be interpreted for what it really is.As Hengstebeck states in her critique "Selective editing only masks thereal problem." (Hengstebeck 32), another main reason arises about therecognition of slavery and racism. Racism is an ever present idea in oursociety. To ban the book would be to deny students the insight that Twainbrings to the subject. Mark Twain brings a first hand account to thesubject through the character of Jim and how he reacts to his whiteneighbors. Jim, although he is shown to be a rational and mature person,bows down to white authority when he says lines like, "Jim couldn't see nosense in the most of it but he allowed, we was white folks and knew betterthan him"

The perspective that Twain gives through the character of Jim isinvaluable because it takes the concepts of slavery and racism and givesthem life. By making the concepts more real and accessible to people,Twain shows the subject for what it really is. Having this perspectivewould only help people to understand the concept better and deal with itsmany implications. As Morton Fried states "The removal of such literaryworks from the classroom, however, would be a strategy of defeat on the waragainst racism." (Fried) Racism is built on ignorance, therefore banningthe book's insights would only perpetuate that ignorance and be a victoryfor racism and not a loss.

To consider banning this novel simply because it has situations andcharacters that are considered racist is superficial. The novel does showthe relationships between blacks and whites in the nineteenth century andall its overtones. However, it shows these situations not to promoteracism against blacks, but to bring a better understanding of the subject.The character of Jim is shown to be caring, considerate towards Huck andmore mature and human than the society allows him to be. Although he isshown to be this way, Twain shows the irony and hypocrisy of treating amature man like simple property. The novel also shows how a boy, who is aproduct of this hypocritical society, comes to realise the true nature ofhis friend Jim and how screwed up his white peers actually are. In showingthese ironic situations and the transformation that Huck goes through thereader sees racism and its implications in a real life setting. People whowant to ban the book miss the idea entirely. Instead of getting rid ofsomething that is supposedly racist, they only perpetuate racism by denyingothers a good source of material on the subject. Overall, banning the bookwould be doing more harm than good for society because of the denial ofignorance-breaking insight on an everlasting conflict.

Religion, Slavery and Democracy in Huckleberry Finn

All children have a special place, whether chosen by a conscious decision or not this is a place where one can go to sort their thoughts. Nature can often provide comfort by providing a nurturing surrounding where a child is forced to look within and choices can be made untainted by society. Mark Twain once said "Don't let school get in the way of your education." Twain states that this education which is provided by society, can actually hinder human growth and maturity. Although a formal education shouldn't be completely shunned, perhaps true life experience, in society and nature, are a key part of development. In the novel Adventures of Huckleberry Finn, Mark Twain throws the curious yet innocent mind of Huck Finn out into a very hypocritical, judgmental, and hostile world, yet Huck has one escape—the Mississippi

River constantly flowing nearby. Here nature is presented as a thought provoking environment when experienced alone. The river is quiet and peaceful place where Huck can revert to examine any predicament he might find himself in: "They went off, and I got aboard the raft, feeling bad and low...Then I thought a minute, and says to myself, hold on,- s'pose you'd a done right and give Jim up; would you felt better than you do now?

No, says I, I'd feel bad...". Only a few weeks with Jim and still feeling great ambivalence, Huck returns to the river to think. Twain tries here to tell the reader how strong the "mob" really is, and only when totally alone is Huck able to make the morally correct decision. The natural flowing and calm of the river cause this deep-thought, show! ing how unnatural the collective thought of a society can be. The largest and most obvious test of Huck's character is his relationship with Jim. The friendship and assistance which he gives to Jim go completely against all that "sivilization" has taught him; at first this concept troubles Huck and causes him a great deal of pain, but over time, through his life experiences and shared times with Jim, Huck crosses the line upheld by the racist South and comes to know Jim as a human being. Huck is at a point in his life where opinions are formed, and by growing on the river, Huck can stand back from society and form his own. Eventually he goes as far as to risk his life for Jim:"And got to thinking of our trip down the river; and I see Jim before me, all the time, in the day, and in the night-time, sometimes moonlight, sometimes storms, and we a floating along, talking, and singing, and laughing. But somehow I couldn't see no places to harden me against him, but only the other kind...I studied a minute sort of holding my breath, and then I s! ays to myself: 'All right, then, I'll go to hell'...".

After a long and thought-provoking adventure, Huck returns to the raft one final time to decide the fate of his friend. Symbolically, Huck makes the morally correct decision away from all others, thinking on the river. Although it might not be evident to himself, Huck causes the reader to see that "sivilization", in their treatment of blacks especially, is not civilized at all. Every person Huck and Jim come across seems to just be following someone else blindly, as the whole country were some sort of mob. In the last few chapters, Tom Sawyer is re-introduced and the reader is left to examine how different environments: "sivilization" and nature (the river), have affected the children's growth. It is distinctly evident that Huck has turned out to be the one with a clear and intelligent mind, and Tom, although he can regurgitate worthless facts about Louis XVI and Henry VIII, shows no real sign of maturity. "The first time I catched up to Tom, private, I asked him what was his idea, time of the evasion?- what it was he planned to do if the evasion worked out all right and he managed to set a nigger free that was already free before?

And he said, what he had planned in his head, from the start, if we got Jim out, all safe, was for us to run him down the river, on the raft, and have adventures plumb to the mouth...". Huck has always thought of Tom as more intelligent than himself, but he cannot understand how Tom could toy with Jim's life in such a way. For much time, Huck is! without the river and it is though his mind clouds; he follows along with Tom playing a sick game until the end when he is once again threatened with being "sivilized". "But I reckon I got to light out for the Territory ahead of the rest, because aunt Sally she's going to adopt me and sivilize me and I can't stand it. I been there before".

Huck's adventure, if nothing else, has given him a wary eye towards "sivilized" society. When the prospect of settling down with Sally is presented he light's out for the Territory to distance himself from a restrictive, formal education. Twain ends his novel by setting Huck up for a new experience and personal growth. The Adventures of Huckleberry Finn taught an important lesson, one that showed the importance of the self in the maturing process. We saw Huck grow up by having the river as a place of solitude and thought, where he was able to participate in society at times, and also sit back and observe society. Through the child's eye we see how ignorant and mob-like we can all be. Then nature, peace, and logic are presented in the form of the river where Huck goes to think. Though no concise answer is given, the literature forces the reader to examine their surroundings, and question their leaders. This essay will realise the themes of religion, slavery, and democracy in the book Huckleberry Finn by Mark Twain. By exploring these themes that lie behind the book's veneer, we can understand Twain's objective for writing this book.

Religion is sarcastically reflected in Huckleberry Finn by Twain's sense of storyline and the way his characters talk. A predominant theme, and probably one of Twain's favorites, is the mockery of religion. Twain tended to attack organized religion at every opportunity and the sarcastic character of Huck Finn is perfectly situated to allow him to do so. The attack on religion can already be seen in the first chapter, when Huck indicates that hell sounds like a lot more fun than heaven. This will continue throughout the novel, with one prominent scene occurring when the "King" convinces a religious community to give him money so he can "convert" his pirate friends.

Twain's skeptical take on religion can be elicited because superstition is a theme that both Huck and Jim bring up several times. Although both of these characters tend to be quite rational, they quickly become irrational when anything remotely superstitious happens to them. The role of superstition in this book is two-fold: First, it shows that Huck and Jim are child-like in spite of their otherwise extremely mature characters. Second, it serves to foreshadow the plot at several key junctions. For example, spilling salt leads to Pa returning for Huck, and later Jim gets bitten by a rattlesnake after Huck touches a snakeskin with his hands.

Another theme that is dealt with in this book is slavery. In fact, slavery is one of the main topics that has been frequently debated in regards to Huckleberry Finn since it was first published. Twain himself was vehemently anti-slavery and Huckleberry Finn can in many ways be seen as an allegory for why slavery is wrong. Twain uses Jim, a slave who is one of the main characters, as a way of showing the human side of a slave. Everything about Jim is presented through emotions: Jim runs away because Miss Watson was going to sell him

South and separate him from his family; Jim is trying to become free so he can buy his family's freedom; and Jim takes care of Huck and protects him on their journey downriver in a very materialistic manner. Thus, Twain's purpose is to make the reader feel sympathy for Jim and outrage against the society that would harm him. However, at the same time that Twain is attacking slavery, he also pushes the issue into the background for most of the novel. Thus, slavery itself is never debated by Huck and Jim.

Moreover, the other slaves in the novel are noticeably minor characters. Only at the very end does Twain create the central conflict concerning slavery: Should Huck free Jim from slavery and therefore be condemned to go to hell? This moment is life altering for Huck because it forces him to reject everything that "civilization" has taught him. In the end, he makes the decision to free Jim based solely on his own experiences and not based on what he has been taught from books. The themes of thievery and freedom also come up in the book, in that Huck and his gang are free to whatever they want. They are on the wrong side of the law and have no one to tell them what to do.

Consequently, the themes of robbery and freedom are ones that permeate the novel. They are first introduced in the second chapter with respect to Tom Sawyer's band: Tom believes that "there is a great deal of freedom associated with being robbers." This theme can be traced throughout the rest of the book. Huck and Jim encounter robbers on the shipwrecked boat and later they are forced to put up with the King and the Dauphin, both of whom "rob" everyone they meet and free to do as they wish. Tom's robber band is also paralleled by the fact that Tom and Huck both become literal robbers at the end of the novel. They both resolve to steal Jim out of slavery and have the freedom to do so.

In conclusion, many various themes run through this novel. Tom has an anti-slavery sentiment, which tells us what Twain thought of slavery. Also, skepticism of religion is demonstrated through all of the hysterical mockeries Twain makes of organized religion. Additionally, the element of freedom is also encompassed, as the main characters are free to roam as they please.

The Problem with Huck Finn

A person is a product of his or her society and environment. A person grows up learning skills and traits from the people around him. These traits influence and affect the person unconsciously for the rest of his life. For instance if a person grows up with an abusive father chances are he will grow up to be abusive to people around him. But what we learn may not necessarily be right (like what is mentioned above), but the person doesn't know that. What would happen to a person who spent this whole life living a certain way and then came to the conclusion that something different was actually correct. This would totally rock his world.

Huck Finn has this exact problem. Huck was brought up in a world where slavery was normal. Heck even the local priest said the Bible said it was okay. What greater authority to have than Gods. But Huck is faced with a challenging decision. As he becomes more and more of a friend to a runaway slave and helps him in escape his entire moral standards are challenged. But this leaves him with an invaluable lesson.

Huck meets Jim as they both are running away from their lives, for different reasons. Huck and Jim head down the Mississippi. But Jim is a runaway slave and Huck is faced with a decision to help or turn Jim in. Huck comes very close to turning Jim in as he struggles to determine what is correct and what is not correct. Huck throughout the story struggles within him to find out for himself what is right and wrong. He sees Jim's compassionate nature and Good-Will and realizes the institution that is slavery is not moral and is in fact the opposite.

Huck even in one triumphant moment comes over his doubts about the morality of slavery. Huck stats "Alright then I'll go to hell". Huck in this one simple statement defines his opinion. No matter what the consequence of his actions, if it be Hell, or jail or whatever, he will not betray Jim. Huck in his struggle inside of himself comes to realise the right thing to do and in doing so becomes a man. A man able to think for himself, and make his own conscience decisions.

One is brought up in a certain environment. Ones personality is shaped and molded off of his environment. But one doesn't have to follow the Norms and standards of ones societies. In Fact it takes more courage and strength to be an individual and to be a free-thinking person. Huck becme this and Huck became a Man when he stopped and thought about the institution of Slavery.

The Adventures of Huckleberry Finn-Inappropriate for Children

The Adventures of Huckleberry Finn by Mark Twain is, not andshould not, be considered a child's story. A story like this may corrupta young child's mind. It deals with adult themes and concepts that aregenerally not suitable for young children. Als o, if used as a child'sstory it may confuse them or give them the wrong idea about slavery andthe terminology of the time.First of all, The Adventures of Huckleberry Finn is extremelyinappropriate for children because it may put bad ideas into a youngimpressionable mind. At the young age of about twelve, Huck is roamingaround the woods all by himself and later on is flo ating aimlessly downthe Mississippi River with a bunch of criminals. Huck is living what mayappear to the children to be a very exciting and glamorous life. Mostparents would never steer their children the wrong way in life, don't wantto tell childr en about a kid around their age or little older than theyare that is homeless and basically cheating and stealing to survive.

Thisnovel explains in depth about various scams such as the Wilks brothersscam, and the teaching schools like the dancing sch ool or "yellowcution". In addition to the royal nonesuch plays which teach childrenthat all you need to do is take the money and run like the King and theDuke did. After reading this novel the majority of children won't go outand try to scam their n eighbors. However, it may seem like an appealinglifestyle for them. It may also give them the impression that being a conman for a living, or being homeless and wandering is a wonderful andglorious carefree lifestyle, and because your Mommy or Daddy tells it toyou, it must not be the wrong thing to do.

In addition to giving the wrong idea about life, it is a brutaland vulgar book that children should not be exposed to. There are acouple of deaths like when Colonel Sherburn kills a harmless town drunknamed Boggs. Earlier on Huck is staying with a the Grangerford familythat is in the middle of a feud with the Shepherdson family. Buck, theyoungest child, is about Huck's age. Buck speaks of murdering all of theShepherdsons for a reason he doesn't even know of. Eventually Buck iskilled by a She pherdson right in front of Huck's eyes. The King and theDuke are tarred and feathered later on and Huck doesn't really think twiceabout it. Huck also encounters a wreck on the river with two criminals onit that are going to leave a third one on thereto die. Not to forget the alcoholic and abusive father that is killed ina whore house. Which is just another example of how vulgar this story is.

Furthermore, not only is the plot very adult, the language is alsounsuitable for children. The Adventures of Huckleberry Finn takes place inthe pre-civil war south. At this time slavery is very common and iscondoned by society. Black people were tho ugh of as property and treatedextremely poorly and inhumanly. When Huck makes up the story on why he,"Tom", was late getting to Aunt Sally's house he explains that a cylinderhead had blown up. When Aunt Sally asked if anyone was hurt "Tom" saysthat nobody was hurt, just a couple of niggers were killed. Aunt Sallywas relieved and said "good, because sometimes people get hurt". This isan example of how black people were treated. Not as real people but asproperty or luggage. Huck would have gott en a similar reaction if hetold her that someone had their suitcase broken. The "niggers" were leftto live in shacks near the Phelp's house. Treating black people that wayis not a setting a good example for today's youth.

We've all made mistakes and the United States made a huge one withslavery, reading to your kids about "niggers" being killed and treating"niggers" as servants is not helping us teach today's children thatslavery and racism are a bad thing. Another th ing that is unsuitable forchildren is the excessive use of the word "nigger". This was a bookwritten a long time ago and nigger may have been a common term to use.However, we shouldn't teach children in today's society to call blackpeople niggers.

In conclusion, Huck Finn is not a child's book and shouldn't beread to children. They are too young to comprehend the book in a matureway. Also, they are too impressionable to take in that kind ofinformation and not be affected in some way by it, an d the only way HuckFinn can be interpreted is in a negative way that gives children the wrongidea about life. The Adventures of Huckleberry Finn should never betaught to young children.

Huckleberry Finn: His Role Model

Mark Twain's The Adventures of Huckleberry Finn is written from the view point of the boy Huckleberry Finn. He tells about the adventures he is having on the Mississippi River with a runaway slave, whose name is Jim. It becomes apparent early in the book that there are a couple of people who play major roles in Huck's life. One is Jim and the other is Tom Sawyer, the person Huck wishes he could be like.

Tom Sawyer is a leader to Huck from the very beginning of the book, when Huck is living with the Widow Douglas. She is raising Huck because his father is a drunk and is not in the area. Huck is doing fine living with the Widow Douglas for awhile, but he soon tires of her way of life. Huck does not like having to stay clean all the time and having to wear neat clothes. He also doesn't appreciate her attempting to civilize him, so he puts on his old rags and leaves.

Tom Sawyer is the one who is able to convince Huck to come back to the widow and "be respectable". Huck wants to be a part of Tom's gang, so he agrees to go back. It takes a certain type of person to make Huck willing to go home because it is a lifestyle he really doesn't like. Tom has that kind of control over Huck's decisions.

Another reason that Huck looks up to Tom as a role model is that Huck feels Tom is more intelligent than himself. Huck is amazed by how brilliant Tom is. "What a head for just a boy to have! If I had Tom Sawyer's head I wouldn't trade it off to be a duke, nor mate of a steamboat, nor clown in a circus, nor nothing I can think of". It isn't simply that Tom is smarter. It is that Tom often makes Huck feel he isn't as smart. One example is when the two boys are trying to free Jim. Huck doesn't understand why they have to do things the hard way. That is when Tom says, "Oh, shucks, Huck Finn, if I was as ignorant as you I'd keep still". Tom also says, "Why, hain't you ever read any books at all?". It is true that Tom has more schooling than Huck, and this also plays a role into Huck's belief that Tom is smarter. Even when Tom's ideas seem silly to Huck, he still believes that Tom is correct. Huck feels that he just doesn't have enough knowledge to understand Tom's intellectual ideas.

Huck also looks up to Tom because he has a better family background than himself. Tom's family isn't aristocratic, but compared to Huck's family it is, and it's "worth as much in a man as it is in a horse". Huck's only family is his drunk father who never has any money. Huck's father even agreed that some people were born "better" than others. Huck sometimes wishes that he came from a better family, like Tom's.

Huck desires Tom's companionship on the adventures throughout the book. The first time Huck wishes Tom is there is when Huck fakes his own death. When Huck is finishing up his own "murder", he says, "I did wish Tom Sawyer was there.". Another time is when Huck and Jim see the steamboat that has wrecked. Jim does not want to explore the boat, but Huck on the other hand finds it to be an adventure. Huck says that there is no way to go by the wreck because "do you reckon Tom Sawyer would ever go by this thing? Not for pie, he wouldn't. He'd call it an adventure...". Huck continues by saying, "I wish Tom Sawyer was here.".

Tom is always able to glorify things that aren't so great and make them exciting. Tom knows just how to add colour to their "adventures" to make them better. This was a quality that Huck finds very admirable because not everyone is able to do it. While faking his murder, Huck says, "[Tom Sawyer could] throw in the fancy touches. Nobody could spread himself like Tom Sawyer in such a thing...". After finishing his "murder", Huck critiques his performance in comparison to what Tom would do.

Later on, Huck was in the company of two con-artists who were claiming to be a king and a duke, and the two cons are pulling one of their scams on some girls. They are claiming to be the girls' long, lost uncles and have come to take care of their dead brother's daughters. What they are actually trying to do is take all the girls' inheritance. Huck starts out helping the king and duke but soon realizes the scam is wrong. Huck knows they aren't royalty and doesn't like taking advantage of these girls, so Huck works up a scheme to catch the two cons. This will leave Huck and Jim free to go without the cons tagging along. Huck proclaims that he has done so well that "Tom Sawyer couldn't 'a' done it none neater himself.". This makes Huck feel proud because he meets what he thinks to be Tom's standards, which is something he strives to do.

The greatest example of Tom's style comes at the end of the book, when Tom and Huck are together at Aunt Sally's. The two boys are trying to free Jim, who is a prisoner and is going to be sold back into slavery. Huck just wants to do it the easy way and get it over with, but Tom says they can't. Tom states that it is too easy. "We need to get up a difficult plan". Tom feels this will make them famous and help them receive praise for their heroism.

Throughout the story, Tom's role in Huck's life can be seen. Tom is Huck's leader. Tom is also a figure Huck tries to be like. Huck measures himself and what he does by Tom's standards and what he feels Tom would think. In Huck's eyes, Tom is perfect. He is brought up well, yet has a free will with a fun side. Tom is an intelligent, creative and imaginative child, which is everything Huck wishes for in himself.

Language and Dialect in Adventures of Hucklebery Finn

Mark Twain's use of language and dialect in the book

"Adventures ofHuckleberry Finn" helped him to bring about the overall feel that heconveyed throughout the book, allowing him to show Huck Finn's attitudesand beliefs concerning the nature of education, slavery, and family values.

When the story begins, Huck is seen as a young boy who is not veryeducated nor wishes to be. He does not seem to care very much for theattention that is given to him by the Widow Douglas, who had taken him infor her son, and her sister, Miss Watson. Huck's moral values were not onlythe product of his ignorance, but there is relation seen between Huck'sattitude and the attitude of his father when Huck is confronted by him.Huck's father is disgusted at the way that Huck seems to be becoming moreand more civilized. He states "...they say you can read and write. Youthink you're better'n your father, now, don't you, because he can't?"Perhaps this statement shows disgust in Huck through not following themoral values of his father, or perhaps this is just merely jealousy on hisfather's part. Huck's father warns Huck about going to school any more, yetHuck goes anyway, showing great willpower in the character of Huck in thathe was gaining an education that he never really wanted in the first place,but soon came to realise that it was something actually useful, and in thefact that he was disobeying his father's orders.

Huck's feelings about slavery are shown when he helps Jim, MissWatson's slave, to escape. Huck's constant statement that "Jim talks likehe is white inside" shows that Huck was unique amongst the society in whichhe lived in the fact that he saw beneath the colour of a person's skin andsaw the person that was truly there. Jim seems to be the only person thatHuck can trust other than Tom Saywer, Huck's best friend. Huck Finn feltthat slavery was a cruel injustice because he had gotten to know Jim andfound out that there was more to him than just being a slave. Huck hadfound that Jim was a human being just like himself. Through these ideas,Mark Twain subtly conveyed his own feelings about slavery that existed inthe south by using Huck as an example.

Mark Twain not only challenged the topics of education and slavery,but he also criticized the very society in which he lived. Social criticismappears in Twain's picture of the feuding Grangerfords and Shepherdsons,two families upon which Huck stumbles while on his travels. The twofamilies show the foolheartedness of the pre-civil war society that existedin Twain's lifetime. Twain tried to convey the point that society had noneed for civil feuds such as the one illustrated, or even the Americancivil war.

Through Mark Twain's use of language, he succeeded in showing thethoughts and beliefs of Huck Finn and the world that surrounded him. Heaccomplished this by showing these beliefs through Huck's realisticattitude, creating the framework to tackle the then-present andcontroversial issues of slavery and nationalistic values that accompaniedpeoples' thoughts on the subject.

Bad Habits in Adventures of Huckleberry Finn

Picking just one bad habit is like getting only one piece of candy at Sweet Factory. Once I finally picked my bad habit I realized how badly I needed to work on it. Huck had a bad habit he needed to work on too. Maybe we didn't know about it or thought we could get rid of it easily. But were either of us going to work it out? In the book Adventures of Huckleberry Finn by Mark Twain, which we were reading in class, the main character Huck had many bad habits as well. But his one main bad habit was lying to himself and by doing this he broke the law, his moral code and the law of God. It all started after he fakes his own death and runs to an island where he finds a run away slave, Jim that worked for Miss Watson, his guardian's sister.

Next they leave to find Cairo but as they float down the river they run into many hardships. While this is happening Huck is doing most of his lying to himself. This is very similar to my bad habit because during my month of trying to quit fighting with my mom I went through some very hard times holding back what I wanted to say. This was a very big hardship of mine. So I realized Huck and I had a lot in common. Huck's bad habit was first shown to us in chapter VIII when Huck tells Jim, "Well I did. I said I wouldn't, and

I'll stick to it. Honest injun I will." He is telling Jim he wont tell anyone that he ran away which means Huck is breaking the law of the land. We knows this because Huck also says "People would call me a low sown Ablitionist and despise me for keeping mum-but that don't make no difference." Huck again lies for Jim in chapter XVI when he is about to tell the men on the raft that Jim is with him but his conscience comes into play. When this happens he lies to these men and this is just adding more to his bad habit. Also in this chapter Huck breaks his own moral code. When him and Jim miss Cairo he says "There warn't anything to say.

We both knowed well enough it was more work of the rattle-snake skin; so what was the use to talk about it?" This is breaking his own moral code because he didn't believe that a rattlesnake could bring bad luck. Then he broke the law of God in chapter XXXI when he said, "You can't pray a lie-I found that out." This is when Huck realized that he doesn't think what he was doing was wrong. Last in chapter XL Huck realizes that the colors of the skin really don't matter. So at the end Huck breaks through his bad habit. Well my bad habit basically started when my mom started telling me no. And I just wasn't going to take it. So I started talking back and I wouldn't stop until I got my way or hurt my mom. Which is really something I don't want to do.

That's why I was hoping by trying to break this bad habit I wouldn't have to do it anymore. It started out pretty good I would be ready to fight or say something that might hurt my moms' feelings and I would catch myself. It started feeling better right away and my mom even noticed the change. But then I began to think less and less about it and it all started back up again. So I wrote in my journals about the change and how I didn't want it to go back but before I knew it my mom and I were fighting and it was the end of the month. Huck and I were alike because I broke my own moral code by being rude to my mom. I also broke the law of God because in the bible it says honour your father and mother and I don't think what I'm doing is considered that. Huck and I were different because Huck no longer had a bad habit and I still do. Well

Huck worked his bad habit out and is probably feeling pretty good. However I'm still working on mine and I think maybe one day I might be free of this. So I'm going to keep on trying and if I ever do make it through this I will make sure tc tell you. But until that day comes I'll always go for as many candies as I can get.

Importance of the River in The Adventures of Huckleberry Finn

In the novel The Adventures Of Huckleberry Finn the setting has a largeinfluence on Huck's character. The period of time that Huck lived in was adistinct era. The country was changing rapidly. During this period steamengines enabled rivers to be used as mass transportation, an idea that had neverbeen explored until now. Waterways were the first way in which large amounts ofgoods could be transported efficiently. This drastically changed much of thenation's economy. Huge factories were built in the north and southernplantations tripled their production by using machines. There were many traitsof this era that can be seen by looking at the components of Huck's character,his language, actions and thoughts. Some of these traits are sutle and can beeasily missed but others are very obvious and powerful. This period of changewas the setting of Huck's childhood.

One trait that is indicative of the era is the social class of Huck andHuck's language. It is greatly affected by his social class and setting. Thebroken English is a sign of Huck's low social class. In addition it also showsthat he is from a southern river town. This can be seen from his expressionsand accent. The language of the novel also assists the reader to get into thelaid back, southern mood of the book. By doing so the story is brought to life.It seems as if someone were to bring you back to the time when the novel and theevents in it occurred.

Because of the rules of the time that Huck's character is governed upon,Huck was never educated. During the early 1800s there was no law that requiredchildren to go to school, therefore his low intellect has a strong impact onHuck's character. It gives him a "plain and simple" outlook on life, thistrait can been seen throughout the book in Huck's character. One specific areait affects is Huck's plans for his future. Huck only thought about what he wasgoing to do for present. Huck had an incapable father. He was thought of asthe town drunk, and would often come home intoxicated and abuse Huck. At onepoint his father locked Huck up in a small room without food or water for days.The setting is important here because if Huck's father were to treat his son inan abusive manner today, he would lose custody of his child. A good example ofHuck's unloving relationship was Huck's reaction to his father's death. Whennotified of his death he was relieved and felt safe! This detail can be used toillustrate the abuse that Huck went through in the beginning of the book, whileliving with his father. Because of Huck's father's irresponsible actions, Huckran away at a young age in the hope that someday he would find freedom from hisfather and society. By running away Huck saved himself from abuse and beingtaken advantage of. One of the things Huck saved himself from was having 6,000dollars, that Huck was awarded for the capture of two criminals in Tom Sawyer,being stolen from him by his father.

Huck's separation from his father is also the reason for his free thinking, responsibility and innocence. These times of hardship formed him into a mature person and helped contribute to his independent personality. Without the influence of the setting Huck would have never been able to achieve the freedom that he had by being independent.

When Huck ran away he joined up with Jim, who was also running away, but from something different. Jim was fleeing from slavery, a common practice of the time. Huck's relationship with Jim contributed to Huck's non-prejudicethinking. Another factor that gave Huck a understanding of how the slaves musthave felt was the prejudice that he experienced himself, being part of thelower class. Huck was infuriated when people looked down upon him for somethingthat was no fault of his, he was born into the class because of his father'ssocial status. For these reasons Huck always treated Jim as an equal, makingHuck ahead of his time. Jim knew that Huck respected him, as a result Jimrisked his own life to save Huck.

Huck's independence and lack of education resulted in a mind that wasnever influenced by adult's beliefs. This allowed Huck to have thoughts basedon what he believed in, not traditions that are simply carried on by messengersof the past's beliefs. Although traditions are often good they prevent newideas from entering people's minds. This made Huck original, thisindividuality could be seen with his relationship with Jim. During this periodof American history slaves were looked down upon, but Huck, being anindependent thinker, looked up to Jim for who he was, not for the colour of hisskin. This was made obvious by their moon lit conversations on the raft. Onthe raft Huck and Jim talked about their past and future, friends and how theyplanned to avoid trouble that could result from their next adventure. From theraft conversations the reader was able to see how Jim longed for freedom and hadfeelings just like everyone else, especially Huck.

As the novel progressed Huck's relationship with Jim grew stronger. Inthe beginning of the book Huck often called Jim "Nigger Jim." This was notbecause of any hatred that Huck had towards Jim. It was only a term commonlyused to refer to blacks. But by the end of the book Huck would only call Jim byhis name. This change in dialogue clearly illustrates how the relationship grewstronger during their adventures. By the end of the novel Huck risked his ownlife to free Jim in the final escape attempt. This happened when Huck and Tomfreed Jim from a holding cell. They were spotted, chased and then shot at bythe men who had captured Jim. If the story were to take place in another time,where slavery did not exist, it could have hid Huck's individuality that slaveryshed light on.

During the river adventures that Huck and Jim shared Huck realized thatbecause of his economic status he was dependent on the river to survive. Thiscan clearly be seen by looking at the origin of his name "Huckleberry". He wasgiven this name because at a young age he had been eating huckleberries. Hisdependence made him loyal to the

Mississippi River. The personification of theriver that Huck uses clearly shows his feelings and thankfulness to the river.The personification also helped show how important the river was to not onlyHuck but to all of the river towns. Social Themes in The Adventures of Huckleberry Finn

The Adventures of Huckleberry Finn is a novel that will continue tobe read for decades to come. Why? The novel by Mark Twain, or SamuelClemens, has many themes that relate to society today. Even today societycontinues to talk about whether the novel should be read amongst high-school curriculums. Society is also continuing to deal with racism, andits effects on the lives of African-Americans. Another theme that isprevalent in society is lying among American children.

Huck Finn is a self taught liar, and a very good one at that. Onthe raft, while floating down the Mississippi, Huck has an opportunity toexercise his gift for lying. The boy enjoys mendacity; he lies for thesake of lying and keeps the reader turning the page piling on one fictionafter another. Just before the runaways get started, Huck visits aneighboring town to get information and encounters a farmer's wife. He isdressed in an old dress and is pretending to be a young girl searching forher relatives. The woman suspects his sex and tries various devices toascertain if her suspicions are true. Among these is threading a needleand throwing a bar of lead at the rats which swarm around the house.Finally she makes Huck own up that he is a boy. In any case, this is agreat example of a young boy lying until his nose is a foot long. Lying isprevalent among today's children as well.

Racism has an obvious connection to today's society. In the novelHuck says many "racist" comments. In this scene Aunt Sally hears of asteamboat explosion.

"Good gracious! anybody hurt?" she asks.

"No'm," comes the answer. "Killed a nigger."

Aunt Sally later refers to the "nigger" as if they are not even a person, regarding the death as if it did not even matter.

"Well, it's lucky because sometimes people do get hurt."

At first glance at the novel Huckleberry Finn, many would protest to the explicit use of the "N" word which was used over two-hundred times.As a result Huck Finn, one of the greatest American novels is noteworthy.This book was not written to besmirch the blacks of any rights or defametheir character. This book was written to prove a point about the racialtension in the South before the Civil War. Therefore, Twain had nointention of being racist. In fact the message Twain is sending isanything but racist. Today, racism has nearly disappeared from our lives.There are still many individual racists but for the most part this diseasehas been cured. As in the book, most people described as racists are not,for they are just mistaken.

There are school districts across the nation that are debatingwhether to ban their children from reading Huckleberry Finn. If this bookis taught, the novel can open student's eyes to the racial tension thatignorance causes. The students will become aware of their history. Theywill not be deprived of a lesson in their past that describes what theirgreat-grandparents went through. We have to remember that Huck Finn waswritten fifty years before Martin Luther King Jr. was born. During thosetimes it was acceptable to lynch an African American man, and acceptable touse the "N" word. If this book is taken out of high-school curriculumswhere would students learn about the history of racism?In conclusion, the many themes present in Huck Finn will always berelevant to modern society. I believe that Huckleberry Finn will foreverbe regarded as a literary classic and as a novel that should be read andenjoyed by people of all ages.

Importance of Creativity in The Adventures of Huckleberry Finn

What would you do if you were a young teenager traveling down theMississippi River, not knowing where to sleep that night or find food foryour next meal? That is the dilemma faced by Huckleberry Finn, and Huckalways found a lot of trouble. When most people are in trouble they eithertake the easy way out and lie, or they use their creativity and wit. Theprotagonist of The Adventures of Huckleberry Finn, by Mark Twain, uses morewit than most fourteen year old kids use in their lifetime. Whenever lifehits Huck with a problem, he always conquers it by using awareness,cleverness, and insight.

Before Huck starts his adventure down the river, he must fake hisdeath to "escape" from pap. The first thing Huck did was to make sure thatpap was far away before starting his getaway. At this point, many childrenof Huck's age would merely get in a canoe and head down stream, most likelygetting caught the next day. Huckleberry Finn is smarter than that. Huckwanted to make sure that no one would come down the river looking for him,except to make his corpse rise. First, he collected all the supplies thathe could find and loaded them into a canoe. After that, he went into thewoods and caught a wild hog. He brought the hog in the Cabin, andslaughtered it, making sure that it left behind a pool of blood on the hardpacked dirt ground.

He disposed of the dead hog by throwing it in theriver to float downstream. Huck also opened a sack of corn and left atrail leading to a shallow lake nearby. Before leaving the cabin, hefilled another sack with rocks, and made a path toward the river. This wasdone to simulate the trail of the robbers dragging their bounty to theriver bank. Huckleberry hoped that pap would think he was killed by agroup of robbers that stole all his possessions. After using these tacticsto avert any search parties, he floated down the river to Jackson Island.Huck made every attempt to make sure that he could sail down the river inpeace. As Huck had hoped, his plan worked beautifully.

While on Jackson Island, Huck mistakenly met up with a "friend" ofhis, Jim. After they settled on the island, Huck wanted to find out whatwas happening at the town across the river. Jim knew that Huck needed to adisguise, and they decided that Huck would dress up as a girl. Afterputting on a gown and bonnet, Huck took the canoe across the river, andfound the house of a stranger. Because he had to keep a low profile for awhile, it was important that it was a stranger. As he knocked on the door,he reminded himself to act like a girl. The lady invited him in. Theytalked about Huck's home town, Tom Sawyer's 20,000 dollars, and inevitably,Huck's murder. The lady soon became suspicious of Huck's femininity. Shefinally asked Huck, "What is you real name? Is it Bill, or Tom, or Bob?-orwhat is it?". Huckleberry finally admitted that he was a maleby the name of George Peters. He continued on to weave a tall tale sayingthat when looking for the town of Goshen, and had received directions froma drunken farmer. Instead of telling the lady his name was HuckleberryFinn and risking the possibility of getting caught with Jim, he extendedhis lie. To keep his story realistic, he told the lady that both hisparents had died, and he left because his new guardian treated him poorly.This was a very good choice because not many strangers will question aperson their parent's death. Huck Left the lady's house with a snack andthe directions to Goshen. Without being overly inquisitive within thisshort visit, Huck learned what people thought of his death and possibletrouble happening back on the island.

After Huckleberry and Jim outwit their "friends", the king and theduke, Huck lost his best friend and possession, Jim. While floating downstream alone, he spots a young man and asks if he saw any n——— dressedin a funny manner. The boy replies that he saw a n—— going towards thePhelp's place. When the boy asks why Huck wants to know where the n——was, Huck replied that the n—— threatened to cut out his liver. Thisnaturally encourages the boy to tell Huck more about Jim's whereabouts andcondition. Huck learned that an old fellow "nailed him", and Jim is justwaiting at the Phelp's farm. Huck starts talking innocently about thereward. The young boy expressed that he would wait seven years to collectthe 200 dollar bounty. This is another example of Huck's discreetinquirings. After leaving the boy, he most likely forgot about thesituation because Huck didn't pressure information out of him. He onlyasks in a nonchalant manner, therefore acting innocent and politeHuckleberry learns that he can only trust a few people. When he isin trouble, he can use his wits to either get out of, or go deeper intotrouble. In Huck's case, he usually goes farther into trouble until he canescape. Huck also learns that he can get a lot of information out ofpeople with well worded, yet innocent questions. This is a lesson thatpeople should learn. When in trouble, we have two choices. We can eithertell the truth, or have fun and try to use wit, cleverness, and a littlebit of luck to save ourselves.

The Role Model in The Adventures of Huckleberry Finn

"The Adventures of Huckleberry Finn" gives a visual look at the time inwhich the author Samuel Clemens lived. He explains how he felt about his lifethrough the eyes of a young boy named Huckleberry Finn. Huckleberry Finn hasmany adventures that teach him life lessons we can learn from today. Althoughthere are differing opinions on whether Huck Finn is a good role model fortoday's young people, I will explain why I think he is.

Huck is a good role model for several reasons. First, he believes thatslavery is wrong. He believes in treating people equally regardless of colour.When Huck sees the widow's runaway slave Jim on Jackson's Island, he has mixedemotions about what he should say and do. He feels badly that the widow isgoing to sell Jim and separate him from his family. Huck decides against betterreasoning to help Jim escape down the Mississippi River to Cairo.

Another example of good role modeling is Huck's faithfulness to those heloves and cares for. Huck lies to protect Jim on several occasions. Lying isnot the best thing, but to Huckleberry, the truth is not always a black andwhite issue. He is faithful to his friends and chooses friendship instead. Heknows that Jim's family needs him. In today's language, Huckleberry's reactionto Jim's situation would reflect what Spock of Star Trek says, "The needs of themany outweigh the needs of the few."

An illustration of another positive side of Huck shows us that he has agood and true heart, and the best intentions even though they may not turn outright. For example, the widow tells Huck to pray for the dinner they are having.Huck's interpretation is, "God thank you for the meal and if you get the chance,please let me catch a big catfish." The widow tells Huck that he shouldn't prayfor material things. Huck disagrees because his Sunday School teacher teacheshim to pray to God for what you want, and it will be granted. The widow tellshim that the teacher is talking about spiritual things. He still disagrees, andis sent to his room. Even though his intentions are the best, he still comes upshort; but he keeps on trying.

Finally, Huckleberry Finn thinks life is precious and shouldn't bewasted. This is the most important lesson he can teach today's young people. Heand Jim find themselves in a situation as they are floating down theMississippi River in the fog. All of a sudden, they see a ferry boat and Huckjumps off of the raft to avoid being hit. He swims to shore and meets a familynamed the Grangerfords. Huck stays with the Grangerfords and gets to know them.The Grangerfords have been feuding with another family named the Sheperdsons.

One day a fight breaks out over love between the Grangerford's daughterand the Sheperdson's son. Huck watches from a tree in terror as the twofamilies fight each other to the death. He realizes from this awful experiencehow easily life can be taken away, and that people should try to come togetherand work out their problems before they get out of hand. Throughout "The Adventures of Huckleberry Finn," there are manyinstances of positive role modeling behaviour for young adults in my view. Atfirst sight Huck's actions look questionable to many. I choose to look at Huckas a kid without a lot of adult supervision and support who tries to make hisway in the world. He is only human and makes mistakes, but I think he learnsfrom them, and that is all that any of us can try to do.

Huck Finn's Roles as Defined by the River and the Shore

Whenever Huck Finn steers his raft from the free currents of the river to the brambles on the banks of the Mississipi he renews his interaction with the society of the American south. When Twain's narrative comes ashore with Huck, the narrative becomes centered on the roles Huck is expected to play, and the roles everyone around Huck is trying to play. Everyone seems knows what the roles are, but they are less sure if the people around them are filling the roles accurately. Speech becomes the primary means through which people investigate roles. The role-less river life becomes defined by silence in contrast to the constant questions on the shore.

The roles played by the people Huck meets are centered around "the legend" that W.G. Cash speaks of: "the assumption that every planter was in the most rigid sense of the word a gentlemen," and that any upstanding citizen was as well. The form of the gentleman was well defined, but no one's position as a gentleman was so defined. According to Cash, the people had an uncertainty that comes with making an assumption about one's own identity; the people of the south had "an uneasy sensation of inadequacy for their role." They needed to "drive home the perception of their rank and value". Equally important was determining the rank of those around them, or the role they were trying to play, if it was not that of gentleman. Each time that Huck alights on shore there is almost immediately an interview of some sort, where his identity is mined. There is never a community in which he is allowed to stand as himself, quietly. At each town Huck is forced to verbally construct an identity for himself.

Thus, the land is not defined only by speech, but by the interrogative pattern of speech; perhaps, as Cash says, "the Southern fondness for rhetoric". Huck's interactions with adults are always interrogatory‹from Judith Loftus, the first woman he meets on his journey, to Sally Phelps, the last one. This quality of his interactions extends even to his relationship with other children. Huck tells us that the first moment Buck Grangerford gets Huck alone, he "asked me what my name was," and soon after "asked me where Moses was when the candle went out". While Buck may not be aware of his efforts, the riddle he asks allows him to place Huck in his understanding of the Christian chivalric code that Cash discusses. The first time Mary Jane Wilks speaks to Huck, she opens a long chain of questions with, "Did you ever see the king?". The constant interrogative dialogue of the shore is thrown into juxtaposition with Huck's life on the raft. Here there are no questions, and no sound. he days on the raft "slid along so quiet and smooth and lovely". Without dialogue, time on the raft has less form than time on the land, both for Huck and for Twain's narrative. Both Huck and Twain have the freedom to look around them.

Whereas time on the land is filled with words, time on the raft is filled with sights. Huck goes into extended melodious descriptions beginning with lines like, "the first thing to see, looking over the water, was a kind of dull line". The visual world opens out from here. When roleplaying does invade the raft, in the form of the King and the Daupin, the interrogation of the land comes with it. After the faux-royalty's finish sharing their own stories, they immediately, "asked us considerable many questions; wanted to know what we covered up the raft that way for, and laid by in the day-time instead of running‹was Jim a runaway nigger?". The King and Dauphin clearly have the shore disease of needing to place Huck and Jim in their rigid understanding of people. Because of the form given to shore life by the dialogue, Huck's voice is frequently made peripheral during his forays off the raft. It is chained to explaining his identity in response to the questions of the townspeople, or describing in detail the behaviour and anecdotes of these people.

In the scenes where Sherburn delivers his diatribe to the town, Huck's voice is merely a conduit for Sherburn's voice for pages at a time, and we hear none of Huck's thoughts. Interestingly, it is only when Huck is allowed to be silent, when he reaches the raft, that his own voice is liberated. It is on the raft that he is allowed to look naturally at the world around him, rather than at the complicated systems of behaviour being played out on the shore.

The Truth of Huck Finn

Throughout the classic novel, The Adventures of Huckleberry Finn, Mark Twain continuously and loosely uses the word "nigger." In the society of the year 2002 that word has become one of the most evil and hated in the English language. It is thought of as so bad that it is rarely even spoken, as people prefer to be politically correct and say "n-word" in it's place. The use of this word has caused the book to be banned and censored by many schools across the country, as people want to shield children from the supposed racism of the novel. It was found to be the fifth most challenged book of the 1990's. This word is definitely terrible and has no place in the current society, but it is important to examine Twain's motive behind the inclusion of this word in the story. The book should not be dismissed as cruel and racist before all of the facts are examined. Before forming a wrong opinion, the evolution of the word and the reasons behind it's use in the novel should be examined. After learning all of the facts, the use of the word in the book shouldn't be looked as evil, but as a reminder of how far society has come.

This novel was written in a time very different from today. It was first published in 1884 and is set some years before in the early 1800's. At this time slavery was common practice in the southern part of the United States. People grew up believing there was nothing wrong with it. People in this time spoke almost identically to the language presented in the book, including referring to African-Americans as "niggers." Twain explains the dialects he was trying to present before the story even begins. In an explanatory he says he was using "the extremist form of the backwoods Southwestern dialect" and "the ordinary Pike County dialect." Both of these types of speech would have included this word. Twain did not use this word to be derogatory toward black people but for the story to remain authentic. The appearance of the word in this book should be looked at as a reminder of a bad time in history. It should be viewed as a chance to realise that people were wrong and their mistakes are still trying to be fixed today. Should slavery not be taught in a history class because it shows the racism of America's past?

It must also be pointed out that Mark Twain was not a racist. This is amazing to think of for a white man who grew up in the state of Missouri in the 1800's, where racism was widespread. Many people claim Twain was expressing his personal ideals in the racism of certain characters. This is ridiculous to believe when you consider that the main plot of the novel is a boy overcoming his racist upbringing to realise that slavery is evil and becomes friends with a runaway slave. Why would he write such a novel if he didn't believe in the views he expressed through Huck? It is also often said that Jim is portrayed as an inferior human being. This is another incorrect idea. Twain portrays Jim as a caring and compassionate character. Jim is shown to be unintelligent, but this is another thing that makes the book authentic.

A slave would not have had access to education and most of them were not very smart. Jim still overcomes this to be a person of great personal character. He was a courageous and loving man who risks his life and freedom to help his friend Huck. Even well respected African-Americans like Booker T. Washington and Ralph Ellison have expressed their pleasure with Jim's character. Ellison once said that Twain gave Jim "dignity and human capacity." Washington stated that with the character of Jim he "exhibited his sympathy and interest in the masses of the Negro people." All of this gives indisputable evidence that Mark Twain was not racist and did not intend his use of "nigger" to invoke such thoughts.

The evolution of how this word is interpreted should also be examined. Today it has become a racial slur that is used by people who still carry a racist point of view. As most people would attest, it is probably one of the worst things a person could ever say. During the time in which Twain wrote the book and especially when the book was set, this word was not seen as evil, but merely a name for slaves. This is shown by the word's first appearance in the book. In the beginning of chapter as Huck and Tom sneak away they see Jim. As Huck says "Miss Watson's big nigger, named Jim, was setting in the kitchen." This is a great example of what the word is used for. It was simply what Huck called the slaves. He does not say it in a mean or derogatory way. It is simply how white people in Missouri referred to slaves. It is not meant to be malicious but only to enhance the realistic feel of the story.

The Adventures of Huckleberry Finn is one of the greatest and most important books in the history of American literature. Another great American author, Ernest Hemingway, once said, "all modern American literature comes from

Huckleberry Finn." This does not sound like a book that should be banned and censored in schools because of the use of one word. The word may be evil and hated now, but people must understand its importance to the novel. People should not try to hide from the past but embrace what we can learn from it. This novel showed the stupidity of slavery and racism in a society when these were common place. This is probably the best novel ever written by an American and for people to try to dismiss it as a racist book is absurd. Twain had numerous, excellent reasons for using "nigger" in the story. Hopefully someday everyone will appreciate this novel for what it really is and stop dwelling on false claims of racism.

Huckleberry Finn-Brotherhood

" Batman and Robyn are the ultimate dynamic duo....", In the novel The Adventures of Huckleberry Finn, by Mark Twain, Twain describes a "Batman and Robyn", like relationship that is formed by two of the main characters, Jim and Huck. Mark Twain brings the characters relationship to life with descriptive details of their attitudes and feelings towards each other. Jim, a fleeing slave, and Huck, who fakes his own death, are on a crusade for Freedom from different individual struggles. Throughout their journey they undergo many incidents that construct their relationship to become a treasured togetherness. Mark Twain's, The Adventures of Huckleberry Finn, reveals Jim and Huck as individuals growing together to mold a relationship which is extremely valid throughout the novel.

Jim's relationship to Huck endows devotion, sensitivity, and brotherhood. Jim cherishes Huck as if he was his offspring, and presents Huck with the possibility of seeing him as a guardian. Throughout the novel Jim proves to be protective and caring as a father would be. Jim and Huck come upon a floating house boat, where they inspect the findings of a decease man on board, "Come in, Huck, but doan' look at his face" (Twain 50). Jim doesn't want Huck to stare at the dead man's face, which is a clear example of Jim shielding Huck from the ghastly sight. This also indicates Jim is concerned about Huck's response to the dead body and he uses a protective father portrayal to indicate this. One more significant illustration of the sprouting relationship between Jim and Huck is the amount of emotion Jim shows when he believes that Huck is gone forever.

Huck performs a horrible prank on Jim, by pretending that he never was separated from him which contrasts with Jim's parental disposition, "Heart wuz mos' broke bekase you wuz los' en I didn' k' yer no mo' what become er me en de raf" (twain 86). Jim is overcome with joy at the site of Huck, he begins to weep. Jim feels that Huck has taken advantages of his trust and friendship and Jim decides to confess to Huck that he would give anything up for him including his life, despite the fact that Huck is on opposing sides of society. This makes Huck feel very ashamed and he promises not to play anymore pranks on Jim. Jim grows more aware of the fact that Huck is honestly regretful of his prank, Jim is more aware of Huck's loyalty and friendship towards him.

Huck's relationship to Jim is based on risks sustained by Huck for Jim, respect, and the internal dispute Huck has with himself. Huck assures Jim that he will not reveal Jim to the authorities, even though he is a runaway slave. "people would call me a low down Abolitionist and despise me for keeping mum-but that don't make no difference" (Twain 43). Huck ignores his morals and upbringings. He realizes that a promise is a promise, in spite of the fact that harboring Jim is against all of society's belief. Another example of Huck's feelings for Jim is the risk he takes against his own safety, to keep Jim secured and out of danger. Huck is informed that the people of their old town, believe Jim murdered him, and the townsmen are looking for Jim.

"Git up and hump yourself! There ain't a minute to lose they're after us" (Twain 63). When Huck finds out that Jim is in distress, he disregards society and acquires Jim to safety. Huck places Jim's safety above his own unconsciously and Jim and Huck's struggle for freedom becomes one. In addition to these examples of Huck's relationship with Jim, Huck plays a prank on Jim which hysterically perturbs him tremendously.

This effects Huck directly because he knows that Jim truly cares for him, "It was fifteen minutes before I could work myself up to go and humble myself to a nigger-but I done it and I warn't ever sorry for it". In Huck's society an apology to a slave from a white person is not only uncalled-for, it is outrageous. This shows how much regard Huck has for Jim. Huck does not repent his apology to Jim. He learns that Jim is loyal and a true friend to him, which is more than Huck could ever say of the society.

The World today is quite different from Jim and Huck's era. There are no longer slaves of any kind. Huck does not understand that by harboring Jim, he is doing a heroic deed, not something that should make him feel guilt. Although he feels guilty for harboring Jim, Huck is actually brilliant in the way that he is surpassing the intellect of ignorant adults of his generation. In the world today there are still people who are prejudice but society does not force an idea of slavery or hatred, in the direction of African Americans or any other race.

Flaws in Twain's The Adventures of Huckleberry Finn

Mark Twain's novel The Adventures of Huckleberry Finn is by any means a classic. However, there are several flaws. First of all the coincidence that everything happens with in my mind detracts some from the story. The other

major problem is that the book seems to drag on and on the closer you get to theend, as if Twain had a page quota to fill and was not worried about the story.The other problem brought up on our hand-out was Huck's lack of seriousness inwhat was a very serious situation for Jim.

As for the coincidence part, it appears most obviously as you readtowards the end. For example Huck ends up at Aunt Polly's, and I was thinking,yeah...right those chances are about one in a million. And then after Hucktells Aunt Polly that he is Tom, Tom shows up...uh-huh, I bet. It is thingssuch as those I just mentioned that make it very difficult for me to read a bookwithout becoming frustrated. It is probably because I am used to real life andlike it or not real life is just not that perfect.

My other gripe was that Twain seems to ramble on and

on and on an.....To me it seems as if the story that he was writing became faint shortly afterthe time when Huck says, "It's me. George Jackson, sir". I do have togive him that the feud was interesting filler, but you can only take so muchfiller. Then when John Wayne (The Duke) and Elvis (The King) come along thereseem to be four or five stops along the river that except for one little detail,are the same. Please excuse the jump back, but how coincidental is it that youhave a Duke and a King on the same raft in the middle of the Mississippi river(yes I do know they are not really royalty but that does not matter)? Evenduring all of this complaining I have done I did find humour in such things aswhen Huck was observing some local "loafers" and their discussions aboutborrowing and lending chewing tobacco. "Here, gimme back the chaw and you takethe plug.". I can just picture four or five guys laying aroundchewing tobacco with spit/tobacco juice running down their chins, probably indirty overalls with no shirts on underneath and boots, to complete the look,three or four days of beard waiting to be shaved, and oh yeah, a nice old strawhat. The picture of this I have in my head is just so vivid that it disgusts menow. I think that is one of the reasons this is such a great book, the imagery.

The final thing mentioned was Huck's lack of seriousness or that he wastoo humorous or too wrapped up in fantasy for the situation both he and Jim werein. Here as opposed to the things I attacked above I will have to be on theside of the defence. My foremost reason is that I do not think Huck realizesthe seriousness of the predicament. Huck is a boy that lives in Hannibal, MOduring the times of the Civil War, he probably does not know any other ways todeal with anyone who is a slave or is trying to escape. Put yourself in hisshoes once and think of the trouble you might have. Then think how you woulddeal with these problems. Would it be in the way many kids do, with a bit offun to try to alleviate some of the tension? Take the time when Jim thinks Huckis dead and he shows up scaring Jim to the point of carrying out a conversationwith a "ghost". Jim says " I alwuz liked dead people, en done all I could for 'em. Read that section over and see if it does not seem to be ingood taste, if you can call anything done by Huck "tasteful". I think it does.My final task is to come up with a new ending. I think my ending goes like this: Huck and Jim find the mouth of the Ohio river as planed and ventureupstream by any means available. As they continue up the river the bond betweenthe two runaways becomes ever stronger. When they reach the free states and Jimis officially free. After waiting around a while the two begin to get money inany way they can.

When it is enough Jim buys his wife and children out ofslavery, and Huck takes a cut (not too much, just enough to get home). Oncehome Huck starts all over with his ever interesting plots (not without the helpof Tom Sawyer). Time passes and over the years Huck misses Jim and eventuallyembarks on a quest. The quest to find Jim. This journey would be much like thejourney he and Jim took just a few years ago. This time though, there is noJohn Wayne and Elvis to make the story drawn out and boring towards the end.Then Huck finds Jim, meets the wife and kids, and goes back home to lead anormal (or as normal as can be) life working as little as possible and livingoff his $6000.

The Metamorphosis of Huckleberry Finn

With his novel about a young adolescent's journeys and struggles with the trials and questions associated with Huck's maturation, Mark Twain examines societal standards and the influence of adults that one experiences during childhood. The Adventures of Huckleberry Finn have been condemned since its publication, usually focusing, especially in modern times, on its use of the word "nigger." While this could be a valid argument had the author portrayed Jim negatively, I find another reason to argue against the novel, especially by school boards and parents groups: because it subverts the ideals that many parents wish to instill in their impressionable youth. Reading this book for the first time since high school and my departure from my parents three years ago, watching Huck live without parental controls made me realise how impressionable one is to the values instilled by his constant role models. Without being forced to conform to societal standards, Huck is allowed to use his own logic to realise what is good and bad, rather than blindly following his elders' "wisdom."

At the beginning of the novel, Huck shows his skepticism of the values that society imposes when the Widow Douglas attempts to civilize him, running away to his freedom until his friends threaten to expunge him from the gang. Given the option of loneliness or independence, Huck chooses to return. When his father returns and takes custody of him again, Huck is deprived of his friends against his own will. Locked alone in the cabin, Huck is given plenty of time to consider his options. If he remains in the cabin, he will continue to be powerless to the will of his father. If he escapes and returns to town, he will only be returned to his drunken father, who will certainly beat him. He realizes that escape is his only solution. By staging his own murder, Huck kills himself to society's influences and enables his own uninhibited personal growth.

Now free of society's rules and standards, Huck is able to approach life in a way that most adolescents wish were possible. He is fortunate enough to have Jim along for companionship, removing the loneliness that prevented his earlier flight from society. Unfortunately, this friendship has already been tarnished by society's influence on Huck. Fortunately, free of society's rules and standards, Huck is allowed to begin to undo his misperceptions of slaves and begins the slow realization that Jim is just as human as he is.

During the first few chapters that they are together, Twain quickly shows the beneficial effect that the two have on each other. Jim's contribution to Huck is an adult presence, one that while expressing a life's experience, is not overbearing, due to Jim's inferior status. In addition, Jim provides protection for Huck from both physical and emotional pains. Twain quickly gives examples of both forms of protection in Chapter 9. Within a few days of their union, Jim's life experiences enable the pair to prepare for the torrential storm that hits the island, which Jim forecasts. Had it not been for Jim and his ability to notice the change in animal behaviour, Huck may have been caught on the river when the storm began, and possibly drown. Following the storm, Jim, as we learn at the end of the novel, postpones Huck's knowledge of his father's death until it is necessary. While it is true that Huck's father beat him and inhibited his development as a normal member of society, the fact remains that any child, especially at an impressionable age, is usually severely affected by the loss of a parent. Even if news of his death would not affect Huck, actually viewing a disfigured corpse is something that most people would prefer to be protected from experiencing.

Continuing with Huck's realization of the problems in society that are better understood from outside of it, the experience he has with the Shepherdsons and the Grangerfords opens his eyes to the problems of blindly following tradition. As we have seen, many people have tried to persuade Huck to follow this path, rather than allow him to make logical decisions for himself. We witnessed it when his father reprimanded him for learning to read and write, arguing that no one in their family was literate, so why should Huck. This experience with the feuding families exemplifies why people should not blindly follow tradition like sheep. At this point, we meet Buck, a representative of an adolescent mind destroyed by adults.

Though the same age as the protagonist, Buck's judgment has been destroyed by his family's ongoing feud with the Shepherdsons. He admits to Huck that the feud began because of a lawsuit between people who died long ago. Through generations of teaching the young children hatred towards the other clan, both families demonstrate an extreme of what can happen by following blindly. For this refusal to rationalize logically, they are all killed for nothing. Whether consciously or not, Huck realizes his fortune in that he has been relieved of many of the preconceived notions that society would have forced on him, as they had on his dead friend. For this reason he cries as he covers the face of the boy who was not given the opportunity to realise the error of his ways.

Huck's next encounter with society and its values furthers his cynical realizations, as he and Jim meet the Duke and the

King. Huck soon realizes that these men are frauds, not only to the people that they con, but also to their companions. They represent the lowest morals in society, which interestingly Huck already attributes to leaders. This is why he does not convey this knowledge to Jim, even though he knows that they are lying about their positions. During the two men's tenure on the raft, we are given glimpses of how morality, when left unchecked, can quickly spiral downward, especially when greed is involved. At first, the men simply con entire towns out of small change, charging a small admission to see the men poorly perform scenes from a Shakespeare. Desiring more and seeing how easy it is, though the already have prior experiences, they advance to charging more for an even less entertaining show, The Royal Nonesuch, exhibiting how easily people are swayed by advertising.

In their final two acts of inhumanity, the royal duo seem to abandon all sense of decency and attempt to steal all of the inheritance money from three girls who are in mourning, then sell Jim back into slavery after that plan is foiled by the men they are impersonating. Even though they succeeded in their earlier ventures, Twain causes these ones to backfire. With regards to the inheritance, Huck steals the money, which the real family finds in the coffin, and the con men barely escape punishment. They do not learn, though, and when they choose to make $40 more important than Jim, they are finally punished, as he informs Mr. Phelps of the scam and the men are tarred and feathered and run out on a rail. This is one of Twain's most striking blows against slavery, for the men are punished, even though they do what society was teaching at the time: that slaves are property to be bought and sold.

After Jim is captured, Huck comes to the conscious realization that many of society's rules are to be broken. Left alone, away from the distraction of society and the misdirection that it gives, he is given time to think on his own, reflecting upon what he has learned throughout his experience on the outside of civilization. He thinks back to all of the people that he has encountered in his life. In retrospect, he can not find another person who is kinder to him than Jim, no one who is more representative of the good portion of the human race than his friend, a man that society does not even deem a man. He knows that he has been taught that slaves are property, and essentially that freeing Jim is stealing from someone else, but he realizes the greater evil, one that only his experiences away from mankind's influence could make him see. For this reason, in the climax of the novel, he chooses to free Jim from slavery. Tom's return to Huck's life provides complication for his goal, though, as Tom, as Huck's friend, is allowed to reanimate many of the notions that Huck was able to overcome during his freedom. Tom, unlike Huck, views Jim as sub-human. For this reason, he does not tell Huck or his family that Jim is now a free man, but rather goes along with helping Huck "free" him so that he can have an adventure. Had Jim not been a free man, we can even question whether or not Tom would have helped Huck. Huck certainly does when Tom agrees, as he can not understand how a boy from a family respected by society could help steal a slave. By making Jim free when Tom helps, Twain shows us that Tom is just another member of society, blinded by tradition.

The final chapter sums up the book well, clearly finalizing many of the lessons that Twain previously informed us in the books' Notice are not in the book. Huck is completely freed of the fear of his father, as Jim realizes that it is time that he learns the truth about his death. Jim is now a free man, showing that Miss Watson realized the error of her ways right before death. Most importantly, Huck realizes how his life has changed throughout this experience and chooses that the society that he was born into is in many ways corrupted by the people within it. Fortunately, because of the money and lack of legal control, he has the ability to retire from it, as he plans to "light out for the Territory ahead of the rest" before mainstream society has the ability to come and ruin it with the misguided traditions and beliefs.

An Analysis of Mark Twain's Novel The Adventures of Huckleberry Finn

I can always remember being younger when I just

wanted to runaway. I would lay in bed and say "this place sucks, I just want to leave" In the novel, The Adventures of Huckleberry Finn by Mark Twain, a young boy, Huck Finn, learns what life is like growing up in Missouri and his troublesome' childhood leads him to runaway from home. Throughout the story Huck learns that in order to escape and run away from home, others need help running away too. Huck lies in order to keep Jim, Huck's companion, safe along the trip. In this novel, Twain uses the Mississippi river as a symbol of freedom for both Huck and Jim.

Huck was raised in a different way, much different from his friends. Huck's father was a drunk and his mother passed away. For a while Huck had the life of doing whatever he wanted. Huck becomes very sheltered because he moves in with Miss Watson and Widow Douglas. These two ladies believe that Huck must attend school, learn religion, and how to be a gentleman. Huck gets tired of living this way and wants to be free. Once he escapes from Miss Watson's, his dad finds him, making Huck live all alone in a cabin. When Pap Finn comes home, he is drunk and beats Huck. Huck figures out a way to fake his death and escape once again. He floats down the Mississippi river and lives the "freedom life." Huck retreats to Jackson Island where he meets Jim, the slave on Miss Watson's ranch.

Huck and Jim decide to team up and escape together. Huck learns that Jim has run away because he may be sold to another ranch, being and slave or possibly being killed. "I hear ole missus tell de widder she gwyne to sell me to OrleansÉ". Floating down the river, Huck uses his lying skills to keep slave hunters away from Jim, " 'Well the five niggers run off tonight, is your man white or black?' ' He is white sir'". Huck lies are used as a survial tool for both Huck and Jim.

When Huck and Jim are on the raft they live a peaceful life, except they are unable to escape the evils of society from the outside world. In their route to freedom, they come upon a couple of con men, the duke and the dauphin. These two "scam artists" use their knowledge to make money for their own freedom, until they sell Jim to a ranch, to once again be a slave. Huck becomes very angry and wants to free Jim. Huck once again lies his way through and gets to the ranch where Jim is. Huck decides to write a letter to Miss Watson, telling her about Jim and where he is; Huck changes his mind again. Ironically, the ranch where this particular scene is written, is the Phelps' ranch; Tom Sawyer's aunt and uncle; and Tom is one of Huck's friends. As Huck mingles his way around the ranch, he finds Tom, and they decide to set Jim free. In their attempt, Tom is shot in the leg. This causes much controversy, enough for Huck's aunt to come fix the problem. Once there, Tom reveals that Miss Watson had died and freed Jim in her will. Jim is now free, so Huck overcame his "lying problem" and travels west.

The Story of Huckleberry Finn is very moving and it is a well-written book for all ages. I enjoyed the book very much cause of the humour and the fact of "trying to survive." It took some time to adjust reading the slang terminology. There are many school districts across America that want to ban their children from reading Huckleberry Finn because of the unmoral values and the use of the "N" word. In my mind students who read this book will become better informed of their history and what teenage life was like in the 1800's.

Laws vs Morals in Huck Finn

"What is right is not always popular and what is popular is not always right." Whether he knows it or not, the character Huck Finn is a perfect example of the truth in this quote. His struggle between knowing in his mind and what is legal, but feeling in his heart what is moral was predominant throughout the novel. Today, we'll examine three examples of situations when Huck had to decide for himself whether to follow the law, or his heart.

When the story begins, Huck is running away to enjoy a life of solitude on the river, but finds himself in a whirlwind adventure to help Jim, a runaway slave, to freedom. Huck begins the adventure caught up in the moment, and without much thought of what he is really doing. All this changes at one moment in the story when Huck realizes that he is breaking the law. Huck is taking Jim away from his owner who did nothing to him. Why should he help Jim escape? What is in it for him except trouble? At a suspenseful turning point in the story, Huck is prepared to report Him to two men on the river when he has change of heart. "True Blue Huck Finn" backs down and realizes that there's more to helping Him escape than trouble: there's a special kind of friendship that Huck's never known before.

Along the river, Jim and Huck run across two scam artists who claim to be a runaway King and Duke. Their raft is overtaken by these two men who force Huck and Jim into their dangerous, yet comical scams. Their last scam proves t be too much of Huck. The King and Duke claim to be the brothers of a quite wealth, but conveniently deceased man. Because of their acclamation, the two men are guaranteed a large inheritance. However, when Huck falls for the beautiful heart and kindness of one of the dead man's nieces he can't imagine stealing the money form her. Huck tells the niece the whole story, and admits who the "brothers" really are. The King and Duke are eventually discovered by the town to be impersonators, and are tarred and feathered.

At another turning point in the story, Huck's guilty conscience gets the better of him. He is granted another opportunity to report Jim. At this time in the story, Huck and Him have been though a lot, to say the least. They have been in and out of trouble and on the edge of discovery countless times. However, at this instant, Huck's hope have been washed away with feat. He's not sure if they can go on much longer. Huck decides he must pray and ask for forgiveness for disobeying God Huck believes he'll go to hell if he keeps up with breaking the law and all. In an attempt to ask for forgiveness, Huck just can't do it. He's not sorry, and decides he'd rather go to hell then turn Him in. Jim was huck's best friend and only father figure he'd ever known. Even though there wasn't a law against these feelings, it was basically a crime against society to feel this way. But Huck had a wiser mind and deeper heart.

Huck Finn tells the story of Huck's maturity and path to

understanding things about society. But Huck didn't like what society understood to be right. Huck had different ideas. Some may call Hucks' views naïve or innocent. But they're wrong. Huck was much wiser then society. He was ahead of his years. About 150 years to be exact.

Huckleberry Finn–Social Conflicts

Mark Twain was known as a humorist and in fact, humour was a tool he used to strengthen his points about what he saw as the major problems of the day. Living at the time of the Civil War, he clearly saw and chose to address such problems as slavery, child abuse, religion and feuds. In Huckleberry Finn, Mark Twain expresses his loathing for some of these serious social problems and yet in general, he never loses his humorous touch. Nonetheless, when he deals with the ills of society that particularly anger him, he chooses not to use humour; rather this is reserved for other areas of his work.

One of the social problems that Mark Twain addresses in Huckleberry Finn is child abuse. Huck is abused by Pap many times during the book and is even locked into a cabin by Pap. Pap also tries to steal Huck's six thousand dollars, and beats Huck frequently, which results in Huck running away. Pap puts down the idea of Huck getting an education. Twain does use humour in his descriptions of some of the interactions between Pap and Huck. For example, the scene when Pap agrees to reform and stop drinking, but ends up getting drunk and falling over is actually funny, but tells us a lot about Pap's character. Twain generally found the kind of behaviour he described through the character of Pap to be disgusting, and by painting a humorous picture of the situation he emphasized his dislike of it. The humour perhaps made Pap seem even less sympathetic.

Another social problem that Mark Twain addresses in the book is slavery and treatment of black people in general. Jim, who is a black slave, is treated like a piece of property. For example, he is forced to practice Christianity, which actually seems to be the opposite of Christian values. Jim is also forcefully separated from his family and has no legal recourse to get them back. Jim is very superstitious, and Huck, who knows this, puts a dead snake, (representing bad luck) at the bottom of Jim's bed and Jim gets bitten. Even Huck, at this point in the book, threats Jim as less than human. illustrates Jim's actual humanity by contrasting him and Pap as parents. He portrays black values as more humane than white ones.

In the novel, it is suggested that one must flee in order to gain freedom. Both Huck and Jim are fleeing from tyranny, which is a dangerous process and too serious for Twain to portray humorously. Huck, himself is conflicted throughout the novel between his feelings for Jim and his sense that he is breaking the law for helping Jim escape. When Huck plays the last joke on Jim, with the trash, he comes to realise that Jim is an equal. Finally, Jim informs Huck that if he and his children do not become free then he will get an abolishonist to help him escape. Huck is first very upset by this and feels he must turn Jim in, but changes his mind as he sees Jim as a person worthy of respect. To the modern reader Huck's dilemma problems may seem funny, but in fact, he is torn between following the laws, however cruel they seemed, and doing what he comes to think was morally correct.

Thus, although Twain is generally known as a humorist and does indeed occasionally make use of humour emphasize his points, when he addresses issues that make him furious like child abuse and slavery he is very serious. Once in a while he puts in a memorable funny scene, but in general, he seems to find these issues too important to risk having people laugh, and therefore not realise the cruelty Huck and Jim, as representatives of parts of society, must face. Cruelty, in any form, in Twain's views is not something to be laughed at.

Values, Morals, and Ethics in Adventures of Huckleberry Finn

In Mark Twain's Huckleberry Finn, the values of Huck and Jim traveling down the Mississippi River are contrasted against those of the people residing in the southern United States. Twain satirically portrays organized religion and society's morals throughout the novel. The freedom and tranquillity of the river gives way to the deceit, greed and prejudice of the towns lying on the shore of the river, causing them to disguise themselves and keep their identities hidden. These two runaways - one a slave, the other a beaten boy - attempt to build a sanctuary from civilization upon their raft, but the influence of the shore values continue to find their way into the thoughts, actions and feelings of both Huck and Jim, which becomes the major theme of this novel. While traveling down the Mississippi upon the raft, Huck and Jim's sense of freedom subordinated all others.

Jim was a "runaway nigger" running from the law, yet he was free, while on the raft, to live and think as any white man. According to the rest of society, Huck was dead, murdered and thrown into the Mississippi; but on the raft he was alive. Both lived an idyllic life on the raft and as Huck put it, "...it's lovely to live on a raft". Later, when the Duke and Dauphin came aboard and they agreed to all be friends, Huck was relieved and felt that everybody should "...feel right and kind towards the others..." while living on a raft. Throughout their travels on the raft, honesty, kindness and equality prevailed, but whenever they touched shore, they encountered the deceit, greed, and cruelty of rural Southern United States.

The idyllic life on the raft was contrasted with the hatred, cruelty, and distrust felt amongst the inhabitants of the shores of the Mississippi. Two feuding families, the Grangerfords and the Sheperdsons, are a satirized look at the lives of Southerners and of organized religion. The two families had been fighting for thirty years and no one knew the reason. When Huck asked if it was caused by land, Buck Grangerford responded "I reckon maybe-I don't know". Both families very hypocritically took guns to church and discussed with a fervor the sermon reported by Huck to be "all about brotherly love". Twain portrayed Mississippi River society to be a greedy, distrustful civilization in which the values were all twisted and where the church was more of a form of entertainment than a religion. Huck and Jim's 'Eden' upon the raft was breached when two frauds found their way onto it. The Duke and Dauphin were continuously lying, deceiving and taking advantage of others. The influence of these two was the cause of many unwanted encounters with the towns and people along the Mississippi. Huck immediately realized they were "...just low-down humbugs and frauds". When Huck was able to slip away from the Duke and Dauphin and resume his journey with Jim, he revealed his relief when he said it's "...so good to be free again". When the Duke and Dauphin returned, Huck "...wilted right down onto the planks... and gave up...", exposing his dislike of the values which they brought onto the raft. The Duke and Dauphin provide an insight into the lives and values of the shore, and a deep contrast between Jim and Huck and the rest of society. Mark Twain contrasted the values of the shore and the river in a way which positively portrayed the river values and the lives of Huck and Jim, and negatively and often satirically, portrayed the values of rural Southern United States. Twain gave freedom to Huck and Jim and showed that all races of humans share like feelings and should all be treated as equals. Throughout the book Huck contends with the influence of society's values and in the end makes a decision to embrace that of equality.

There were many heroes in the literature that has been read. Many have been courageous and showed their character through tough times. Through these tough times they were forced to make important decisions and this is where you get the real idea of who is deserved to be called a hero. The most influential though of all these was Huckleberry Finn. Through the innocence of childhood he is able to break through the societal pressures that are brought on him and do right.

In Mark Twain's The Adventures of Huckleberry Finn you meet a rebellious young teen named Huck Finn. Huck is not your everyday hero especially in the beginning of the novel but slowly through the story his mature, responsible side comes out and he shows that he truly is the epitome of a hero. Huck is forced to make many crucial decisions, which could get him in serious trouble if not get him killed. Huck has natural intelligence, has street smarts, which are helpful along his adventure, and is assertive. Huck has always had to rely on himself to get through things because he is from the lowest levels of white society and his dad is known more or less as the 'town drunk." So when Huck fakes his death and runs away to live on an island he is faced with yet another problem, which revolves around the controversial issue of the time of racism. While living on the island he meets Jim who was a slave but Huck soon learns that he has ran off and now in the process of making his way up north to Canada. Here Huck is faced along with his first tough decision, to go with Jim and help him, or just go and tell the officials of a runaway slave and get the reward. Huck reluctantly joins Jim and promises him to get him to free land for the sake of a good adventure but he still feels guilty to be conversing with a runaway slave let alone help him escape. Along the way Huck has many challenges, which are just like this one. This is truly remarkable for a child to be able to break away from the influence of society and go with his heart and do what is right especially when it was considered wrong.

The thought of helping a slave and actually treating them like a normal human being was totally unheard of at the time, down south. That's why this story is so great because a boy is able to ignore all that has been taught to him about blacks and go do whatever he feels is the right thing. Huck's decision in his moral confliction truly impressed me with how courageous Huck was for the sake of his friendship and how he didn't take any regard to the law. Twain shows that there is hope for the future and that if an ignorant child can realise how awful slavery was then someday the nation will wake up and put a stop to it. In conclusion, Huck Finn through all the trials he was put through voluntarily for his friendship with a runaway slave, Jim, proves just why he deserves to be called a hero. Huck had many difficult, moral choices which he was forced to make along his journey and for those reasons Huckleberry Finn is able to be called a hero.

Cruelness in Adventures Of Huck Finn

Throughout the tale of Huckleberry Finn as told by Mark

Twain (Samuel Clemens), almost every character for his or her own reasons lies. This can be considered a commentary on the morality and ethics of man kind by Mr. Clemens. Almost no person exists that has never uttered at lease one untruth. That is one of the wonderful things about this novel. It closely mimics real life. There are characters that lie for personal gain. There are also those that lie only in hopes of helping others. Though both are lies, one can be considered courteous or even heroic at times, where the other can only appear greedy and wrong no matter what light it is viewed in. Mark Twain often uses the river to denote freedom and purity, however just as many lies are told on the river as off. This is because Twain doesn't make the assumption that all lies are wicked, and can thus attach them to his symbol of pure good.

Practically every "good" character in Huckleberry Finn lies. Huck himself lies on almost countless occasions. Miss Watson lies on at least one occasion. Jim tells several lies during the tale. Tom Sawyer is practically unable to speak the truth. Yet none of these characters are seen as morally corrupt. The villainous characters lie on a constant basis in the course of the story. The king makes lying an art at times, while the duke lies without pause for his entire appearance in the story. Pap makes up numerous tales during his time in the book. All these characters are considered evil and wrongdoers.

The difference is the fact that the latter characters lie in hopes of personal gain, while the first characters lie to help others, or in order to entertain. Nearly every character lies in Huckleberry Finn; it is their motivation for their lies that defines their character to the reader. Huckleberry himself tel
many a lie during the story. Perhaps his biggest lie
he fakes his own death, and makes the wh
his "dead carcass".

This caused the widow and
amount of heartache and concer
escape by telling men on a passing b
raft was his father who "got the small
away slave. Although the first lie hurt sc

interprets it as Huck's only choice and therefore doesn't "mark him as a bad person". The perception of Huck is that of a hero, so no matter the moral choices he makes, we tend to see him as such. Miss Watson, a picture of Godliness tells a terrible lie. She swore to Jim that he wouldn't "sell him down to New Orleans," while she had full intention to until he ran off. This lie was the type that held gain for Miss Watson, but negative affects for others namely Jim. Yet even though she is seen as somewhat of an ogre until she eventually releases Jim, she is not seen as one of the villainous characters of the book for this lie.

This has to do mostly with her being introduced with Huck's interests apparently as her main concern by giving him directions for his own good such as "sit up straight" and the like. By being brought into the reader's view as a role model, the cruel lie she told is diminished and barley even dwelled upon by most readers. Tom Sawyer is a professional liar. Tom however is considered imaginative rather than a liar for the most part. He is known well for his lies amongst the other characters. When Huck fakes his own death, Jim comments that "Tom Sawyer couldn't get up no better plan" since Tom is constantly lies. Tom also takes part in the scheme to steal Jim out of captivity; the whole time lying to Huck that Jim isn't free when he knows perfectly well that Miss Watson freed Jim on her deathbed.

Tom's character is a diabolical liar and is yet seen only as a mischief-maker and not a true threat to anyone. Even the lovable innocent Jim will lie for personal gain. His "innocence is lost" when he successfully scams unwitting Huck . He manages to trick Huck out of a quarter for the use of his "magic hairball" that tells the future. This lie was only designed to get Huck's money, not to hurt anyone. This and the fact that Jim is practically ignorant account for his being a "hero" in the story even though he lies to his friend and steals himself out of slavery.

The King and the Duke are dubbed villains for their lies. Even the only names the reader is able to call them by are frauds. The "Duke", purely to receive preferential treatment from Huck and Jim claims he is a descendant of the "Duke of Bridgewater". Inspired by the duke's lie, the king tells his own tale. He claims to be the long lost "King of France" "Dauphin". This is clearly not true to everyone except for trusting old Jim. Huck however treats them as royalty so as not to anger them. These men only lied in order to escape work and receive favors from Jim and Huck. They later deceive entire towns with their makeshift theatre presentation "The Royal Nonesuch" for financial gain.

Also they play with the emotions of two girls that recently lost their uncle in order to steal his money. The king and the duke lie only to "please themselves", this is why, unlike other liars throughout the story, they are pegged as the criminals and eventually ridden out of town on a rail. The river and the shore often have meanings in Huckleberry Finn. The river can represent purity and freedom. The shore almost always represents the things that are wrong with society and captivity. Even so, both contain an equal amount of lies. This suggests that the lies themselves are not necessarily evil, so much as the person telling them may be. The king and duke lie to Huck on the river on many occasions. This illustrates the fact that all the characters lie; it is just a question of their character that denotes the nature of the lie. Had all lies in the story been evil, Clemens never would have had any occur on the utopian Mississippi. While all characters and for the most part all people lie, it is the motivation behind the lie and the moral fiber of the person telling it that causes harm or good. The fact that a character in the story lies does not make them a bad or evil character, simply more realistic. The focus of Clemens through the social graces of his characters and their dialects was to create a true to life story. By adding the complexity of honesty to good or evil ends greatly contributes to this theme of realism.

Social Ills Exposed in The Adventures of Huckleberry Finn Mark Twain wrote The Adventures of Huckleberry Finn in 1883. The novel deals with many problems of society. Huck Finn "can't stand" hypocrisy, greed and "sivilz"ation, qualities that are still present today.

One trait shown in Huck Finn is hypocrisy. In Twain's other novels, as well as Huck Finn, Twain is very critical of the hypocrisy of organized religion. Early in Huck Finn, Huck is confronted with two different versions of heaven. Miss Watson's view of heaven is not appealing to Huck.

In her heaven, all that one does is sing and play the harp. Huck does not like Widow Douglas' much either, but it is better than Miss Watson's. Huck would rather be free to do as he pleases. Slavery is also hypocritical with Christianity. Slave owners would make slaves believe that God loves all people, which is contrary to the belief that slaves are inferior. The southern view of gentlemen is also hypocritical. These "gentlemen" are supposed to be noble, yet they own slaves and kill each other. They take part in feuds, even when they cannot remember the cause. They kill each other in duels for no reason, but say that it was in the name of honour. All of this hypocrisy makes Huck want to rebel against this society.

Hypocrisy is still present in society today. There are many reported cases of clergy having affairs or molesting children. For instance, Reverend Baker has had relationships with prostitutes. He always apologizes, but then he does it again. One of the precepts of the Catholic religion is to follow the instructions of the Pope. Many Catholics however, do not follow the Pope's instructions on birth control or abortion. Government officials are also hypocritical. They preach family values, yet often they do not follow these values. Senator Packwood resigned from the Senate for his actions. Dick Morris lost his job and his respect over an affair with a prostitute. Most aspects of today's society involve hypocrisy.

Another trait that Huck hates is greed. He is kidnaped by hisgreedy, alcoholic father. Huck's father beats him for his money whenHuck's wealth is discovered. While on the Mississippi, Huck and Jim comeacross a boat full of thieves. They are so greedy that they conspire tokill an associate to get his money. Their boat sinks and they die beforethey can kill their associate. Huck could have saved them, but does not.Later, Huck meets the King and the Duke. They are "con artists." Theyswindle innocent people out of money. They

. government or obscene arerestricted. In general, attempts civilize or reform people are for thegood of society, but .hey often restrict personal freedom.Mark Twain's The Adventures of Huckleberry Finn deals with manyproblems of society. These problems are still relevant today and willcontinue to be so.

Huckleberry Finn–Rejection of Religion

One of the main themes, and probably one of Twain's favorites, was the rejection of religion. Religion is one of the most constant targets of Twain's satirical pen. In Adventures of Huckleberry Finn, Mark Twain portrays contemporary religion as shallow and hypocritical. He criticizes the hypocrisy of conventional religion by comparing it with the true religion of Huck. Twain tended to attack organized religion at every opportunity, and the sarcastic character of Huck Finn is perfectly situated to allow him to do so. The attack on religion can already be seen in the first chapter, when Huck indicates that hell sounds like a lot more fun than heaven.

This will continue throughout the novel, with one prominent scene occurring when the "King" convinces a religious community to give him money so he can "convert" his pirate friends. Mark Twain also used the contrast between the characters of Tom Sawyer and Huck Finn to illustrate a romantic and realistic imagination. Tom is spectacularly imaginative in the boyish, romantic sense. Tom has filled his head with romantic adventure novels and ideas; this has shaped Tom's worldview and feeds his fantasies, which he is constantly trying to act out. After reading about gangs and highwaymen, Tom decides to build a gang wishing to rob people and become successful highwayman.

Tom's gang would kill or ransom the men and get the women to love them. Often times Tom's romantic imagination is not just silly, but downright dangerous. An example of this dangerous romantic imagination was when Huck wanted to free Jim and Tom was enlisted to help. Tom, knowing full well that Ms. Watson had released Jim prior to her death, did not disclose this information to Huck; he wanted to have an adventure helping Jim "escape". During the elaborate escape, Tom wanted Jim to train animals in his prison and have a coat of arms. Tom also sent Jim's captors warning of the upcoming escape attempt. Tom didn't know of the necessity to get Jim out now and not later.

Because of Tom's dawdling, Jim's life was put in danger when they finally did escape. As they were running away, bounty hunters were chasing them and shooting at them. Knowing the reader would be in need of a breathe of fresh air between Tom's elaborate schemes, Twain created Huck. Huck's desires are indeed remarkably few and simple. Huck wanted only to be wild and free. Huck often escaped from Ms. Watson by running to the woods and going exploring. Ms. Watson tried to "sivilize" him, but he didn't like to learn about dead people or other such "nonsense". He saw no point to education other than to spite his father.

Huck would rather be out fishing or playing in the woods. The final, and best, example of Huck's desire to be free was the ending line in the book. "I reckon I got to light out for the territory ahead of the rest, because Aunt Sally she's going to adopt me and sivilize me, and I can't stand it. I been there before." Huck hates to be oppressed by society and their views on life. This opinion reflects on Huck's own realistic attitude and how it allows him to view people as equal. Huck's realistic view on life is evident when he tears up the letter he had written to Ms. Watson about helping Jim escape. He began to remember all of the times Jim had been at his side, being a father figure to him. He realized how they had suffered together and had fun together, Huck was not about to turn his own brother in because of his skin colour. Huck tore up the letter and said he'd rather go to hell than to betray his friend. By reading about Huck and Tom and their contrasting views on life, allows the reader to have a breathe of fresh air in between the elaborate schemes of Tom.

Good Vs. Evil in The Adventures Of Huckleberry Finn

On important theme within The Adventures Of Huckleberry Finn is thestruggle between good and evil as experienced when Huck's personal sense oftruth and justice come in conflict with the values of society around him. Theseoccurrences happen often within the novel, and usually Huck chooses the trulymoral deed. One such instance occurs when Huckleberry realizes that he is helping arunaway slave. His moral dilemma is such that he is uncertain whether he shouldor should not turn this slave, named Jim, over to the authorities. Societytells him that he is aided a criminal, and that is against the law. However, hehas grown quite attached to Jim, and is beginning to realise that Jim is areally good person. He would also never hurt him.

This illustrates the conceptand symbolism of Jim's freedom and societies influence on Huck. At one point, Huck convinces himself that the nest opportunity hereceives, he will turn Jim in, and clear his conscience. The opportunity becameavailable when slave hunters meet them on the river. Huck had an absolutelyperfect chance to turn him over. However, he made up a story that his fatherwas sick and needed help and asked the slave hunters for help. They immediatelyassumed that his father had smallpox, and he wanted nothing to do with Huck orhis father. Thus, he had saved Jim, and actually felt good about it. Furtheralong in the book, Jim becomes a slave again. Huckleberry, with the aid of TomSawyer, free's Jim. Once again, Jim's escape and freedom are more important toHuck than societies viewpoint.

The river is also important. The river is symbolic of freedom. It isalso symbolic of good. When Jim and Huck are rafting down the river, they arefree of society. They have no laws. This is not to say that they are lawless,however, the laws they obey are there own. This is in direct contrast to beingon land, where society reigns supreme. Land is evil. This contrast also seemsto make the river a character in itself. It's at time's calm and relaxed, andat other times fast and dangerous, and sometimes foggy and confusing. However,it's always moving. Always taking Huck and Jim to new adventures, and to newplaces. It is their backbone.

So you see, that the concepts of escape and freedom within the book and the ways in which these concepts are symbolized are extremely important. They not only define what this book really is about, they single-handedly make the book worth

Friendship in Adventures Of Huckleberry Finn

In the novel The Adventures of Huckleberry Finn, by Mark Twain a young boy by the name of Huckleberry Finn learns what life is like growing up in Missouri. The story follows young Huckleberry as he floats down the Mississippi River on his raft. On his journey he is accompanied by his friend Jim, a runaway slave. Throughout this novel Huckleberry Finn is influenced by a number of people he meets along the way. Huckleberry Finn was brought up in an interesting household. His father was rarely ever home and if he was, he was drunk, his mother had passed away so Huck had no one to really look out for him or take care of him. Huckleberry had the life that many teenagers dream of, no parents to watch you or tell you what to do, but when Huckleberry finds himself in the care of Widow Douglas and Miss Watson things start to drastically change. Widow Douglas and Miss Watson are two relatively old women and think that raising a child means turning him into an adult. In order for Huckleberry to become a young man, he was required to attend school, religion was forced upon him, and a behaviour that was highly unlike Huck became what was expected of him by the older ladies. Not to long after moving in, Huckleberry ran away.

When he finally came home he respected the ladies wishes and did what they wanted, but was never happy with it. When Tom Sawyer enters the picture, he is the immediate apple of Huckleberry's eye. Huckleberry sees Tom as the person that he used to be and was envious of Tom's life. Huckleberry saw freedom and adventure in this young man and soon became very close friends with him. Huck then joins Tom's little "group" to feel that sense of belonging and adventure that he misses out on due to living with the two older ladies. Soon enough Huck realizes that all of Tom's stories are a little exagerated and that his promises of adventure really are not that adventurous. Tom gives Huckleberry a false sense of excitement and eventually Huck leaves Tom's gang. Later on Huckleberry 's father, Pap, enters the story and tries to change everything about Huckleberry that the two women have taught him. Pap is a very unkempt person and his outward appearance is definitely the epitome of the saying," What you see is what you get." Pap's comes in and demands that Huckleberry drops out of school, stops attending church, and that he stop reading and learning. After a couple of months of avoiding his father, Pap kidnaps Huckleberry and takes him to a small cabin in the woods far from civilization. Once again Huckleberry is given all of the freedom that he wants and once again Huckleberry becomes dissatisfied with the life that is bestowed upon him. Huckleberry comes to the conclusion that in order for him to stay alive, he must run away from his father and make his father and everyone else believe that there is no way of finding him. Huckleberry decides to stage his own death while his father was away on one of his drunken bouts. After he stages his death he leaves for Jackson's Island in the middle of the Mississippi River.

After Huckleberry leaves he meets up with Jim, Miss Watson's slave. They ran into each other after Huckleberry's arrival on Jackson's Island. As it turns out, Jim ran away because he overheard a conversation saying that he was to be sold to people in New Orleans. Jim makes Huckleberry feel comfortable about his decisions and about being himself. Huckleberry also realizes that he can learn a lot from Jim. Jim knows how to how to tell the future, how to tell the weather forecast, and is a very good judge of character. Huckleberry feels a need to be with Jim and feels very safe when they are together. Huck's new found friend prompts the decision to float down the Mississippi on a raft together. Jim gives Huckleberry a sense of security but also allows him to have enough space to do his own things. As opposed to Tom, Jim is very intelligent and truthful. He accepts Huckleberry the way that Tom did, but Jim does not have to lie about what promises will come of their friendship to make Huckleberry stay.

Jim also gives Huckleberry a sense of freedom, like Pap, but shows Huckleberry that he cares about what happens to him. Huckleberry finally found a living situation in which he feels comfortable in and likes to be in. In the novel The Adventures of Huckleberry Finn, there are many outside forces trying to impose their way of life on the young Huckleberry Finn. Coming from a broken home, Huckleberry is left in the care of Widow Douglas and her sister Miss Watson. These two elderly women try to make Huckleberry become a perfect gentleman by forcing him to attend school and church. Huckleberry feels trapped and uncomfortable with the expectations that the two ladies have and eventually runs away. He then meets up with Tom Sawyer who proves to be a boy full of adventures that prove to be the work of a vivid imagination. Huckleberry becomes bored with the relationship and decides to go back to the two older ladies.

After he comes back, his father, Pap kidnaps him and tries to return him to the life that he knew before. Huckleberry soon became unhappy with his new life because he felt that no one cared about him or what he did. His father was always drunk and forced him to drop out of school and stop attending church. Huckleberry finally becomes apart of a worthwhile relationship with a slave boy named Jim. Huckleberry and Jim are immediately inseparable as they decide to float down the Mississippi River together. In the end Huckleberry proves to have found a friendship worthy of having. A friendship that gives him all of the aspects of all the earlier relationships, but one in which he feels comfortable being a part of.

Survival in The Adventures of Huckleberry Finn

In literature, authors have created characters that have traitsthat contributes to their survival in society. The qualities of shredders,adaptability, and basic human kindness enables the character HuckleberryFinn, in Mark Twain's novel The Adventures Of Huckleberry Finn to survivein his environment. The purpose of this paper is to depict the importanceof these traits or qualities to his survival.

Huckleberry Finn is able to confront complex situations because heis shrewd. Nothing is more natural or more necessary than his ability tolie. In certain situations I will discuss how he must lie because thecircumstances forced him to deception and lies and evasions are the onlyweapons he has to protect himself from those who are physically strongerthan he. The creativity, common sense, and understanding of people ofdifferent classes give him the edge he needs to survive in a rather harshsociety. Living with Ms. Watson and Widow Douglas, Huck has adjusted hislife to that of a civilized society. Huck illustrates his shrewd thinkingwhen he see signs that indicates his father is back. Being afraid of hisfather, he gives all of his money to Judge Thatcher to avoid beingpersecuted by his father. Protecting himself was his number one priority;he knew that if his father got the money he would get drunk and in returnwould abuse him. His father drunkenness become a threat to his life lateron in the story and by stopping him from getting the money, he stopped hisfather from being an abuser at that point and time.

Pap, Huck's father returns to town to get custody of his sonbecause he here of Huck's fortune, finally resorting to the kidnapping.Huck is locked in the cabin when Pap is not around; once he was locked upfor three days. At this point and time Huck was being neglected and abuse;his father had no idea what his abusive behaviour was doing to Huck until heescapes. Pap became so abusive(not realizing it because of he is alwaysdrunk), that he almost kills his son in the cabin, thinking he was theangel of death. This incident forces Huck to realise that his father is animmediate threat to his life and he must escape. His plan to escape is oneof common sense combined with shrewdness and imagination. He creates abloody scene with the blood of a pig he shot, smashed the door, left somehis hair on a bloody ax, and left a trail of food, creating the impressionthat he was killed by robbers; his plan is a success.

Huck must enter the world after his death in disguises, born as anew person repeatedly to conceal his real identity. Dressing as a girl togo ashore to gather information is just one of the identities he mustassume through out his whole journey. This example shows how ingenious andinnovative Huck is in creating a creditable story that will camouflage hisreal identity.

In the act of meeting a lady who had recently settled intown, he dresses as a girl, makes up a name and a convincible story, "trusting providence to put the right words in my mouth when the time come."He finds out that her husband was going to Jackson Island to see if hecould find Jim. He is fortunate enough to get this information or else theywould have been caught by suprise.

The capsizing of Jim and Huck's raft, creates a situation in whichHuck must go ashore. He finds himself in the midst of barking dogs in frontof the Grangerford's home. Trusting providence again, he introduces himselfas George Jackson and that he fell overboard from a passing steamboat. Heis welcomed into the Grangerford's home because his identity and story isconvincible. After a day there, Huck forgets his new name. UnderstandingBuck, the youngest of the family, desire to show off, Huck gets him tospell his name revealing his new identity. Getting Buck to spell his namebecause he understands his personality, is just one of Huck's qualitiesthat help him to survive on the frontier. The adaptability of Huck Finn is marked throughout the novel. He is extremely adaptable and can tolerate living with the widow, his father, and in the Grangerford's home. Toleration of the best and worst situations seems to be one of his best qualities. Huck did not like the burden civilized society placed upon hisshoulders. Even though he did no like the restrictions of society, helearned to accept the ways of the widow; he wore the fancy clothes, atedinner at a table, did not curse or smoke, and decided to get an education.He benefited from living with the widow and he saw that it was somehownecessary to follow her rules; abiding by her rules were hard at first, buthe reached a point where he "was getting sort of used to the widow's ways,too, and they weren't so raspy on me."

A father is suppose to wish the best for his children, but Papseems to dislike the idea that his on is getting an education, becomingbetter that who he was. Huck's father hears of his fortune and returns toget custody, ultimately kidnapping Huck and putting him a locked cabinacross the river. Pap would beat his son quite frequently. In the woodsHuck felt free of the civilized world because he would smoke, curse, andeat at any time of the day because Pap had no objections, yet his freedomwas altered by the presence of his father. Huck was abused, but he made thebest of a terrible situation. He got to a point where he "didn't see howI'd ever got to like it so well at the widow's." He got used to the woodsand had no desire to return to civilization.

At the home of the Grangerford's, Huck quickly adapts to a relaxingand luxurious environment. He is impressed by their furniture and most ofall, the great food they had to offer him. Huck realizes that staying here,he will benefit from this generous family. Huck is also a person whom responds sympathetically human beings, even to the least of society. He protected Jim, a slave, the duke and king, cunning thieves, the robbers on the Walter Scott, and to the Wilks girls. Basic human kindness enables Huck to become a better person, it especially helps the relationship between Jim and Huck.

In some parts of the novel, Huck saves Jim, a runaway slave frombeing caught. He save him on Jackson Island and saved him from bountyhunters on the Mississippi. This quality shows Jim that Huck cares deeplyabout him as a friend. In return Jim treats Huck as a friend or even as hisown child although he is a slave. Jim would take Huck's watch at nights onthe raft and do other things for Huck that made his life on the raft not sohectic at it would have been if Jim was not around. It is fair to say thatHuck being kind to Jim, makes his living or survival on the raft a peacefulone.

In conclusion the qualities of shrewdness and ingenuity, basichuman kindness, and adaptability contributes equally to the survival ofHuckleberry Finn in his environment. Adaptability empowers Huck to survivefrom the best, living with the Grangerfords, and the worst, living with Papin the woods. Huck becomes a person of moral values and have goodrelationship with Jim, realizing he is also a human being, not just anotherslave because he is sympathetic to the least of society and relinquishedthe values of a severe society. Shrewdness and ingenuity helped Huck toneutralize situations that could not have been resolved by just anyone.Huck's sympathy for other human beings, adaptability, and his shrewdnessand ingenuity are among the qualities that makes Huck one of the greatcharacter in American fiction.

The Tall Tale in The Adventures of Huckleberry Finn

In Mark Twain's timeless American classic, The Adventures of HuckleberryFinn, the narrator often finds himself in undesirable situations.

Thesesituations, which are far-fetched even for the nineteenth-century, provide muchhumor to the novel and demonstrate Huck's cunning. Huck's adept use of the talitale becomes a survival tool on this adventure. In the novel, Huck sees lies as more of a practical solution to problemsthan as a moral dilemma.

He rationalizes that he has "never seen anybody butlied, one time or another". Unlike the lawless adventurer of the frontier,Huck does not use his knack for selfish purposes. He, instead, uses his liesstrictly as a means of escaping misfortune and never for his own profit. At onepoint in the story, Huck uses his skill to fabricate a story that keeps a skiffof slave-hunters away from Jim: " 'Well, there's five niggers run off to-night,up yonder above the head of the bend. Is your man white or black?'...'He'swhite' ". Huck's tall tales are used for the survival of both Huck andJim, and Jim knows this.

Huck's stories are usually believed, but even when doubted, he managesto change his fib just enough to make it believable. An example of this is whenhe is caught as a stow-away on a raft and his original story is not believed bythe crew: "Now, looky-here, you're scared, and so you talk wild. Honest, now,do you live in a scowl, or is it a lie?". Huck then changes his storyjust enough to make it believable, displaying his unique ability to adjust histale to within the parameters of believability. Throughout the novel Huck foolsmany intelligent people. His youth gives him a mask of innocence, that peopledon't want to disbelieve. Stretching the truth comes naturally to Huck Finn. Although his lies may seem to show a lack of good ethics, it is the lies themselves that truly show his virtue.

The Controversy of Reading Huckleberry Finn in Schools

"All modern American literature comes from one book by Mark Twain called Huckleberry Finn," according to Ernest Hemingway. Along with Ernest, many others believe that Huckleberry Finn is a great book, but is the novel subversive? Since this question is frequently asked, people have begun to look deeper into the question to see if this novel is acceptable for students in schools to read. First off subversive means something is trying to overthrow or destroy something established or to corrupt (as in morals). According to Lionel Trilling, " No one who reads thoughtfully the dialectic of Huck's great moral crisis will ever again be wholly able to accept without some question and some irony the assumptions of the respectable morality by which he lives, or will ever again be certain that what he considers the clear dictates of moral reason are not merely the engrained customary beliefs of his time and place." Trilling feels that Huck Finn is such a subversive character that this will not make people believe in something totally again, because they will fear being wrong like the society in Huckleberry Finn was. I believe this and I think the subversion in the novel is established when Mark Twain begins to question the acceptable morality of society. Twain uses humour and effective writing to make Huckleberry Finn a subversive novel about society in the 19th century.

Huck Finn, a boy referred to as "white trash," is a boy that has grown up believing totally what society as taught him. This passage shows an example of how society teaches him. "...And keep them till they're ransomed." "Ransomed? What's that?" "I don't know. But that's what they do. I've seen it in the books, and so of course that's what we've got to do." "Well how can we do it if we don't know what it is?" "Why, blame it all, we've got to do it. Don't I tell you it's in the books? Do you want to go to doing different from what's in the books, and get things all muddled up?" This is a conversation between Tom Sawyer and his gang of robbers. This shows how the boys are influenced by society and believe they most follow exactly what is in the books, because that is the right way to do things. In today's society, ransoming someone is a huge crime and is totally unacceptable. In this book, Twain makes ransoming a humorous issue. In fact, throughout the novel Twain makes violence a humorous issue and does not act upon it as a serious issue. This goes with the whole theme of the novel that there is no moral. The way Huck has been raised, he has no clue that what Tom's gang wants to do is ludacrist, and should be totally unacceptable. Twain uses this conversation also to show the beginning of questioning throughout the novel. This will show a pattern of how Huck questions things to learn. Whatever Hucks hears, he believes is the right and acceptable answer. Tom's Gang of Robbers was a part of humorous violence in the novel, but Huck would run into real violence as well. Huck faked his death, and headed down the river, and he decides to go ashore and stays with a stranger family named the Grangerfords

Huckleberry Finn–Moral

The Adventures of Huckleberry Finn by Mark Twain tell the story of how a young boy learns how to overcome the idea that colored folks are less equal then white folk. Regardless of the positive lessons portrayed throughout this book, it has been miss represented even from the very day that it was published. In fact, it has been said that this "book has been controversial since it was published it 1885" in a Los Angeles Times article written by Henry Weinstein in 1998. The Adventures of Huckleberry Finn is a classical story which was written for enjoyment and future education. This book was not written to encourage any derogatory slurs to any ethnic groups. Even though Jim, the colored friend of Huckleberry Finn, felt that every white person though of colour people as less equal, his friendship with Huck should be an inspiration to everyone to overcome differences. America has become a country that has given every one of its citizens an awesome privilege to be equal. Along with this privilege to be equal, America citizens have the opportunity to learn and become educated. The schools that provide this education should had the right to teach people how this country has evolved into a great nation. This right should include an ability to examine both the good and the bad and it should include a proper response to both. The Adventures of Huckleberry Finn provides an excellence chance for teachers to explain to young people how America has now treats everyone equal.

Many times in the friendship of Huck and Jim, Jim's idea that all white people treat colored people as less equal then white people show up. Jim, who is a run-a-way slave, was always trying to avoid any contact with white people of town. One specific example of how Jim thought about white people was when he stumbled across a dead man on the river in a house. Jim did not what to tell anyone, not even Huck. He thought that if anyone found out they would blame him for murdering the fellow. Jim was always in hiding. He thought that if a white person saw him, he would be sent back to his owner and punished. Jim only really came in contact with on the Mississippi, as Russell Backer wrote, were "drunkards, murderers, bullies, swindlers, lynchers, thieves, liars, frauds, child abusers, numskulls, hypocrites, windbags, and traders in human flesh." Because of the people that he meet, he formed an idea of what all white people might thing of all colored people. Jim should not have stereotyped white people like this. At the same time schools should not stereotype Huckleberry Finn as a derogatory book because of the thoughts of early southern Americans.

The friendship of Huck and Jim in The Adventures of Huckleberry not only is a good example of how people of different ethnic background should treat each other, but it is also a good encouragement to readers to have loyalty to friends. Huck was feeling guilty for not telling on his run-a-way slave. He even wrote a note that would get Jim in trouble. After some time, Huck decided that his friendship was important to him. Huck ripped the note and never told on Jim.

If examined improperly, this classic story includes an offensive word. People must consider many other situations in history that could include offensive literature. In history, Semitic peoples were treated terribly by Adolf Hitler. If schools in America do not have the right to discuss, explain and read about history, how will young people learn what is good and what is bad. Should every history book be banned from schools because Hitler was anti-Semitic? No! Rather people need to learn how to "think critical about offensive ideas" as Reinhardt once said in a Los Angeles Times article in 1998. Also, how will young people know why or how they now have the privilege to be a citizen of a county that gives all ethic group equal rights.

Huckleberry Finn–Morality

Society establishes their own rules of morality, but would they be accepted in these days?

For example, throughout the novel "Huckleberry Finn ", Mark Twain depicts society as a structure that has become little more than a collection of degraded rules and precepts that defy logic. This faulty logic manifests itself early, when the new judge in town allows Pap to keep custody of Huck. "The law backs that Judge Thatcher up and helps him to keep me out o' my property." The judge privileges Pap's "rights" to his son over Huck's welfare. Clearly, this decision comments on a system that puts a white man's rights to his "property"—his slaves—over the welfare and freedom of a black man.

Whereas a reader in the 1880s might have overlooked the moral absurdity of giving a man custody of another man, however, the mirroring of this situation in the granting of rights to the immoral Pap over the lovable Huck forces the reader to think more closely about the meaning of slavery. In implicitly comparing the plight of slaves to the plight of Huck at the hands of Pap, Twain demonstrates how impossible it is for a society that owns slaves to be just, no matter how "civilized" that society believes and proclaims itself to be.

In addition, childhood has been described by the author, as an important factor in the theme of moral education: only a child is open-minded enough to undergo the kind of development that Huck does." It was a close place. I took...up [the letter I'd written to Miss Watson], and held it in my hand. I was a-trembling, because I'd got to decide, forever, betwixt two things, and I know it. I studied a minute, sort of holding my breath, and then says to myself: "All right then, I'll go to hell"—Em dash intended here? and tore it up. It was awful thoughts and awful words, but they was said. And I let them stay said; and never thought no more about reforming..."It, describes the moral climax of the novel. Jim has been sold by the Duke and Dauphin, and is being held by the Phelpses spending his return to his rightful owner. Thinking that being at home in St. Petersburg, even if it means Jim will still be a slave and Huck will be a captive of the Widow, would be better than being in his current state of peril far from home, Huck composes a letter to Miss Watson, telling her where Jim is. When Huck thinks of his friendship with Jim, however, and realizes that Jim will be sold down the river anyway, he decides to tear up the letter. The logical consequences of his action, rather than the lessons society has taught him, drive Huck. Huck decides that going to "hell," if it means following his gut and not society's hypocritical and cruel principles, is a better option than going to everyone else's heaven. This is Huck's true break with the world around him. At this point he decides to help Jim escape slavery once and for all, and he realizes that he, Huck, will not be re-entering the civilized world: he has moved beyond it morally.

Since Huck and Tom are young, their age lends a sense of play to their actions, which excuses them in certain ways and also heightens the profundity of the novel's commentary on slavery and society. Huck and Tom know better than the adults around them, but they lack the guidance that a proper family and community should have offered them.

Furthermore, Huck and Tom encounter individuals who seem good (Sally Phelps, for example), but Twain takes care to show us that person as a prejudiced slave-owner. "Preacher be hanged, he's a fraud and a liar". The shakiness of the justice systems that Huck encounters lies at the heart of society's problems: terrible acts go unpunished, yet frivolous crimes, such as drunkenly shouting insults, lead to executions Sherburn's speech to the mob that has come to lynch him accurately summarizes the view of society given in this book: rather than maintaining collective welfare, society is marked by cowardice, a lack of logic, and profound selfishness.

Bibliography

Baetzhold, Howard G. "Samuel Longhorn Clemens." In Concise Dictionary of American Literary Biography: Realism, Naturalism, and Local Color, 1865-1917. Gale, 1988, pp. 68-83.

Bridgman, Richard. Traveling in Mark Twain. Berkeley: University of California Press, 1987.

Camfeld, Gregg, ed. The Oxford Companion to Mark Twain. New York: Oxford University Press, 2003.

Chadwick-Joshua, Jocelyn. The Jim Dilemma: Reading Race in "*Huckleberry Finn.*" Jackson, Miss: University Press of Mississippi.

Fishkin, Shelly Fisher. Was Huck...